S0-BCM-375

NOV 1 1 1992

FEB 2 3 1996
MAR 1 7 1996
APR 1 0 1997

AUG 2 1 2003

THE POLITICAL ECONOMY OF
URBAN TRANSPORTATION

Kennikat Press
National University Publications
Interdisciplinary Urban Series

General Editor
Raymond A. Mohl
Florida Atlantic University

DELBERT A. TAEBEL / JAMES V. CORNEHLS

THE POLITICAL ECONOMY
OF
URBAN TRANSPORTATION

National University Publications
KENNIKAT PRESS   //   1977
Port Washington, N. Y.   //   London

Chapter 1 is a revised and expanded version of "Urban Transportation: A Typology of Ideological and Policy Perspectives," *Traffic Quarterly* 29 (Oct. 1975). Copyright © 1975 by Eno Foundation for Transportation, Inc.

Chapter 4 is a revised and expanded version of "Politics, Regulation, and Urban Transportation Priorities: The Triumph of the Auto Society," *Antitrust Law and Economics Review* 7, no. 3. Copyright © 1975 by Antitrust Law and Economics Review, Inc.

Chapter 6 is a revised and expanded version of "The Outsiders and Urban Transportation," *Social Science Journal* (Apr. 1976). Copyright © 1976 by the Western Social Science Association.

Chapter 8 is a revised version of "Citizen Groups, Public Policy and Urban Transportation," *Traffic Quarterly* 27 (Oct. 1973). Copyright © 1973 by Eno Foundation for Transportation, Inc.

Chapter 9 is a revised version of "Urban Mass Transit: What Are the Limits?" *Consulting Engineer* 42 (Mar. 1974). Copyright © 1974 by Technical Publishing Co.

Copyright © 1977 by Kennikat Press Corp. All rights reserved. No part of this publication may be reproduced, stored in a retrieval system, or transmitted, in any form or by any means, electronic, mechanical, photocopying, recording, or otherwise, without the prior written permission of the publisher.

CONTENTS

LIST OF TABLES AND FIGURES

TABLES

FIGURES

PREFACE

Transportation is widely regarded as one of the critical elements in today's urban crisis, while congestion and traffic jams are often seen as the principal barriers to a healthy urban transportation system. Reflected in the many books and articles on the urban transportation problem, this particular thrust is exemplified in the comments of two scholars: "That a few Americans orbit the globe in less time than it takes others to get to work illustrates the urban transportation problem."[1] A further elaboration of this theme is made by George Smerk, who maintains that the urban transportation problem is "universally understood to be traffic congestion, or simply too many vehicles trying to pass through the same place at the same time."[2]

If congestion and its attendant problems constituted the major dimensions of the transportation problem for American cities, this book would not have been written. Although there is ample evidence that this problem exists, it is a problem which diverts our attention from the more critical issues of urban transportation. Indeed, we would contend that mobility problems for most urban dwellers are quite minimal.

The technological capability of the urban transportation system as it exists today in American cities is a major achievement. In general, the urban resident can move farther and faster today than at any time in the past. The transportation system as we now know it gives the urban citizen the kind of mobility his forefathers never dreamed of. Congestion appears to be on the decline, and traffic engineers have made great strides in devising schemes for improving the flow of traffic.

Yet, the proposition that congestion is the principal problem in urban transportation persists. This entrenched viewpoint would be quite harmless if it were merely confined to rhetorical pronouncements. But, unfortunately, it is embraced by many of those in policy-making positions.

One must keep in mind that the way we define a problem determines the policy alternatives, and we can explore for a moment the implications of the "congestion" syndrome. If congestion is the problem, then presumably "noncongestion"—the absolute freedom of movement along some right-of-way—is the answer. Congestion, then, implies some restraint on the freedom of movement.

For purposes of further analysis, let us conceive of the metropolitan area as a series of rings, with the inner ring representing the central city and the outer ring representing the suburbs. Let us also assume that the space devoted to traffic arterials is the same for each but that the population is greater in the inner ring than in the outer ring. Under these conditions, the inner ring would experience a greater degree of congestion than the outer ring. One way of resolving this problem is to construct additional arterials in the inner ring. Now, two things may happen. In the first place, the people who live in the inner ring could be displaced and move to new locations in the outer ring. If they work in the inner ring, it is true that their journey to work will be less congested. However, the trip will be quite a bit longer, and the net effect based on time may be zero. Furthermore, by moving to the outer ring, they will increase the congestion on the arterials in the outer ring.

It may be, of course, that due to the increased mobility in the inner ring, the families displaced by the new arterial construction will not only stay in the city but that those from the suburbs may also move to the city. If this were the case, then the new arterials will soon become congested again, and the net effect based on time may be zero.

Congestion and density, then, are concomitant phenomena. For policy scientists, primarily political scientists, the objective is a spatial readjustment which expands the size of the metropolitan area. Economists, on the other hand, tend to adopt a cost-benefit perspective, and when it is suggested that alternative modes of transportation, such as rapid transit, might well reduce congestion, they are quick to point out that such a policy is unfeasible because of low density.

Thus a paradox emerges: Given the transportation system we now have with congestion viewed as the major problem, the only feasible solution is to construct more highways so as to reduce density, but because of low density rapid transit as an alternative is unfeasible. In sum, density is too high for an auto system and too low for the rapid transit system.

In contrast to this fixation with congestion, the thesis of this book is that the transportation system in American cities today creates a whole series of problems and that these problems constitute the critical dimensions of the urban crisis in relation to transportation.

To provide the reader with a kind of "road map," we have sketched out in the first chapter various policy approaches employed by scholars and practitioners in the analysis of urban transportation. This guide might not only aid the reader in a fuller appreciation of our perspective but also might provide a valuable framework in the analysis of the other literature on urban transportation.

The transportation system in American cities is the focus of the second chapter. To understand where we have been and where we are today provides the student with the basis for determining where we ought to go.

How we got where we are in terms of both policy and institutions is the subject of the next three chapters. Governmental policy and fiscal measures are outlined in Chapter 3. The economic institutions and their role in transportation policy are explored in Chapter 4. The next chapter examines the political structure, the linkages with economic institutions, and the barriers to change.

The impact of our urban transportation system, especially its deleterious impact on urban design, pollution, and the poor, will be explored in the next two chapters. These adverse impacts, of course, have generated considerable reaction by various citizen groups, which provides the focus for Chapter 8.

Finally, we will assess mass transportation as an alternative to our auto-oriented system. There have been many claims that mass transportation will cure many ills in our cities. These claims will be examined, and we will attempt to find out which values can be achieved and which seem less likely to be achieved.

THE POLITICAL ECONOMY OF
URBAN TRANSPORTATION

1

APPROACHES TO
URBAN TRANSPORTATION

In the past several years, numerous articles and books have been written about the problems of urban transportation.[1] The literature is quite extensive and far-reaching in its thrust but tends to be rather chaotic. Urban transportation researchers represent a wide variety of disciplinary and professional practitioners, including traffic engineers, political scientists, urban planners, sociologists, economists, and environmentalists. Because the transportation system in cities so obviously affects virtually every other facet of urban life, the literature frequently crosses disciplinary lines, and this, of course, contributes to the chaos. These efforts, however, have been worthwhile: The literature covers almost every facet of urban transportation; thus, an extensive body of knowledge is now available, ideas that may help to solve urban transportation problems.

Yet, there is at least one important caveat. There are few, if any, organizing principles for the study of urban transportation. Furthermore, the available literature tends to cover the waterfront so extensively and in such detail that it is almost impossible to find any focus, theme, or common ground for discussion of crucial issues. Indeed, the issues themselves are difficult to distinguish. Although this is no doubt a reflection of a transitional stage in the analysis of urban transportation, it creates a dilemma: there seems to be no appropriate place to begin and no place to end. We need some overall organizational scheme or framework to facilitate interpretation of this mass of research and policy analysis. Otherwise, we may be overwhelmed by more information than can be digested or used.

The purpose of this chapter is to develop a preliminary framework for understanding the various approaches taken by scholars and practitioners who have been concerned with urban transportation. As the study of this subject matures, classification schemes will become more complex and more sophisticated. But the need for organizational and evaluative premises is obvious today and will become more acute in the future.

Although there are many possible bases for developing a classification system, we believe that one of the most useful is the identification and definition of the normative orientation of transportation research and policy analysis. Accordingly, the classification scheme adopted here can best be described as ideological.[2] Most urban transportation studies have a decidedly ideological basis even though there is often an exaggerated show of objectivity. In fact, it would be surprising if this were not the case, since the issues surrounding urban transit are significant policy matters, which places them squarely in the center of the political arena.

SEVEN IDEOLOGICAL DIMENSIONS

Seven ideological "approaches" or analytic dimensions are found in the current literature. Of these seven approaches three are favorable to an automobile society; one is anti-automobile; one advocates the expansion of mass transit; one stresses the concept of "balanced transportation"; a final, somewhat heterogeneous, category may be referred to as the "ecological approach." These approaches, of course, tend to overlap, but for the most part each has certain clearly distinguishable characteristics. Therefore, they will be presented as: (1) the auto monopolists; (2) the auto apologists; (3) the social engineers; (4) the trustbusters; (5) the transit technicians; (6) the balancers; and (7) the ecologists.

1. THE AUTO MONOPOLISTS

The main proponents of this approach are associated with economic organizations directly involved in the production of automobiles and petroleum. They are buttressed by the construction and trucking industries. The most articulate exponents of this viewpoint are drawn from the ranks of the "highway lobby." This viewpoint is effectively communicated through a variety of channels—public meetings, professional associations, newspaper articles, advertising, and consistent professional presence at hearings before legislative bodies considering measures potentially affecting the lobby's interests.

Of course, the private economic organizations advocating this view are staunchly supported by the Federal Highway Administration and the powerful state highway departments,[3] and even at the county[4] and city levels. Although these highway agencies are direct allies of the economic interest groups, they can speak openly without being branded as private interest groups. Indeed, some of the most vociferous spokesmen of this position are "public servants."[5]

The principal values of the advocates of this approach are quite straightforward. To them the automobile is the primary symbol of modern industrialized society. The great era of industrial expansion, the introduction of the assembly line, automation, and literally thousands of derivative industries are all regarded as inextricably linked with the emergence of an automotive society. Their implicit (and sometimes explicit) national goals are usually two cars in every garage, a gasoline station on every corner, and cities devoted overwhelmingly to streets, parking lots, and maintenance facilities for the auto. Progress is measured in terms of car ownership and highway and street mileage. If the cities seem choked and under strain, the solution is to improve and expand car-carrying capabilities.

There is also the strong underlying suggestion that the automotive industry is virtually indispensable to the continued economic prosperity of the United States. If not indispensable, it is at least a very desirable component of a healthy, prosperous economy. With nearly 20 percent of the gross national product closely linked to the automotive industry, far too many jobs are at stake. Thus they argue that the shock waves sent through the economy by the demise of the automobile and truck as the dominant means of transportation would be economically and politically unacceptable. American industrial might would be crippled, and the enormous capital loss and new investment requirements involved in the transition to a new system would be foolish and unattainable.

The idea of "free" choice, however, is the paramount value of the auto ideology; it is presented as "the Democratic Way." Free choice, of course, turns out to be choosing the automobile, largely because there is nothing else to choose. Notwithstanding the absence of alternatives, there is an almost messianic belief among many exponents of this outlook. They believe that even if all the true costs of auto transportation were known, and even if safe, efficient, and pleasant transportation alternatives were available, the average American still would choose the automobile.

The automobile, moreover, is defended as a great and powerful symbol for Americans. It epitomizes the American way: free men and women freely choosing that most individual and uninhibited way of getting about, all brought about by the interplay of market forces in a free enterprise system; a populace unbeholden to any "public" authority that might dictate departure schedules and available routes. This is the ideology expressed so fervently in one of the latest Madison Avenue jingles:

> Driving in your car,
>> It's all there in your hands,
> You've got *room* to go,
>> And the whole wide world to see;
>
> There's something in the feeling,
>> Of a really fine machine,
> That *turns you loose,*
>> That really *sets you free.*
>
> It's *a better way,*
>> It's a better feeling,
> When the wheel belongs to you,
>> The road goes *anywhere you say;*
>
> It's a better way,
>> It's the *feel of freedom.* . . . [6]

The message is clear: the automobile is peculiarly well suited to American life-styles. The suburban, spread-city development coincides with America's rural roots and its space-loving, open style of life. Footloose, mobile Americans want to feel free to cruise all over the landscape, to move often and to be able to go anywhere—to work, play, or mall—at a moment's notice.

The automobile is championed as the ideal answer to this life-style. It is instantly available, allowing flexibility in choice of residence and office. It provides individual service at the least "apparent" cost. Even if it doesn't minimize costs, argue the auto advocates, Americans are generally affluent and have the ability to pay for the convenience afforded by personal transportation.

Finally, they claim that Americans will reject anything but personal transportation. The evidence for this is supposed to be so overwhelming that it is rarely cited. But the constant decline in bus riders, the phenomenal growth in auto ownership, and the defeat of legislative proposals curtailing auto use are taken as facts that preclude serious consideration of alternatives. What exists is what Americans want; if they wanted something else, the market would have provided it.[7]

For the proponents of auto ideology, government is merely an instrument that expresses the American preference for automobiles. Since it is inconceivable that transportation consumers would choose anything but the car, it is logical to assume that one of the primary—possibly the primary—functions of government is building roads. Debate about automobiles is discouraged, and attempts to reopen discussion are met with incredulity. Hence, "The business of government is business" becomes the motto of the auto monopolist.

2 . THE AUTO APOLOGISTS

Although this approach is similar to the one just described, there are some significant variations. The automobile is seen as socially desirable because it epitomizes free choice and hence consumer welfare. Yet, there is some recognition of the need for public transportation. Many proponents of this position admit that the automobile has limitations, especially external diseconomies; they believe that public transportation would benefit cities.

Three major dimensions distinguish this viewpoint from the auto monopolists. First, although its exponents see transportation primarily in terms of economics—especially the journey to work—they understand that the costs of owning an automobile may be beyond the financial capability of some urban residents. Furthermore, the size of this group may not be large enough to support a useful public transportation network without some form of public subsidy. Second, recognizing that there may be built-in imperfections in the market process, the apologists also realize that industry may need unskilled labor for many of its jobs, thus providing employment for those who might otherwise end up as welfare recipients, which would necessitate even greater public outlays. Third, the apologists are aware of the need to relieve center city congestion. With downtowns dying and even office space moving to suburban locations, and with increasing demands for air quality standards, some form of public transportation is acceptable and inevitable. Of critical importance are the quantity and the form of future public transportation. They want to limit public transportation to what is "absolutely necessary" and to forms that require a minimum subsidy, preferably no subsidy at all, and few large public capital outlays. It is not surprising, therefore, that the apologists usually subscribe to a motorized highway transportation system, principally buses.

Auto apologists come from two different groups. Many of the fringe members of the highway lobby recognize that the day of uncontrolled growth of private auto ownership and use may be over. If there are going to be changes in the urban transportation system, they reason, it would seem prudent to support motorized public transportation. After all, buses can be viewed as large automobiles, and they certainly run on roads and highways. Then too, the giant automobile corporations either produce buses now or have the capability of producing them. The other group linked with the apologist approach is the highway engineers. Reserved bus lanes open the door for new construction, and many other modifications in the highway system will foster additional contracting work. The preservation of the street and road network is of crucial importance: as long as there are streets and highways available, it is always possible for automobiles to travel along them.

The apologists enjoy considerable support from certain segments of the academic community. These sophisticated spokesmen are generally transportation engineers or economists who agree with the goals and values supported by the auto apologists. Their expertise is primarily employed to refute arguments for rapid mass transit with the cold, hard logic characteristic of their models. Their prime weapon, one used by auto monopolists, is the "density argument," in which it is claimed that an efficient, economical rail transit system can only be operated in a city with a highly dense population. Through cost-benefit models (which usually avoid any but measurable economic costs and benefits) they are persuasive proponents of a motorized public transit system.[8]

3. THE SOCIAL ENGINEERS

The social engineers adopt the dictum *In the long run we are all dead.* Short-run goals are the only important considerations. The only immediate changes that can be made are those which lie within the existing transport system. Long-range changes in transportation systems may be desirable, but the overriding concerns of the social engineers are immediate benefits for the needy. They see the automobile and other motorized transportation as a means for improving the lot of various groups in the urban community who are at present either ill-served or not served at all by the transportation system.[9] These are primarily minorities, the elderly, the handicapped, and the poor. Hence the social engineers are humanistic auto monopolists.

Economic realities are of utmost importance for the social engineers. They see the lack of adequate transportation as the major barrier in securing employment; their immediate objective is to bridge this barrier. Social engineers do consider other modes of transportation, such as rail rapid transit; they are also aware of the undesirable effects of the automobile on the city. But the needs of the poor and underprivileged are so compelling that immediate action is necessary.

In a sense, social engineers adopt the same perspective as advocates of income redistribution. Some of them want to redistribute transportation by encouraging the government to provide cars for the poor.[10] Still others hope to see increased use of taxis and jitneys,[11] with the possibility in some cases that public transportation service would be provided free of charge.[12]

Proponents of this perspective are drawn mainly from the academic community, though officials from various social welfare agencies are also spokesmen for the approach. The social engineers seem to have tacitly accepted the auto monopolists' belief that the automobile will not be deserted by affluent Americans. They also tend to see the city in terms of haves and have-nots, and transportation as a key factor in making everyone haves. Their views are similar to those of minority capitalists, who advocate a "piece of the action" for the disadvantaged. Providing transportation for the underprivileged thus becomes a temporary governmental policy pending the entry of many of these groups into the mainstream of economic life. And the few who can never be expected to enter will still be enabled to get about much like everyone else.

4. THE TRUSTBUSTERS

Although the word *trust-busting* refers primarily to the efforts of those who would like to dismantle the Highway Trust Fund, the term represents an approach that is much broader in its orientation and negative in its thrust. In principle, a trustbuster is anyone who is opposed to the primacy of the private automobile. Before any real progress in altering transportation priorities can be realized, they argue, the self-perpetuating nature of automotive taxes must be halted. Society cannot afford the resources already allocated to auto transportation plus those required for mass transit.

In general, the trustbusters see the automobile as the prime culprit in the decline of the American city. They view urban sprawl, suburbanized isolation, noise, air and visual pollution, disparities in job opportunities, and the isolation of subgroups (minorities, the elderly, and the handicapped) as direct consequences of the automobile. The highway lobby and highway engineer are exposed as the enemy, and the first and only task is the total defeat of the highway lobby. Numerous books in recent years reflect this viewpoint —Leavitt's *Superhighway-Superhoax,*[13] Mowbray's *Road to Ruin*[14] and Ayres's *What's Good for G.M.,*[15] for example. Articles recounting the efforts of local citizen groups to block highways also exemplify this approach.[16]

Trustbusters come from a variety of groups and organizations. Environmentalists have become some of the more vociferous opponents of the automobile society at the national and local levels.[17] Neighborhood groups have largely confined their activities to a specific highway project threatening their area.[18] Yet, the movement has gained a considerable number of supporters. Indeed, the Highway Action Coalition serves as a lobby for trustbusters in Washington and even publishes a journal, *The Concrete Opposition.*

5. THE TRANSIT TECHNICIANS

The transit technicians, like the auto monopolists, favor a transportation monopoly. Rather than favoring a total automobile society, however, they want a total mass transit society. They would like to see one monopoly replace another. These views are seldom articulated in journals and books.

More frequently, they are expressed at the meetings of the various trade groups in the mass transit industry. To some extent, they are also buttressed by their principal governmental sponsor, the Urban Mass Transportation Administration (UMTA). UMTA is to the transit technicians what the Federal Highway Administration is to the auto monopolists.

There is one group of supporters who are not the direct operators of transit agencies but who nonetheless would like to see the advent of a mass transit society. Engineers and vehicle design professionals, as well as their industrial sponsors, are the chief champions of futuristic systems, such as TACV and the monorail. Although some of the major auto producers have some interest in these efforts, other corporations, especially those from the aerospace industry, have become keenly aware of the potential market. The most notable publicity effort of these designers to date was the glittering spectacle "Transpo 70." It was sponsored by UMTA, and several futuristic designs for mass transportation were unveiled by various industrial corporations.[19]

Many hard-core "mass transporters" are operators of local transit systems. They often have the same engineering perspective that is entrenched in state highway departments. Furthermore, they consider themselves "hard-headed" businessmen who see problems of mass transportation from an operational perspective. Their conferences are devoted to such matters as marketing, schedules, maintenance problems, fiscal arrangements, and more efficient equipment. Although they may be sensitive to such urban problems as the environment, minorities, and urban design, they are more concerned with the day-to-day problems of the revenue box and the operational status of their equipment.

A large segment of transit operators, the bus companies, occupies an uneasy position. While representing mass transit, their functions are, paradoxically, tied to the continuation of the automobile. Although buses are considered mass transit, they run over roads—roads that would not exist were it not for the automobile. Notwithstanding, in the face of increasing transit deficits and forced municipal take-over, the aim of this group is still firmly fixed on providing smooth, quiet, attractive, air-conditioned buses that attract new customers. For them, the dreams of city planners and scholars for improving the transportation system in the urban community are diversionary ploys. The real problem for the transit technician is to make sure that bus No. 202 is working and on time.

6. THE BALANCERS

The idea of a "balanced" transportation system for our cities is enjoying a considerable vogue in journals and public meetings. Obviously, the terminology invoked is of some importance in itself and designed to take the wind out of the sails of those who advocate other solutions. The opposite of balanced is imbalanced, and it seems somewhat preposterous that anyone would advocate anything imbalanced. Of course, like beauty, balance may reside in the eyes of the beholder. As Smerk points out, "the rhetoric of mass transportation is replete with fuzzy goals and meaningless phrases. The winner is probably the 'balanced transportation system,' a term attached to programs combining highway and transit improvements in some nebulous way. . . ."[20] Unless the idea of balance is accompanied by some criteria for determining when it occurs, it may be a wholly spurious and diversionary idea. Of all the ideological positions, that of the balancers appears most vulnerable to this criticism.

The balancers are in the same ideological camp with the advocates of the mixed economies. They give preference to the private sector (automobiles) while maintaining a keen perception of the need for public services that the private sector either cannot or will not produce. Why can't we, they seem to say, have our cake and eat it too? Like the auto monopolists, they are enamored with the lofty ideal of free choice, but they are willing to concede that free choice may not work too well in practice. The balancers, ever attuned to acceptability, have the further advantage of appearing to agree with everyone: they appeal to reason and avoid conflict.

In principle, balancers recommend curtailing the use of automobiles and expanding the role of public transportation. Although the term *balanced* is employed, this group would seldom insist that there should be complete parity between the automobile and public transportation. Each serves an important purpose, and there should be an appropriate "mix."

Among the advocates of this approach are numerous political scientists and liberal economists.[21] They contend that the costs of social diseconomies cannot be internalized to private producers and users of transportation; therefore only public authority can compensate the losers. These balancers provide a part of the analytic rationale for the professional city and regional planners whose conception of the physical plan for the city coincides with the "balanced" system.

Center city, its residents and its businesses, are dependent on an internal network of mass transit facilities correlated with radial, high-speed commuter lines, and these in turn are serviced by a network of bus feeder and park-and-ride facilities along the suburban fringe. The models conceived by balancers to develop these systems make extensive use of such concepts as trip generation patterns stemming from existing or proposed uses of land, modal split concepts, and gravity models. The models are designed to give the distinct impression that the planners know exactly what to expect from their designs. If the planner wants to encourage the industrial development of a certain area of the city, he knows that various other facilities will be required, such as highway egress or rail links. By manipulating the mix and shape of these facilities, he can determine the actual design of the area and predict its impact on the total transportation network. It is the American dream, a solution that allows everyone to do exactly what he wants.

Even though city planners consider balanced transportation as a viable means for restructuring the city, there are limitations to the practical value of the balanced viewpoint. In the first place, the city planner is stuck with his city as it is, and the historical development of that city is a major constraint. Second, the planner is wedded to a highly rational model. Although "comprehensive planning" receives the same adulation as a "balanced transportation system," planning as it now operates in most cities is "incremental" and hardly comprehensive.

7. THE ECOLOGISTS

The most recent approach to the study of urban transportation is the most amorphous and for its proponents the most frustrating. Although the term *ecology* is employed, this position does not specifically refer to the environmentalists and conservationists, though many of them may be advocates of this approach.

Ecologists see the transportation system as extending far beyond the narrow objectives of moving people and goods, of efficient and well-integrated transportation networks, or even of urban design. They see transportation as only one major subsystem operating in the urban environment, but one that is capable of exercising a profound influence on the design and function of the city itself, one that is capable of affecting the physical environment and the wise use of land and natural resources to preserve beauty and life. Costs and benefits of transportation are reflected far beyond the farebox, service to patrons, traffic congestion, effect on the downtown area, right-of-way acquisitions, and capital outlays. Benefits may be realized in the diversity and pleasantness of neighborhoods and landscapes, in the impact on political representation, in the attractiveness of the city to new residents, and in the diminution of current social costs, such as crime, social disaffection, polarization, and racism. The ecological perspective is total in scope, holistic in content, and heuristic in design. It seeks to encompass all the other major subsystems in the urban community, to examine all the effects of transportation on the interrelated parts of the system, and to foster an open systems model for analyses capable of including each new discovery.

The magnitude of this approach frequently leads to immobilization and paralysis. Indeed, this frustration has led many to a total rejection of the current urban system. In this sense, the ecologists may be likened to the trustbusters; but whereas the trustbusters reject only the automotive society, some ecologists argue that the automotive society is merely one more manifestation of what is wrong in numerous areas of American urban life, such as housing, health care, and education.[22] For others, the solution is not quite so clear and hardly so simple. If there are basic flaws in the various spheres of urban society, the task is to identify these trouble spots and at least to postulate systems to cope with the problems.

For the ecologists the benefits from transportation occur collectively, not individually. For instance, an individual will benefit if all of his neighbors stop dumping their wastes in the water while he continues to discharge his own insignificant wastes. Likewise, an individual will benefit from having everyone else use public transit while she or he uses the now uncluttered roadways to drive a private automobile. Only groups, through democratic action, as in the control of contagious disease, can be relied upon to obtain the maximum social benefits of transportation.

The ecologists would have us avoid the trap of believing that freedom means the unrestrained right to inflict great social harm, however unwittingly or unintentionally. As someone has aptly remarked, man may have the inalienable right to go downtown, but that right certainly does not include the right to take 4,000 pounds of metal with him.

SUMMARY AND EVALUATION

In this introductory chapter, we have outlined seven general approaches or analytical dimensions for the study of urban transportation. The themes we have touched upon will be elaborated more extensively throughout this book. For example, the social engineering approach is evident in our discussion in Chapter 6 concerning "The Outsiders and Urban Transportation," and Chapter 8 on "Citizen Reaction" will recount in greater detail the strategies of the trustbusters. For summary purposes, however, Table 1-1 portrays the major characteristics of each approach. These various categories are not meant to be exhaustive or complete in their treatment. Furthermore, there is some overlap between some of the categories. Our purpose here is to provide a starting point; this classification system should be considered primarily as a tool.

Having identified several approaches and having indicated the confusion this can create for the student of transportation, we would be unfair if we proceeded without some evaluation and an indication of our preference. Because this is a book on urban transportation, we have drawn on a wide variety of sources which exemplify each of these approaches. But our

TABLE 1-1

Summary of Approaches to Urban Transportation

Approach	Major Proponents	Modal Bias	Economic Ideology	Political Perspective	Purpose of Transportation
Auto monopolists	Highway lobby, especially contractors, highway engineers	Automobile	Darwinian capitalism	Government as instrumental supporter of auto	Economic growth, free choice
Auto apologists	Fringe members of highway lobby, large-scale employers	Auto with some transit	Welfare economics	Government as transportation provider of last resort	Full employment, work-trip emphasis
Social engineers	Social service agencies	Auto for short range	Redistribution	Government intervention on behalf of underprivileged	Economic opportunity for poor
Trustbusters	Muckrakers, planners, etc.	Implicitly mass transit	Anti-monopolists	Anti-highway lobby	
Transit technicians	Transit agencies	Mass transit	Marketing	Government as instrumental supporter of mass transit	Efficient service, development of CBD
Balancers	City and regional planners	Depends on situation	Optimization	Government as determiner of transportation system design	Optimal choice, development of city
Ecologists	Individualistic; no major group identity	Mass transit, nonmotorized movement	Social control	Government as determiner of ideal urban community	Socio-functional integration

perspective most closely parallels the ecological outlook. Even though we have noted several serious weaknesses in this approach, especially its unboundedness, it provides a rationale for examining a wide range of phenomena about our cities. Finally, it alters the nature of the basic question. Instead of asking: What kind of transportation system do we want, it posits a more fundamental question: What kind of city do we want?

2

THE URBAN
TRANSPORTATION SYSTEM
IN RETROSPECT

*Every country in the world faces the danger of being terrorized by
technology.*

Albert Speer, former Nazi official,
at the Nuremberg Trials, 1946

The kind of city we live in today is largely a product of the transportation
system. Housing patterns, land utilization, and employment and commerce
centers are all shaped by the transport system. Even a casual observer can
note the impact of transportation on the design of our metropolitan areas.
As he approaches an urban center, he first sees the isolated subdivisions, the
single-family houses on rather large tracts, the country estates. Suburban
towns imperceptibly blend into one another. Then older houses, the suburbs
of yesterday, appear. Strips of neon signs and commercial centers emerge
and disappear, and gigantic parking lots loom out, inviting the motorist to
stop and pause and—it is hoped—spend some money. Restaurants, motels,
and a whole phalanx of gas stations crowd the route. Stoplights bound out
at the driver in rapid succession until the auto is dwarfed by gigantic buildings and bridges, captured in the shadows of the city. Houses cluster along
newly developed streets, commercial activity tends to be located at major
intersections, and industrial and manufacturing plants are frequently found
at railheads and ports. The location of facilities and their concomitant
activities is influenced by the transportation network.

The rise and fall of cities throughout history and especially in the United
States can also be accounted for largely through changing technology in
transportation. The ghost towns in America today are the result of changing
transportation patterns. As rail transport declined in importance, many

cities that previously enjoyed a certain degree of economic prosperity fell on hard times. Indeed, when rail service was closed down completely, the towns located along the route withered. In contrast, the boom towns of America today are frequently located at the intersections of the major interstate highways. Small, sleepy towns in the hinterland suddenly were converted into major market centers with the development of interstate highways, and the population growth of these boom towns has increased at a staggering rate. The irony of the situation, of course, is that *urban man*—at least by conscious design—had little to do with the development of the city or its decline. Rather, the city dweller, especially in recent times, has been a victim of the technological changes that have been wrought in transportation systems. The purpose of this chapter is to describe how early transportation systems affected the development of American cities and how the automotive system drastically altered the face of the city. We will then briefly examine the major dimensions of the automotive society and review alternative modes of urban transportation. Finally, we will evaluate the consequences and implications of our current transportation system.

SYNTHESIS AND ANTITHESIS IN URBAN TRANSPORTATION

In early America, water transportation served as the primary link between urban centers. The emergence of our early cities illustrates the relationship between transportation and urbanization.[1] Cities along the Atlantic were the first to develop, because as seaports they linked the New World to the Old. But water routes also were of significance in the development of inland cities. River and canal transportation "determined the pattern of settlement, the direction and volume of commerce, and the ease and speed of the occupation of the West."[2] Land transportation, on the other hand, was not only expensive and time-consuming, but nearly impossible at certain times, especially in the winter and spring, when land routes turned to quagmires. River technology, however, was still primitive. Although the sailing schooners that plied the oceans were relatively efficient, they were useless on inland water routes. Barges, flatboats, and keelboats were most frequently used for transportation on inland waterways, but they were slow and unwieldy. Although rivers served as the major water routes, the development of canal routes offered new possibilities for the development of inland cities. The Erie Canal, which connected Lake Erie with the Hudson River in Albany, was completed in 1825, and its success led to the construction of other canals through the Atlantic and Midwestern states. By 1850, the canal system covered some 4,460 miles. The development of the steamboat was a major technological breakthrough. Steamboats exploited the extensive river and canal network[3] and led to the rapid development of cities along these routes, including Cincinnati, Pittsburgh, and St. Louis. As a consequence, the steamboat became the primary mode of transportation and maintained its dominant position until after the Civil War. Although the steamboat served as a primary impetus in the development of inland cities, it was of limited utility, since many areas in the United States were not accessible to water routes.

With the chartering of the Baltimore and Ohio Railroad in 1827, a new transport mode that overcame this limitation was introduced, and the United States embarked on the feverish task of constructing railroads. Many small settlements in the Midwest and West became boomtowns, including Minneapolis, Dallas, Chicago, Fort Worth, Omaha, and Denver, and the competition to build routes to various locations was carried on with embarrassing zeal. Federal, state, and local government added their blessing to this rapid development by offering massive land grants to the railroads as well as cash and credit. In Illinois, more than 2.5 million acres of federal land was given to the state, which in turn passed it on to the Illinois Central Railroad. In all, some 131 million acres of public land were given to the railroads as inducements for developing additional routes. The federal government also provided direct loans to the railroad companies, and local and state governments gave encouragement by providing free land and tax exemptions. Even though government grants added enormous wealth to a small group of railroad barons who exercised tremendous power over the destiny of the United States, the government's generosity spurred the rapid development of new routes. In the first decade after the chartering of the Baltimore and Ohio, more than 2,800 miles of track were laid, but the major development occurred between 1850 and 1900. The 9,000 miles of track in 1850 were expanded to almost 31,000 by 1860, and by 1890, more than 163,000 miles of track were completed.

Water and rail terminals shaped the modern city by providing central locations for industrial and commercial activities. But the internal design of the city also was influenced by other modes of transportation. For the most part, people in the city walked to their places of work. Factories and houses were jammed together, and both workers and managers lived near the factories. For example, Boston—even by 1850—was primarily a "city of pedestrians," and "the area of dense settlement hardly exceeded a two-mile radius from City Hall."[4] As a consequence, cities were characterized by a highly dense and heterogeneous population with factories and housing in close proximity.

There were, of course, a few wealthy people who could afford horse-drawn carriages to move about the city. Still, this type of transportation was highly limited and unavailable to most residents in the city. With the advent of public conveyances, however, the city began to expand at an increasingly rapid rate.[5] The omnibus, a horse-drawn wagon first employed in the 1820's, carried from twelve to twenty passengers, but it was relatively slow. Shortly thereafter, the horse railway was a significant improvement over the omnibus, since it provided for a much smoother and faster ride. The horse car "hastened the expansion of a city's dense, built-up area and acted as a separating agent that allowed middle- and upper-class citizens to move to their own fashionable neighborhoods."[6]

The electric streetcar was the next major innovation in urban transportation, and "acted as an inexorable force in molding American cities."[7] The streetcar, while expanding the city boundaries, served as an integrating mechanism by "creating a focus for a whole city in the central business district."[8] In this sense, the streetcar preserved "the centralized communication of the walking city on a vastly enlarged scale."[9] Even with these major technological improvements in transportation, however, there were still severe problems. In the first place, every major advance in transportation merely made the streets more crowded. Second, the social reformers hoped that the streetcar would open up the suburbs to the poor, but "the poorest remained the least mobile, locked into their ghetto areas."[10]

The demise of the streetcar in many American cities was brought on by two events, First, in their haste to build new streetcar lines and obtain new franchises, the owners borrowed so heavily that they were forced to sacrifice maintenance and service. As a consequence, patrons became exceedingly hostile, and efforts to regulate the franchises further exacerbated the financial situation. Second, the automobile first made its appearance on the scene at the time when the streetcar franchises were in their greatest trouble. As one observer claims, "The Golden Age of electric railways was killed by the automobile. But its demise was hastened by the attitudes and machinations of many owners and managers who acted as if no alternative would ever be found to mass-transportation devices."[11]

The introduction of the streetcar and the commuter train did not materially affect the centripetal forces that gave rise to the city.[12] It is true that the character of the city changed due to the radial lines, and it is likewise true that boundaries of the city could be extended due to these technological advances. Yet, most of the routes were designed to serve the center city, and the location of these lines merely spurred additional growth along the routes. As a consequence, these new transit modes complemented the existing centripetal forces at work.

With the advent of the automobile, however, the centripetal forces which held the city together were shattered. As one author notes,

the automobile did more than simply add additional layers to the streetcar suburbs which already surrounded every city. Unlike the fixed trolley tracks, which almost always led downtown and thus encouraged transit patrons to maintain their economic and social ties with the core, the private car encouraged crosstown or lateral movement and, if anything, discouraged travel to the increasingly traffic-snarled city center.[13]

The effect of the auto on the city is analogous to what astronomers call the big bang theory of the universe. According to this theory, the universe is rapidly expanding due to a tremendous explosion at its core eons ago. The auto served as the triggering device for the "big bang" as far as cities are concerned and has been the major centrifugal force in changing the face of the city. The most notable effect is evident in the changing population patterns, especially the fantastic growth rates of suburban areas. The growth of metropolitan areas in the United States continues even when the major cities are losing population. Between 1960 and 1970, for example, the suburbs in the 230 metropolitan areas increased in population by 25.6 percent. In the 14 largest metropolitan areas, however, the population of central cities declined by 3.1 percent. As the population shifts to the suburbs, manufacturing plants tend to follow. But when plants locate in the suburbs, the suburban dweller can move farther out into the countryside, spawning a new suburban ring. The manufacturing plants follow, giving rise to a new exodus and the further dispersion of the metropolitan area.

The physical face of the city also has been drastically altered. "If some of the present trends are extrapolated further," argues James Johnson, "the city of the future will be one in which the central area is of steadily decreasing importance and . . . the city of the future will be cut through by urban motorways with much more space being devoted to road intersections and parking facilities."[14] In much more dramatic terms, Kenneth Schneider claims that an "aerial photo of any American city center reveals devastation as obvious as that resulting from a London Blitz. Saturation bombing is the only adequate comparison. Hundreds of buildings have been wiped out."[15]

But, surely, some will say, there must be a limit to this expansion. Surely, the big bang will dissipate, and the future suburbanization process will come to a halt. Yet a British scholar sees no end in sight. The big bang is leading to "nothing less than the complete disintegration of the city."[16] He foresees "an ugly and planless dispersal of the population" with the oceans serving as the only immediate barrier.

In sum, we have treated the American city as something to be used, something to be exploited for economic gain. Social and cultural values have been largely ignored. If the downtown is paved over to the detriment of inner city residents, that was a small price to pay for economic development, even though the economic gains usually redounded to only a small segment of the metropolitan population and most frequently to those who lived in the suburbs. Although the impact of the auto on the life of the city will be discussed more fully later, our immediate concern is to trace how we got where we are, and we will briefly examine the rise of our automotive society.

THE AUTOMOTIVE SOCIETY

When Henry Ford designed the assembly-line process, it was considered a major breakthrough for the production of automobiles.[17] The only problem with assembly lines, however, is that they do not stop; almost 10,000 cars are produced every day by American auto manufacturers. At the turn of the century, there were some 8,000 motor vehicles registered in the United States. By 1940, there were 32 million, and it is estimated that there are some 118 million registered vehicles today.[18] To look at this pattern from another perspective, one can examine the ratio of cars to people. At the turn of the century, there was one private automobile for every 10,000 people. In 1930 it was one for every 5.3 people, and even with the depression, it dropped to one for every 4.8 by 1940. Today, there is one private car for every 2.3 persons. While the United States is approaching a zero population growth for people, the birth of the automobile is going on at an astounding rate. In the 1960's, for example, the United States gained some 23 million people, but it added 31 million motor vehicles to the public roads. Some 80 percent of American families now own a car, and some 18.5 million have two or more cars. In certain regions of the United States, car ownership is even higher. In San Jose, California, for example, 91 percent of families own one car, and more than 33 percent own two or more. For moving people in metropolitan areas of the United States, the private auto is unchallenged. Some 80 percent of all work trips are made by the automobile in metropolitan areas, and 96 percent of suburban dwellers use the private auto to get to work. In addition, the auto accounts for more than 85 percent of recreational and shopping trips, and the nonwork trips by the auto exceed the work trips on a two-to-one basis. In 1970 alone, it is estimated that United States motorists drove 1,125 billion miles or the equivalent of 4.5 million trips to the moon.

To accommodate the burgeoning of the auto, there are some 3.8 million miles of roads in the United States. In 1921, for example, only 447,000 miles of road were classified as "improved." By 1965, 2,776,000 miles were classified as improved. To counter the argument that highway builders are concretizing America, the engineers argue that there is very little difference between total highway mileage today and fifty years ago. The former federal highway administrator argued that "most of the investment in highways during the last half-century or so has been made not so much for new routes but for improving the existing system."[19] If one considers only linear miles, there is some validity to the claim. But the highway today is a voracious consumer of land. The interstate expressway, for example, uses about 43 acres per mile compared with less than half an acre per mile for the road of 1916.

It is well established by now that the construction and expansion of highways merely stimulates greater use. The argument that we need more roads because of the increase in cars is a never-ending and self-fulfilling proposition. When Congress authorized the interstate system in 1955, there were about 18.5 cars for every mile of United States roads. By 1970, the ratio had increased to about 30 cars per mile, and even with the continual expansion of expressways the ratio is expected to reach 50 vehicles per mile by 1990. In her book, Helen Leavitt provides us with a variation of Parkinson's Law with the proposition that automobile traffic will increase to the maximum limit of road accommodation. As an example of this phenomenon, she cites the New Jersey Turnpike, which was constructed to relieve traffic on U.S. Highway 1. After completion of the turnpike, traffic increased by 5 percent, and the turnpike carried as much traffic as Highway 1 within three years after it was completed.[20] The Hollywood Freeway in Los Angeles is another prime example. With designers predicting that the freeway would carry an ultimate volume of 100,000 vehicles per day, the traffic count exactly one year after it opened was 168,000.

This lemming-like rush into the auto age has not been without its direct costs. Public highway expenditures in 1921 totaled a little more than $1 billion. By 1955, a year before the interstate system was legislated by Congress, annual expenditures were still a rather modest $7 billion. Within ten years, however, expenditures almost doubled to $14,232,000,000,[21] and by 1970 more than $21.5 billion was expended for roads and highways. In other words, it took ten years for expenditures to increase by $7 billion between 1955 and 1965, but it took only five years for them to increase by the same amount between 1965 and 1970.

The per capita costs for this tremendous increase in highway expenditures are approximately $105 per year. But the burden on the consumer for building highways in comparison with other auto costs is quite small. In 1970, for example, almost $78 billion was expended by consumers on transportation, or approximately 12.6 percent of their income.[22] Most of this expenditure went for the private auto, and only 7.1 cents out of every transportation dollar went for some other mode of travel. In 1970 alone some $72.4 billion was expended by consumers on the auto, accounting for 92.9 percent of the total expenditures by consumers for transportation. Personal expenditures for other forms of local transportation accounted for only $2.5 billion or 3.2 percent. The consumer also spent about $3 billion on intercity transportation, or about 3.9 percent of the total transportation bill.

Thus, urban transportation is locked into a one-dimensional transportation system, an auto-oriented system laden with ominous signs for the city.[23] The consumer is viewed by many as the culprit behind the scenes. After all, in a free market, the consumer is merely expressing his preference for the auto, and few have been willing to suggest that his choice be restricted in this matter. When the economist talks about consumer preference, however, it is implicit that there are several options available. Although we will return to this point later, it should be noted that in essence the consumer has no choice in the matter. It hardly seems surprising, then, that in a society with a single transportation system the consumer would opt for the automobile. Although city planners have long pleaded for a more "balanced" transportation system—one which affords options for the consumer and fosters a more viable development of the urban community—the prospects appear bleak.

THE OPTIONS IN URBAN TRANSPORTATION

For the urban planner, public transportation, especially rapid transit, is ordained as the great savior of the city. There is seldom a conference on transportation today in which some form of mass transportation is not ardently advocated. When the federal government established the Department of Transportation, it even recognized the importance of mass transportation. It created the Urban Mass Transportation Administration (UMTA) and gave it equal organizational status to the Federal Highway Administration. When we examine the transportation trends in the United States, however, there is little evidence to suggest that exhortation and organizational changes have accomplished much for public transportation. Table 2-1 indicates the level of motor vehicle registrations and transit riders since 1950. These data make abundantly clear that there is an inverse correlation between automobile registration and transit ridership. While automobile registration more than doubled in the past two decades, transit ridership declined by more than half. This raises a serious question concerning the possibility of achieving any kind of balanced transportation system so long as the growth of the automobile remains unchecked.

In general, there have been two types of public transportation in metropolitan areas—fixed rail, and bus and taxi. Fixed rail includes such modes as the commuter railroad, rapid transit, and the streetcar. The commuter railroad, in contrast to rapid transit, is a multipurpose carrier in that it operates on the same tracks as intercity rail traffic. The commuter train is characterized by high speeds and a high passenger-carrying capacity. One reason it can operate at high speed is that stations are widely spaced.Like other public transportation systems, however, the commuter railroad has suffered a marked decline in many metropolitan areas. In 1935, forty-one

TABLE 2-1

Auto Registration and Transit Ridership
(1950=100)

Year	Registered Motor Vehicles	Transit Riders
1950	100.0	100.0
1955	127.4	66.4
1960	150.2	54.3
1965	183.7	49.1
1970	221.5	42.8

Adapted from Wilfred Owen, *The Accessible City* (Washington: Brookings Institution, 1972), p. 5.

of the larger metropolitan areas had rail commuter service, with 240 separate routes. By 1960, only twenty of these same metropolitan areas had commuter service, and the number of routes declined to 83.[24] Yet, the commuter railroad generally carries passengers from outlying areas to the center city, while rapid transit more frequently operates within the confines of the central city. More recent rapid transit lines, however, reach out into the suburbs. For example, the Bay Area Rapid Transit system (BART) extends out to the suburbs in the San Francisco–Oakland metropolitan region, and indeed most of the stations in the BART system are located in the suburban areas rather than the central city.

In recent years, there has been renewed interest in the development of rapid transit systems for metropolitan areas. One of the principal arguments by the proponents of rapid transit is its tremendous passenger-carrying capability, and it is frequently argued that rapid transit can carry 60,000 passengers per hour, or approximately the same number as twenty lanes of freeway. Yet rapid transit is operational in only six major cities in the United States, Boston, New York, Philadelphia, Cleveland, Chicago, and

San Francisco. New rapid transit systems are under construction only in South Jersey and Washington, D.C.

Only in New York, however, does passenger volume exceed 40,000 per hour per track. (On occasion during peak hours and on the most heavily traveled express routes it exceeds the 60,000 figure.) None of the other rapid transit systems comes close to these figures. For example, on the Congress Street run in Chicago, the passenger-carrying volume at peak hour slightly exceeds 10,000, and on the Cleveland subway it exceeds 6,000 during peak hours. Even the new BART system, with sixty-five seat cars and ten-car trains, reaches only 30,000 passengers per hour. Although the claims for moving passengers on rapid transit might be greatly exaggerated, the fact remains that these systems have the capability for moving great numbers of passengers, and for the most part this has been accomplished with rather outmoded equipment.

Of the three fixed-route public transportation systems, the streetcar and trolley have virtually disappeared from American cities. At its height in 1920, the streetcar carried some 13.7 billion passengers per year, and even through World War II it carried almost 10 billion passengers per year. But the end of World War II signaled the demise of the streetcar. By 1950 passengers carried by streetcars declined to slightly under 4 billion, and by 1970 only 200 million passengers rode the streetcar. The trolley has been of less significance in transporting passengers. It reached its zenith in 1950 with 1.7 billion passengers, but trailed off to the same passenger-carrying level as the streetcar by 1970.

The other forms of public transportation in metropolitan areas are the bus and the taxi. Both, of course, are outgrowths of the auto age and share the same right-of-way as the private automobile. One of the major advantages of the bus is flexibility in changing route patterns. Furthermore, the bus is characterized by a high passenger-carrying volume. On ordinary city streets, a single lane can accommodate from about 150 to 175 buses per hour and can carry from 7,500 to 9,000 passengers. With exclusive lanes, of course, the number of buses can be greatly increased. Nevertheless, bus transportation in the United States has also declined, though the decline has not been as dramatic as that for other modes. In 1949, buses carried some 10 billion passengers, but by 1970 that figure had been cut in half.

Although the taxi is a common form of public transportation in most American cities, data concerning usage are rather meager. Taxis offer the consumer almost the same degree of flexibility as the private auto, but fares are generally high. Although high-income groups use taxis quite frequently, they are often a necessity for low-income groups who are without a private automobile. In New York City, for example, more than 900,000 people per day ride the taxi.

There are, of course, other forms of transportation available to the urban dweller, but most transportation experts ignore them. Walking as a mode of transportation is seldom considered—which might seem strange, since it served as the principal form of transportation at one time. Yet, today walking is a rather dangerous pursuit. In many areas, no sidewalks are provided, and the walker takes his life in his hands on any extended trip. Indeed, "the right of the pedestrian to the use of public ways has been protected throughout recorded history until the development of the automobile."[25] Another form cf transportation and one quite common in many urban areas throughout the world is the bicycle. Again, however, rights-of-way have seldom been provided for the cyclist. Indeed, on the interstate system the cyclist is banned.[26]

The trends in public transportation offer bleak hopes for resurrecting a viable urban transportation system. Since 1945, surface and rapid transit passengers declined from about 24 billion to under 8 billion in 1970. As public transit revenues plummeted, fares increased and service depreciated. Even with this rather discouraging picture, Wilfred Owen argues that "transit trends are about to be reversed."[27] As evidence, he points to the recent construction of rapid transit systems. Only 16 miles of routes were completed in the twenty-five year period following World War II, but between 1970 and 1975, some 76 miles of subway routes are expected to be finished, and for the period 1976 to 1990, another 91 miles are projected. In addition, he notes, many systems have started modernization programs. Moreover, the Urban Mass Transportation Assistance Act authorized $10 billion in aid for public transportation. Extensive research on new concepts in public transportation has been undertaken, and the UMTA has funded a variety of demonstration projects with several catchy names, such as the airmobile, the aerotrain, tubeflight, and the minimonorail. Even in view of these programs, however, it seems somewhat premature to suggest that a major shift in urban transportation is under way. The evidence on this point is not yet in, and what evidence there is fails to sustain an optimistic posture.

TRANSPORTATION AS A SYSTEM

Up until this point, we have been talking about urban transportation as a system without specifying the meaning or the implications. A system can be defined as "a set of parts coordinated to accomplish a set of goals."[28] In this chapter, we have briefly examined the two major components of the urban transportation system, namely, private auto transportation and public transportation. Based on this brief survey, it seems clear that the parts are totally uncoordinated, that one major part has atrophied, and that the urban community is now completely dependent on one form of transportation.

For the systems theorist, "requisite variety" is a fundamental character-istic of a viable and healthy system. Variety in this context means that there are several independent mechanisms available to the system for achieving its objectives. When a system—be it a biological system, an ecological system, or a functional system, such as transportation—lacks variety, when it depends on a single mechanism to achieve its goals, the chances of calamity are greatly increased.

Examples of this threat can be drawn from several sources. If a farmer plants a single strain of wheat, a disease to which this strain is susceptible might completely wipe out his crop. Forests in which there is only one kind of tree are much more vulnerable to extinction than forests in which there are various species.

Variety serves several functions in a society. For the economist, a market in which the consumer can exercise various options will result in a healthy economy. For this reason the classical economist views monopoly as a threat. In a democratic society, variety is also viewed as a major value. There are some who would claim that democracy operates in a society in which the citizen has the right to cast a vote. But if the citizen has no choice when he casts his vote, then voting becomes a meaningless exercise. Even totalitarian systems of government have frequently extended suffrage to citizens.

In conclusion, the urban transportation system qua system is out of balance. For the moment, we are not talking about the external consequences of this system. Rather, our concern is merely with evaluating the implica-tions of a one-dimensional transportation system. For many people in the past, the terrifying thing about the automobile was the spectre that increas-ing congestion would result in the total immobilization of the city. As we noted earlier, however, this prospect seems unlikely. But in an age in which urban America has put its complete and total faith in auto transportation, a more terrifying picture is one in which millions of autos will sit idle, when the wide streets of the city are barren. This prospect may not be too far off, and it won't be that man is trapped in his auto but that he is trapped without it.

3

PUBLIC POLICY AND
URBAN TRANSPORTATION

Politics can be defined as the "authoritative allocation of [societal] values."[1] As with any good definition, the first task is to define the operational terms. *Authoritative* generally refers to those values legitimated by government action, usually through the promulgation of some written document, such as a legislative act or a presidential proclamation. *Allocation* implies some distributive formula, though it in no way indicates that all "values" are equally distributed or given comparable standing in the community. Indeed, the attainment of certain values will necessarily result in the negation of other values. Consequently, politics and political controversy revolve around the question of which values will receive governmental sanction.

In this chapter we will first explore the kinds of explicit and implicit values in the development of urban transportation policy. To provide an overview of the various perspectives employed in the analysis of public policy, we will next summarize some of the major models. Then, we will explore the fiscal and legislative policies which have fostered the kind of urban transportation system we have today. Because of the diversity of state and municipal laws regarding transportation, we will not attempt any analysis here, although certain aspects of these policies are contained in subsequent chapters. Finally, we will summarize the major thrust of urban transportation policy.

VALUES AND POLITICS

The term *value* means some goal, some standard to which people subscribe. The debate and controversy surrounding America's involvement in the Vietnam War provides an illustration. The guiding values of the proponents were national security, treaty obligations, national honor, and international stability. Those of the opponents were humanistic: the sanctity of life and a repugnance for needless killing and destruction. Public laws, of course, are the manifestation of current political values. But what have been the values either explicitly or implicitly involved in transportation policy? There are several obvious and tangible values in the promulgation of transportation policy: for instance, the desire for mobility. Mobility provides individual opportunity for work and play and for the development of an extensive commercial network. A corollary value, especially evident in much of the early legislation concerning government involvement in transportation, was the "opening of the West." Although America was blessed with enormous resources, these resources were of little use unless they could be transported to the marketplace. After World War II, transportation became an end in itself, a value requiring protection. The auto industries, the petroleum industries, and related economic corporations were depicted as the backbone of the American economy. Public policy, it was argued, must in no way diminish these activities, for to do so would create serious unemployment and eventually ruin the American economy. Finally, individual freedom could be greatly enhanced through public policies encouraging transportation growth, especially the growth of automobile use, since the car, more than any other mode of transportation, epitomized the notion of individual freedom.

Since politics involves value conflicts, our auto-oriented legislation reflects a bias against nonautomobile values. There are many, for example, who view the city as an end in itself, as an intrinsic value in modern society. In addition to its marketplace activities, the city represents the richness of a society in terms of culture, art, and diversity. To diminish the value of cities qua cities undermines the greatest achievements of man and degrades the environment in which the highest aspirations of mankind can be fulfilled. Yet as already indicated in the previous chapter, the vitality of cities has been sapped by the centrifugal forces of our current transportation policies. As diversified places, cities also contain many subsettlements, the neighborhoods. These neighborhoods provide identity and meaning to the residents and are thus seen as another important value associated with cities. Yet, in many cases, our federal and state transportation policies have totally negated the value of neighborhood integrity. When a highway goes through a neighborhood, costs are calculated only on the basis of land purchase and relocation expenses. The intangible costs of destroying a group's identity and life-style are impossible to estimate. A third value, which reaches beyond city limits, is the preservation of our environment. Air, water, and land are important components of life, components that should be protected by public policies. It is this value that clashes most directly with the economic growth value. Public policies promoting the quality of the environment tend to impinge upon the auto industry, especially the requirement for exhaust emission control devices. As yet, there is no clear indication as to which value will prevail, though environmental values are under severe attack as a consequence of the energy crisis. The final value implied by debates over transportation policy, especially policies fostering public transportation, is democracy. Freedom is to the pro-auto advocates what democracy is to the pro-public transit advocates. While the pro-public transit advocates acknowledge that transportation provides mobility and opportunities, they subscribe to the belief that it should provide opportunities for *all* and that one's inability to buy an automobile should not serve as a barrier to full participation in a democratic society. In conclusion, these values serve as the benchmarks for debates over transportation policy; they provide the "political" setting for understanding transportation policies. If politics is indeed concerned with the allocation of values, then the foregoing overview provides us with a kind of scorecard; now by examining transportation policy, we can tell the "winners" from the "losers."

APPROACHES TO PUBLIC POLICY

Public policy can be analyzed from a variety of perspectives. Except for one, each of the following approaches has its own biases. Advocates of specific viewpoints argue that their perspective not only serves as a sound empirical base for the analysis of public policy but that it also accords with "democratic government." The seven different approaches described below are the legal-institutional approach, the group-theory approach, the elitist approach, the organizational approach, the rationalist approach, the incremental approach, and finally the systems approach.[2] These approaches are not necessarily discrete or mutually exclusive; yet each emphasizes a different perspective.

1. THE LEGAL-INSTITUTIONAL APPROACH

Until the 1920's almost all analyses of public policy were made in the framework of the legal-institutional approach. Although certain constitutional provisions, especially the "separation of powers" concept, provided a normative base, these studies were primarily descriptive. Law making was viewed almost as a technique, and the most interesting question for the legal-institutional scholars was whether the law accorded with the Constitution. Furthermore, these early scholars were interested in questions concerning the fine balance between the executive, the legislature, and the judiciary. Thus, the government was viewed as a machine. How it decided on which policies to enact or what impact these policies had on American society were of little importance. What was of great importance was how well the machine ran.

2. THE GROUP THEORY OF POLITICS

By 1935, Arthur F. Bentley had already developed a group theory of politics.[3] But his perspective had little effect on the long-entrenched legal-political approach. Not until the 1950's, with the publication of David B. Truman's *The Governmental Process*,[4] was the concept of group theory given the blessing of political scientists. Instead of focusing on governmental institutions, group theory concentrates on contending forces in society that make claims or demands upon government. The rather sterile notion of government as depicted in the legal-institutional literature is still retained, except that government's role is more clearly defined as an arbiter. Since group claims are often in conflict, the task of government is to arbitrate them and negotiate compromises. These compromises are then legitimated through the enactment of laws. The final "governmental process" is then to enforce these compromises and to fill in the gaps through the judicial process.

Public policy, then, is viewed as a dynamic equilibrium between groups. If the group theory serves as an empirical theory for explaining what actually happens, it certainly appears to be suspect on normative grounds. In this framework, what would prevent powerful groups from overwhelming small or minority groups? The group theorists respond by claiming that group dynamics does not mean the end of minority rights. Instead group theory provides a model for an ideal democracy. They admit that there are indeed visible groups vying for political favors; but there is also a large "latent" group, a "silent majority" that subscribes to the basic values of American society, including fair play and constitutionalism. Second, they argue that Americans are inveterate "joiners," that many of us belong to several groups, and that in many cases the values of these groups are in conflict. In other words, no group can command the total and complete allegiance of its membership. As a consequence, each group must be moderate in its claims, and intra-group compromises will compel each group to act responsibly. Finally, even if a group becomes abusive and disregards completely the public interest, countervailing groups will arise, and these groups in coalition with others will offset the power of any individual group.

3. THE ELITE THEORY

A third approach, which has its roots in sociology, is called elite theory; its disciplinary derivation is "stratification theory." This theory views society as a pyramid with a small group of "elites" at the pinnacle; instead of multiple groups in society vying for power, there is a single group. Public policy does not reflect the values of the masses, but rather the values of the elites. The elites stand above the governmental structure and manipulate it for their ends; thus policies flow downward. By their very nature, elites tend to be conservative, with the preservation of the system their paramount concern. Consequently, changes in policy will be incremental rather than revolutionary. Although elites seek to preserve their system, this does not necessarily mean that they totally ignore the interests of the masses. Indeed, some elites may advocate welfare and other visible policies that are in the interests of the masses. But their interest in the masses is primarily paternalistic, and their welfare policies are primarily aimed at appeasement. In this sense, they recognize the *latent* power of the masses and will respond to it through co-optation.

4. THE ORGANIZATION THEORY

While advocates of the previous three approaches all view public policy from a macroscopic perspective, organization theory takes a microscopic perspective. Like the group theory of politics, organization theory sees a variety of groups; but in this case, governmental agencies operate with the intent of delivering some governmental service, whether it be education, police protection, or health care. For most citizens, the major policy decisions are of little importance since they are mainly affected by the "street-level bureaucrats," those governmental employees who directly interact with the individual citizen.[5] Instead of examining policy formation at the national level, organization theorists are concerned with its implementation, with its direct impact on citizens. Organizational theorists contend that it is not the policy per se that needs to be restructured, but the institutional framework for delivery. Organizational theorists argue that in terms of public policy, government agencies should echo Pogo's "We have found the enemy and they is us!"

Bureaucratic characteristics, such as hierarchy, extensive rules and procedures, and professionalism are viewed as the critical problems. They undermine the delivery of public services and thus subvert the original intent of the policy. Because the bureaucracy is interested in maintaining its own position, it has become insensitive to the needs of its clients. What is needed is an abureaucratic, dialectical organization that meets the needs of its clients.[6]

5. RATIONALISM

The rationalist holds that political values can be rationally planned and formulated; it is implicit in the ecological approach discussed in the first chapter. What the rationalist would have us do is first identify the major value preferences of society with some type of weighting. To illustrate this first step, we might take those values related to transportation discussed in the first part of this chapter, though the rationalist would have us consider a much broader list of values. In this process, we would first have to determine the extent to which society values mobility, freedom, economic growth, the environment, cities and neighborhoods, and equality, and then give each of these values a weight. The next step in the rationalist model is to define all possible policy alternatives to achieve these values. For example, one alternative might be a transportation system consisting solely of private automobiles; another alternative might be to have some kind of mix between private and public transportation; and a third might be to have a complete public transportation system. The next step is to forecast the consequences of each of these policy alternatives, especially as each relates to our value preferences, and to determine the ratio between the achieved and the sacrificed values for each policy alternative. The final step is the selection of the policy alternative that maximizes our range of value preferences.[7]

One can immediately see the difficulties of this approach, especially since this example represents an oversimplification of the process. If we included the value preferences in other policy areas, such as education, housing, and health, we would have to determine the impact of each alternative in each policy area on the entire range of values. Therefore it is not surprising that there have been critics who argue that this model is highly impractical. How does one measure *societal* values and how can weights be assigned? How can an official or an expert possibly anticipate all the consequences caused by any policy alternative, especially given our limited base of knowledge on a wide range of problems? Until these and other questions can be adequately answered, the rationalist model, according to the critics, offers little hope for formulating public policies.

6. INCREMENTALISM

If rationalism represents a grand scheme for formulating governmental policy, incrementalism stands at the opposite end of the spectrum. Indeed, incrementalists believe that our knowledge base is limited and that politics is not a rational process. What actually happens, they argue, is that public policy is a continuation of past policies with only minor modifications.[8] Instead of considering a comprehensive set of alternatives, incrementalists focus on a limited set of alternatives, and even these alternatives represent only minimal deviations from past policies. Today's policy is only slightly different from yesterday's and tomorrow's. Given the enormous number of public programs, it is inconceivable that the policy maker could adequately review each and every one; rather, the policy maker tends to accept previous policies and devotes most of his attention to new programs. Even though incremental policy making is highly conservative in its orientation, its advocates argue that there are several advantages. First, by making only minor modifications in policies, no serious damage will occur if forecasts are incorrect; it is fairly easy to retreat. Second, if we abandon one program in favor of another, we might be faced with disaster. If the new program fails, we have no fallback position.

The critics of incrementalism view this model with disdain and offer three major objections.[9] First, they argue that such a policy-making process is suicidal. Because of the enormous problems facing America, the gap between our politics and our problems is widening: incremental policy making cannot deal with this gap. Second, they criticize the incrementalists's injunction against "putting all our eggs in one basket." If we retain a past policy merely to provide a fallback position, we can never adequately develop or fund any new programs. Finally, incrementalism is not only irrational but antirational, according to the critics. If new knowledge is discovered that would yield new, innovative policies, it is absurd to ignore this knowledge, to proceed on a course of action merely because it is similar to past policies.

7. SYSTEMS THEORY

The most popular model employed by policy analysts today is systems theory. There are several dimensions to this approach, including inputs, outputs, the system, feedback, and the environment (see Figure 3-1).[10] The inputs are demands and supports that are transmitted to the system; the system includes those structures and processes through which authoritative decisions are made, such as the legislature, the judiciary, and the executive. The inputs are converted into outputs by the system, and, depending on the impact of these decisions, feedback occurs, generating new inputs. Systems theory, then, subsumes several characteristics noted in the previous models. For example, the environment and input dimensions of systems theory are related to the group theory of politics; the decision-making system is related to the legal-institutional model. Since systems theory also includes feedback as an essential component, it is also related to incrementalism. At the same time, systems theory purports to be a rational approach, since it comprehends a wide spectrum of variables.

Figure 3-1.
The Systems Theory Model.

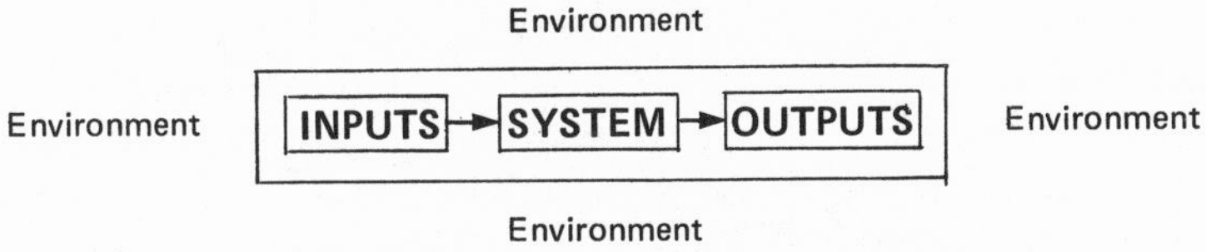

Environment

Environment | INPUTS → SYSTEM → OUTPUTS | Environment

Environment

Although it is a popular model employed by many political scientists, there have been several major criticisms of systems theory. While it may provide a taxonomic framework for understanding the political process, critics complain that it is exceedingly difficult to make the major concepts operational.[11] Many types of political behavior do not fit neatly into one of the categories. Yehezkel Dror lists the weaknesses of contemporary systems analysis studies related to transportation as follows:

Preoccupation with "mix-of-modes" issues and with satisfaction of extrapolated consumer demands, within a cost-benefit framework. Some attention to pollution effects, especially when susceptible to translation into economic values. Ignorance of changes in the values to be served by future transportation, such as transportation tastes, aesthetic feelings, new patterns of leisure use. Neglect of transportation impacts on community life and social interaction. Ignorance of possible positive functions of inadequate transportation. Ignorance of political and power implications of transportation. Inadequate treatment of interfaces between transportation and communication, housing and various aspects of the patterning of human activities in space.[12]

Still, the analysts who apply the theory, not the theory itself, are often at fault. In this book we draw heavily on the systems approach, but we have attempted to incorporate the major social variables which account for our current transportation policy. Furthermore, we will attempt later to show how transportation has impacts on other processes in our urban society. Thus far, however, we have surveyed the major values of urban transportation and have summarized several perspectives for analyzing public policy. With this background, we can now turn our attention to our transportation policies. The next section analyzes the broad outlines of legislative fiscal policy, stressing the financing and finance mechanisms employed, and the role of subsidies. The subsequent section details the historical stages of urban transportation legislation, closing with a summary of the current status of legislation.

LEGISLATIVE FISCAL POLICY

Legislation and fiscal policy are manifestations of the same process. Legislation is ordinarily effected through appropriations. Hence the main directions and the amount of the appropriations are important. But equally important are the various ways in which funds are provided as well as the

TABLE 3-1

Size and Distribution of Federal Appropriations for
Transportation, 1955–1975

Agency or Program	1955	1960	1965	1970	1972	1975*
Department of Transportation			*(millions of dollars)*			
Highway	636	2,978	4,069	4,507	4,923	5,020
Aviation	122	508	756	1,223	1,834	2,120
Railroad	2	3	3	17	57	267
Coast Guard	190	238	367	588	661	903
Urban mass transit	0	0	11	106	327	1,351
Other	0	0	23	−8	22	6
Offsetting receipts	0	0	−20	−16	−19	−
Subtotal	950	3,727	5,209	6,417	7,805	9,667
Other agencies	342	539	818	715	986	1,153
Total	1,292	4,266	6,027	7,168	8,791	10,820

*Already made or planned

Source: *Setting National Priorities, The 1972 Budget* (Washington, D.C.: Brookings Institution), p. 260, and U.S.D.O.T., *A Progress Report on National Transportation Policy,* May 1974, pp. 38–40.

strictures or guidelines placed on the way they may be spent. The resulting amalgam of legislation, appropriations, financing mechanisms, restrictions, and program impact is what constitutes legislative fiscal policy. Table 3-1 illustrates the priorities of the federal government's commitment to different transport modes from 1955 to 1975. In 1970, almost two-thirds of all federal outlays for transportation were for highways. Even more significantly, if aviation, the Coast Guard and "other agencies" were eliminated, leaving only ground transportation, 93 percent of all 1972 federal expenditures went for highways. The 7 percent for other modes of ground transport in 1972 had only reached that level as a result of tripling the allocation to urban mass transit. This was principally due to the Urban Mass Transportation Assistance Act of 1970. In 1970, 98 percent of all federal outlays for ground transport had gone for highways; in 1960 almost 100 percent. The comparison with 1955, when less than 50 percent of total outlays was for highways, highlights the impact of the Federal Aid Highway Act of 1956, which increased federal aid to highways by more than five times in the decade from 1955 to 1965. By 1975, three-fourths of all planned federal expenditures for ground transport were still for roads. While the share for mass transit and railroads increased, the absolute dollar amount for highways also continued to rise. The result so far is not a lessening of the commitment to highways, but rather an expansion of total outlays for transportation, with about 60 percent of the net increase going to mass transit. Another feature of the mass transit component is that a large share of these expenditures will be for buses and transit operating subsidies. As noted in Chapter 1, in some ways buses are not really alternatives to auto transportation. They require the same roadways and suffer many of the same environmental, urban design, and aesthetic handicaps associated with the automobile. They are appendages to the auto/highway system.

The shift from slightly more than $100 million for mass transit in 1970 to $1.3 billion in 1975 has come about principally as the result of two new laws and the amendment of the original Federal Highway Act. The 1973 Federal Aid Highway Act, discussed in greater detail later in this chapter, authorized an additional $200 million for mass transit (buses) to be diverted from the Highway Trust Fund for 1975 and $800 million for 1976. And in late 1974 the Federal Mass Transportation Act became law, authorizing $11.9 billion over a six-year period for mass transit, including operating subsidies for existing systems. At an average of a little under $2 billion per year, this still would leave mass transit well behind the automatic flow of funds for highways. In addition, since there is no mass transit trust fund, there is no assurance that the authorized sums will actually be appropriated. It is a beginning, but only time will tell if the shift represents a sustained policy change.

Some of the main sources of transportation finance and the uses for which these funds are intended are depicted in Table 3.2. Where the money for transportation finances comes from and how it is distributed are matters of considerable importance to understanding the flow of funds for transportation. The Federal Highway Trust Fund accounts for about one-third of road building in the United States annually; states and local

TABLE 3-2

Transportation Finance: Sources and Amounts

Sources and Program	Approximate Yearly Total	Use
FEDERAL HIGHWAY PROGRAM The Trust Fund (1956 Highway Act and subsequent updating)	RATES OF USER TAX 6¢ / gal. gasoline 10¢ / lb. tire and tube rubber 5¢ / lb. retread rubber $3 / 1,000 lb./yr. heavy vehicle use tax 6¢ / gal. lubricating oil 8% of mfg. sale price of truck and bus parts and accessory sales 10% of mfg. sales, buses and trailers	Highway Construction Activities
	$6 billion 90:10 matching*	
URBAN TRANSIT ASSISTANCE General revenue: income tax, excise tax, investments, etc.		
Grants and Aid:		
1961 Housing Act		Coordination of transportation programs.
a. Urban planning assistance in technical assistance to state and local governments for planning, studies, and publication of findings	$25 million (total)	
b. Demonstration grants: 2/3 matching, not long-term capital improvements	$50 million (total)	
c. Loan programs: Low interest, for acquisition, construction, reconstruction of mass transit facilities and equipment, private or publicly owned (comprehensive plan must exist or be in preparation).	($47.5 million was appropriated by Congress)	(continued)

*Formula was the same as the 1944 act: 45% for primary roads; 30% secondary; 25% for extensions in urban areas. Federal amount: 90% of bills.

TABLE 3-2 (continued)

Sources and Program	Approximate Yearly Total	Use
1964 Urban Mass Transportation Act a. Federal financial assistance	$375 million	To improve existing systems
b. Long-range program (2/3 matching; 1/3 if no comprehensive plan locally)		
c. Emergency program		
d. Research and development, and development projects (development of mass transit systems that will not contribute to air pollution)		
e. Relocation requirements and payments		
f. Additional grants for (1) unified urban transportation system planning (2) managerial training (3) higher education research	$10 million over 12-year period	For bus and subway systems
RECENT LEGISLATION a. Urban Mass Transportation Assistance Act of 1970, 1973	$3.1 billion for grants over 5 years	Long-range planning for projects; aid to public systems for capital improvements
b. Rail Passenger Service Act of 1970, 1972, 1973		Created the National Rail Passenger Service Corp. to provide optimum passenger service over a basic route structure determined by the secretary of transportation.

(continued)

TABLE 3-2 (continued)

Sources and Program	Approximate Yearly Total	Use
c. Federal Aid Highway Act of 1973	$1.0 billion over 2 years to be diverted from Highway Trust Fund	Purchase of buses
d. Federal Mass Transportation Assistance Act of 1974	$11.9 billion over 6 years	Capital outlays for new facilities and equipment; operating subsidies

REVENUE SHARING (Public Safety
—not for matching—to cities)
MISCELLANEOUS SUBSIDIES AND/OR
SPECIAL TREATMENT—Source and
amount often hidden)
    Low interest rates on loans
    Preferential tax treatment
    (e.g., oil depletion allowances,
    exempting bonds, etc.)

STATE AND LOCAL FINANCING

Sources and Program	Approximate Yearly Total	Use
Trust Fund (Highway Department) 5¢ gal. gasoline tax (similar to federal user tax arrangement)		Matching money for highway construction and maintenance
Streets and roads and public/ mass transit programs		General Revenue Property tax, sales tax, licensing, fines, fees, etc.
Loans and/or Bond Issuances	General Revenue	Local needs and/ or matching monies
TOTAL STATE AND LOCAL TRANSPORTATION PER YEAR	$12 billion	

governments provide the remaining two-thirds. State and local monies go heavily into maintenance; federal funds are generally for new construction.[13]

Until 1974, legislation shaped by the automotive interests (discussed in greater detail in Chapter 4) had federal finances for transportation strait-jacketed. There were virtually no options to encourage other types of transportation, nor was there any legal authority to use revenue generated for the Highway Trust Fund for other purposes. Even where extensive evaluation and planning by local and regional authorities documented the need for funds for other uses (as was frequently the case), the government's role was fixed by the terms of the Trust Fund's monopoly of revenues. Where meager sums were authorized for mass transit, as in the 1964 Urban Mass Transportation Assistance Act, the two-thirds matching as compared with the 90 percent matching formula for highway funds still placed mass transit at a formidable disadvantage. Until 1970, the federal funds could be used only for new construction, even where older thorough-fares could be modernized or repaired. But the cost to the state or local government for repairs or modernization could quite possibly exceed the 10 percent match required to get a new road. The result: poor quality, ill-repaired secondary arteries and expensive, gleaming new freeway ribbons cutting through the cities.

THE HIGHWAY TRUST FUND

Because extensive documentation of the Highway Trust Fund has appeared in numerous publications over the last few years, the following will provide only a summary of its main features.[14] The fund was created by the Federal Aid Highway Act of 1956. Originally it was supposed to terminate on September 30, 1972, but it has been extended through 1977.

The fund earmarks the revenue collected on those items indicated in Table 3-2 for the exclusive use of the Federal Highway Administration (Bureau of Public Roads) for the construction of the Interstate System and the ABC roads. The latter are (1) roads connecting market centers to urban areas; (2) roads connecting farm to market centers; and (3) an urban fund for the extension of ABC roads into population centers of more than 5,000. The internal distribution of ABC funds each year much be in a ratio of 45%, 30%, and 25% respectively for these three uses. The geographic distribution of ABC funds by states is based on population, area, and mile-age. The ABC roads have received roughly 20 percent of the estimated $70 billion expended from the fund through 1974. The distribution of inter-state funds is based on each state's "need." Need is determined in relation to the cost of completion of the entire Interstate System and the estimated cost of a particular state's share of that cost. Fifty percent of the costs of ABC projects funded must be borne by the states, whereas the federal share for interstate roads is the previously noted 90 percent.

One of the original arguments for the establishment of the trust fund was to insure continuity of funding. It was designed to insulate the highway program from congressional whims and the vagaries of year-to-year appropriations. While it cannot be denied that the fund achieved these goals, it is also true that the fund became immune to the ordinary accountability demanded of most governmental programs. As national needs changed, transportation funding became unresponsive to the demand for alternate forms of transit, and in some cases even unresponsive to serious environmental and social impacts of the highway program.

From an economic point of view, one of the most serious problems associated with financing roads through the mechanism of the trust fund is the absence of full-cost accounting in evaluating the highway program. Related to this is the inability to make meaningful comparisons between different transport modes, based on a full cost-benefit comparison. Costs, in the trust fund sense, tend to be equated with the actual money outlays or cash flows through the system. The cost of the highway is thus money expended on right-of-way acquisition and actual construction of the facility. In addition, from an individual state's point of view (which is where most highway decisions are ultimately made) the true cost of the highway is further diminished to the perceived 10 percent cost, which represents the state's share of actual money outlay.

Although it is not widely publicized, the average state contributes about twice as much for highway construction as does the trust fund. Much state and local funding is also in the form of trust funds: for instance, the use of such trust fund techniques as earmarked gasoline taxes. Sharing of state and federal money with municipalities to cover the costs imposed by road construction would seem justifiable; 54 percent of all passenger travel takes place within urban areas. Yet, Texas cities, for example, had to allocate 19 percent of their expenditures out of property, sales, and other general taxes for street construction and maintenance.[15]

Ignoring for the moment the so-called external costs, such as noise, air pollution, congestion, and ugliness, urban auto users fail even to cover operating costs incurred by the city in the provision of services to auto users. Costs exceed revenues for these purposes by about 50 percent.[16] These data directly contradict a widely held belief that highways are not subsidized because they are financed by user charges. They are subsidized to the extent that new highway construction capital costs, which seem to be covered by earmarked revenue sources, necessitate an increase in the level of operating expenditures.[17]

Subsidies granted and social costs imposed come in many forms. The main problem seems to be that they are extremely difficult to perceive without careful case-by-case analysis. An example of a subtle subsidy, very common in transportation finance and only slightly related to public benefits, is the tax advantage received by some municipal bondholders. The Port of New York Authority is a quasi-governmental agency originally created to provide public mass transit. Over the years it has developed into a business-oriented operation whose principal concern appears to be returning a profit to its bondholders rather than providing effective public transit. The Port Authority has concentrated its transportation investments in autos, buses, and trucks. The tolls from these have so expanded that the authority has diversified into real estate and office buildings, financing the World Trade Center in New York and thus increasing the existing over-abundance of office space in that city. Theodore Kheel describes how these subsidies come about.

The interest the Port Authority pays on its bonds is tax-exempt to the lender. The authority will borrow the money it needs at an annual interest cost many millions of dollars *below* the price private borrowers would pay. Where is the difference coming from? From the federal, state and city governments that would otherwise collect that amount in taxes paid to bondholders. In addition, the Port Authority will pay New York City at least $15 million a year less in real estate taxes than private builders would pay for comparable space. When the World Trade Center is completed in 1972, Washington, Albany and New York may be subsidizing it by a sum approaching $50 million *per year.*[18]

... The Port Authority makes money from the federal government another way. It borrows money at low rates in the municipal bond market because its interest payments are tax-exempt. It invests a part of this in United States Government securities as reserves for the bondholders securities—which, because they are not tax-exempt, pay the higher interest. The Port Authority pockets the difference, a pure subsidy from the federal government.[19]

In spite of this kind of subsidy, the following real social costs of the Port Authority's policies are ignored or shunted aside:

The strangulating traffic its bridges and tunnels bring, the cost of air pollution, street and road maintenance, crowded courts and hospitals, zoning insurance rates, demands on police and sanitation services—these are someone else's problems, not the Port Authority's. The Port Authority complains that riders on the Hudson tubes, now operated by the authority, receive a subsidy of 31 cents per ride. But a man who drives his own car to work in Manhattan for 50 cents via the Port Authority's Lincoln Tunnel may be indirectly subsidized by as much as five dollars per ride. That is a rough estimate of what it may now be costing, in municipal services and lost time to industry, to cope with New York City's traffic problem.[20]

Highway investment decisions and mass transit plans could not be made by a free market mechanism. Motorists have no effective way to express the demand for a freeway or a commuter train where none exists. Roads and transit facilities involve large, risky outlays; roads and rail lines must be built before anyone knows how much they will be used. Once constructed, they can seldom be converted to any other use. Highways and mass transit facilities are thus both public goods. They must be built (funded) by governmental units. Government officials should (though they often do not) evaluate total social costs (air pollution, aesthetics, noise, etc.) and total social benefits (improved health, lower death rates, extension of effective mobility to all) before deciding to construct either. The question is not whether we should have subsidies; we already have them. The real issue is: Are the social benefits derived worth the costs?

ALTERNATIVE FUNDING MECHANISMS

The issues of funding mechanisms and subsidies have led to a variety of alternative policy suggestions. These proposals range from wholly new methods of financing transportation in general, including the creation of a mass transit trust fund similar to the Highway Trust Fund, to proposals for peak load pricing or special taxes on commuters to be used to fund various alternatives. A number of these plans have been designed to deal with specific nonfinancial needs or to counteract special problems. Their usefulness for these purposes is discussed in other parts of this book. Here we are mainly concerned with their financial implications.

One obvious proposal, the one advocated by trust busters, is to terminate the Highway Trust Fund altogether. Those favoring this approach argue that so long as the fund continues to receive revenues, the built-in bureaucratic, economic, and political interests that have developed around the highway program would lobby strongly and effectively for a continuation of business as usual. The evidence that this may indeed take place is already strong. The Interstate System and the trust fund created to finance it were supposed to terminate in 1972. They have been extended twice already, and as of November 1975 the House Ways and Means Committee, while rejecting a proposal to increase the gasoline tax by $.03 a gallon to provide a $3 billion annual transit fund for mass transit, nonetheless voted 17 to 12 to continue the $6 billion a year going to the Highway Trust Fund through 1977. It is also noteworthy that in testimony given before the House Subcommittee on Transportation, former Secretary Brinegar presented data that projected highway expenditures would remain at approximately their present levels through 1980.[21]

Political reality suggests that it is highly unlikely that the gasoline tax will ever be abandoned. The tax is politically acceptable and a source of considerable revenue. Further, the energy crisis, whatever one thinks about its short-range meaning, has certainly strengthened the political ability to retain and even increase the tax with little opposition. Taxing oil is now virtually synonymous with saving America from the foreign "hordes."

Many who are in general agreement with this assessment of political reality espouse tapping the trust fund for mass transit. On the basis of expediency this would seem to be a very reasonable thing to do. Allow the monster that has starved mass transit to provide the sustenance for its revival. It's poetic justice that the users (and abusers) of motorcar transportation should continue to pay a levy used to support mass transit.

One such proposal urged the conversion of the Highway Trust Fund into a "super transportation trust fund" combined with the airport trust fund.[22] Such an idea would certainly stand a better chance of insuring some sort of balance between funding for highway and other forms of transportation. It would presumably force the evaluation of all alternatives in deciding on future specific transportation facilities.

There are problems with this approach, however. First, it could be argued that the main features of the national highway system are now complete and that further federal funding of highway construction is no longer necessary for the foreseeable future. Second, the already well-entrenched highway lobby and the staffs of state and local transportation agencies might be in a position to continue the policy of highway domination through the technical domination of transportation planning. Finally, the concept of the trust fund itself continues to be open to question as a financing mechanism. Why should transportation, rather than, say, housing or health facilities, enjoy a guaranteed source of revenues and insulation from the public scrutiny afforded by congressional budget review?

Another proposal which has been suggested by former Transportation Secretary Volpe himself is the creation of a separate Mass Transit Trust Fund. Various different tax sources have been suggested, including tobacco, but the aim is to secure permanent financing for mass transit facilities comparable to that presently available for highway. The same rationale for a trust fund is used as for highways: continuity of funding is deemed necessary to insure commitment by the cities and to pay for very large, nonflexible capital costs.

Another trust fund exclusively for mass transit might be the only way to achieve parity between highway and mass transit needs. It looks less and less likely each year that the assured funding for highways is ever going to be ended. So from a political outlook, it might be best to get roughly co-equal status for mass transit. On the other hand, the attainment of ongoing funding for mass transit might serve to lessen the demand for greater review and accountability regarding the construction of roads. This could conceivably lock the fund in even more solidly and insulate it from criticism.

The principal argument against the creation of a mass transit trust fund is probably still the same one used to criticize the Highway Trust Fund. It is too difficult to foresee what our attitudes about urban transportation alternatives might be fifteen or twenty years from now. Having seen what the unimodel approach has accomplished in one instance, we might well be chary of a repeat performance. The best insurance against such possibility is regular and critical review. Once a mass transit system is approved, let the federal government guarantee—say, through the posting of a bond— that sufficient revenues to complete the task will be appropriated. But it would seem unwise, in view of past experience, to commit monies that *have* to be used to build mass transit facilities, regardless of whether anyone really wants or needs them.

There appears to be growing agreement that some degree of operating subsidy will be required to keep mass transit in existence. The need for a minimum service level for the many who simply cannot use the present car-exclusive system is basic for an urbanized society. That many of these people are also the urban poor makes it impossible to cover costs out of the farebox without defeating the original purpose of maintaining transit. Only wide usage and the attendant economies of scale would successfully keep fares low enough while covering costs.

It can be argued that maintaining a transit system that excludes certain classes from mobility is subsidizing the users of the system by imposing social costs (externalities) on other members of society. Those who are deprived of mobility are bearing the "costs" that allow auto transportation to be kept at an artificially low level. The cost of automobile *use* should be raised to cover the social as well as the private costs, and these revenues should be employed to subsidize mass transit.

One of the problems, of course, is not merely how to provide transit for those who *must* use it, but to lure some of the auto users back to transit. The only truly successful way to accomplish this would be to simultaneously lower transit fares (costs) while increasing the costs of automobile use. Some balance would have to be reached, one that made it economical for more people to use good quality transit. Presently our policies do not seem to recognize this. We attempt to provide mass transit or public transit at modestly subsidized rates. However, with the exception of increased gasoline prices (about which we had very little to say), we continue to subsidize auto transit and thus keep the price of this form of travel artificially low.

Even with such efforts at finance as those just noted, it will be difficult to lure many auto users to transit because of the peculiar capital-cost financing of private auto usage. Capital costs of cars (unlike subway cars or railcars) are borne by individual consumers. Once an auto is purchased, there is a very powerful incentive to use it as often as possible in order to spread out capital costs.

The question of subsidies also raises issues about efficiency and about who the beneficiaries are. John Higgins suggests that transit subsidies are often ripoffs for city machines and transit operators.[23] He argues that more attention should be paid to performance criteria to insure that transit companies are serving the public well at lowest cost. Different types of subsidies could be tested to determine the best levels to achieve specified ends. These subsidies could also be combined with other transit revenue measures, such as increasing auto traffic tolls and parking fees; the proceeds could be used to defray the cost of the subsidy.

Elaborate schemes for peak hour pricing (road users during rush hours would be billed at higher rates by means of electronic monitoring devices), sliding scale subsidies, and free transit in designated core areas of the city have been devised. Each of these has the same basic purpose, however: to alter the structure of pricing in a way that will shift greater costs onto the automobile while encouraging greater transit use.

In this section we have attempted to show the wide range of fiscal options which are available in transportation policy and the different impacts which might be expected from some of these. In practice, surprisingly few fiscal alternatives have been used, and the result has been a rather one-sided approach to transportation policy. In the next section, we attempt to sketch out the historical development of urban transportation legislation which has accompanied these fiscal policies.

THE STAGES OF URBAN TRANSPORTATION LEGISLATION

Although federal concern with *urban* transportation evolved in the early 1960's, its role in intercity transportation dates back to the early days of the Republic; the Gallatin Report of 1808 serves as an important landmark.[24] For the most part, however, early federal involvement was limited to water and rail transportation. It was not until the early twentieth century that road transportation came within the federal domain, and not until recent times that it expanded its scope to include intracity transportation. The purpose of this analysis is to examine legislation affecting urban transportation. Four stages in the development of federal policy can be identified.

1. THE LAISSEZ-FAIRE STAGE

Prior to the depression, the federal government followed what George Smerk calls a laissez-faire policy[25] or what others may call "benign neglect."

Urban problems were the sole responsibility of the cities themselves. Illustrative of this stage was the Federal Aid Road Act of 1916, which provided funding for intercity and rural roads. Although this act gave great impetus to the development of state highways, urban highway construction was specifically prohibited under its terms, which excluded aid to any city with a population of more than 2,500. The need to develop intercity routes was undoubtedly of some importance, but the act itself reflects the anti-urban bias of the legislature, a bias still evident in federal transportation legislation. In 1928 the federal government took a rather timid step by making funds available for road construction in municipalities, but only along those sections in which houses were more than 200 feet apart. Obviously this restriction would limit federal assistance to roads on the fringes of the city that were sparsely settled. This restriction was the precursor of the government's indirect way of fostering suburbanization. Thus, cities were faced with developing their own transportation systems and to a large extent the various urban transit systems were privately owned, further limiting the control city governments could exert.

2. THE DEPRESSION ERA STAGE

With the onslaught of the depression in the 1930's the Roosevelt administration's primary concern focused on a revitalization of the economy. It is little wonder, then, that legislation emanating from Congress during this period was aimed at providing employment rather than establishing any comprehensive transportation policy.

The road-building programs at this time were part and parcel of the public works effort initiated by the New Deal. Road construction, of course, was highly suited to the New Deal efforts since it required large numbers of unskilled laborers and because of the ubiquitousness of roads. Furthermore, unemployment was most visible in urban areas; thus it was politically feasible to undertake such programs in the cities. Yet, programs starting for one purpose tend to perpetuate themselves even after the purpose is met. This is so because various groups and organizations come to depend on the continuation of these programs, and programs thus serve to generate and sustain a network of interest groups on an incremental basis.

Because of the vast unemployment in the cities, it was essential that federal aid for highways be doled out to the urban areas as well as for the "farm-to-market" roads, and the Emergency Relief and Construction Act of 1932 provided for federal highway construction in the city. In addition, the Hayden-Cartwright Act of 1936 designated federal funding for other highway construction within municipalities, including bridges, costs of surveys, the elimination of grade crossings, and the construction of routes.

This act also served as the precursor of the subsequent Highway Trust Fund by making it "unfair and unjust to tax motor vehicle transportation unless the proceeds of such taxation are applied to the construction, improvement or maintenance of highways."[26]

Aside from serving as an employment stimulant, these programs also resulted in the construction and improvement of a vast network of roads and highways in the urban areas. Wilfred Owen estimates that under these programs some 651,000 miles of highways and streets were constructed or improved.[27]

In sum, the federal programs for roadway construction during the depression were based on expediency rather than any long-range or comprehensive plan. Yet, the absence of any such plan served to destroy and unbalance the urban transportation system.[28] Furthermore, Mertins and Miller argue, "many roads of questionable value were constructed during this time only to become, later on, maintenance cost burdens totally disproportionate with their use."[29]

3. THE HIGHWAYS–ONLY STAGE

Although a virtual moratorium halted highway construction during World War II, two events served to set the stage for a continuation and expansion of the federal government's tunnel-vision policy on transportation. In the first place, World War II brought America out of the depression, and at the close of the war Americans were highly affluent. Second, the auto industry experienced tremendous growth during the war and greatly expanded its capability of producing cars. This affluence, which meant that many Americans could buy their own private automobiles, coincided with an expanded capability by American industry to produce cars.

Even before the close of the war, the federal government vigorously moved to remedy the backlog of highway work. The Federal Aid Highway Act of 1944 authorized the expenditure of $500 million per year for the first three years following the end of the war, and funds were made available to urban communities with a population of more than 5,000. The act provided for federal aid of 50 percent for the cost of construction and one-third for right-of-way costs.[30] Forty-five percent of the funding was set aside for primary roads in the federal aid system and 30 percent for roads in the federal secondary system. A full 25 percent was devoted to roads in urban areas. Although this legislation served as the forerunner for a one-dimensional approach to urban transportation, it at least had the saving grace of rationalizing and organizing the highways by designating a national system. At the same time, the act served as a temporizing panacea for the urban transportation problem.

Without any question, the culmination of the federal government's highways-only approach was the passage of the Federal Aid Highway Act of 1956. In view of the tremendous impact of this legislation on urban transportation, it is surprising that it generated little opposition. The major newspapers of the country, especially the *Chicago Tribune,* strongly supported the measure, and it received bipartisan support in Congress. Yet, since its passage it has served as the focal point of the transportation controversy.

In view of the extensive commentaries elsewhere concerning the scope and implications of this act,[31] only a few brief remarks need to be made at this point. First the act changed the name of the Interstate System to the "National System of Interstate and Defense Highways," and the authors of the act did so "because of its primary importance to the national defense."[32] One must remember that the appeal of national defense and national security has often served as a powerful, if hypocritical, argument for many federal programs.[33]

Second, the act retains the same formula for funding as the 1944 act: 45 percent for primary highways, 30 percent for secondary highways, and 25 percent for extensions of these systems within urban areas. In contrast to the 1944 act, however, the federal government paid 90 percent of the bill for interstate highways, leaving the states and cities to fund only 10 percent of the cost. Third, the major innovation of the act was the establishment of the Highway Trust Fund. Instead of funding highway construction out of general revenues, the act imposed a gasoline tax and certain other highway-related taxes earmarked for direct support of the Interstate System.

In sum, "if any single piece of legislation can be identified as providing the overwhelming force in making urban transportation 'highway dominant,'" argue Mertins and Miller, "this legislation must certainly bear the onus."[34] And as Smerk notes, "if the Interstate System does not turn out to be an extraordinary benefit, it should definitely be classified as man's most appalling wasteful project."[35]

4. THE BALANCED SYSTEM STAGE

Although the highway thrust of federal transportation policy continued unabated during the 1950's, there were several efforts to remedy the highway-only policy. Yet, Congress closed out the fifties with a piece of legislation which further exacerbated the problem. If most of the legislation in the 1950's encouraged the growth of highways, the Transportation Act of 1958 complemented the process by making it easier for the railroads to discontinue commuter service in the urban areas.

In response to this trend, Mayor Dilworth of Philadelphia headed a group of twelve mayors to examine a variety of urban problems including transportation. The report, which asked for increased federal assistance, was further buttressed by the platforms of both major parties in 1960, which recognized the critical state of urban transportation. The Democrats pledged federal aid for comprehensive metropolitan transportation programs, including bus and rail mass transit, commuter railroads as well as highway programs, and construction of civil airports.[36] Finally, the Doyle Report added further support for congressional action with its revelations concerning the position of commuter lines.[37]

After two major hearings in Congress on federal mass transportation policy, Congress passed the Housing Act of 1961, which is considered by many as the first explicit recognition by the federal government of its responsibility in regard to urban transportation. This legislation provided aid to "facilitate comprehensive planning for urban development, including coordinated transportation systems, on a continuing basis," thus recognizing the interdependence of transportation planning and general community planning. It also authorized some $50 million for acquisition and improvement of mass transportation facilities and another $25 million for transit demonstration projects. Only $47.5 million, however, was ultimately appropriated by Congress. One other key aspect concerned agency responsibility. The legislation designated the Housing and Home Finance Agency to administer the program—as the proponents of the act wanted—rather than the Bureau of Public Roads. The comprehensive planning thrust of the Housing Act was also embodied in the Federal Aid Highway Act of 1962. The act calls for the "development" of transportation systems embracing various modes of transport; no highway projects could be funded unless the planning process was continuing and comprehensive.[38]

Planning for a transportation system is one thing; providing money is something quite different. Until 1964 the federal government's contribution was a mere token. The Housing Act of 1961 provided a meager $25 million for demonstration projects, but the major deficiency of the act was its failure to provide funds for long-term capital improvements. To overcome this gap, Senator Harrison Williams introduced a bill calling for $500 million in funds for urban mass transportation systems in early 1963. In his transportation message before Congress in April 1963 President Kennedy maintained: "Our national welfare . . . requires the provision of good urban transportation, with the properly balanced use of private vehicles and modern mass transit to help shape as well as serve urban growth."[39] As finally passed by the Senate, the bill authorized the expenditure of only $300 million over a three-year period. The major barrier to such a bill, however, was the House of Representatives. Although a companion bill had been introduced in the House in early 1963, the bill was bottled up in committee, and it appeared that it would be scuttled. In the spring of 1964, however, President Johnson threw his weight behind the bill, and it finally passed the House in June 1964 by a vote of 212 to 189.

The Urban Mass Transportation Assistance Act of 1964 carried on the thrust of the Housing Act. In addition, it deftly handled the problem of public versus private ownership by providing that any plan "shall encourage to the maximum extent feasible the participation of private enterprise."[40] Although the act's intent was to preclude any massive take-over of private transit facilities, the trend toward public ownership continued.

As finally passed, the act authorized $375 million with no more than $75 million authorized for the two years thereafter.[41] In addition, the act provided that federal funds could be used for a variety of capital improvements, such as purchase of land, buses, railcars, signal equipment, and other items. Yet, the act also restricted the federal share to two-thirds of the cost, and only one-half for areas without a comprehensive plan. This latter provision stands in stark relief to the highway sharing formula of 90/10. As a consequence, the act still retained the warning for cities that if they wanted to achieve a balanced system by opting for other modes than the auto they would be faced with the task of chipping in almost 30 percent more of the funds than for highways.

Between 1964 and 1968 legislation affecting both highways and urban mass transit was minimal. The Mass Transportation Assistance Act was amended in 1966 to provide for additional funding, especially for studies and for training. Of major importance was the provision authorizing funds for technical studies for planning, designing, and engineering of urban mass transit projects. Although no new highway legislation was passed until 1968, highway building continued in full swing. More than $12 billion was collected in the Highway Trust Fund, but urban reaction to highway building started to emerge. Citizen resentment to the Washington, D.C., project brought the matter home for many congressmen, and several struggles ensued in other urban centers, such as the Memphis Overton Park project and San Francisco's Embarcadero Freeway.

The Urban Mass Transportation Assistance Act took into account increasing urban disenchantment with the "highway solution" by changing the quality and quantity of citizen involvement. Public hearings were required under the act to consider the economic, social, environmental, and design implications of the proposed highway plans as well as possible alternatives. The act further liberalized the provisions concerning replacement housing, established a Highway Beautification Commission, and directed the secretary to formulate guidelines to minimize the social, economic, and environmental impact of highways. As a trade-off to rural interests, the act also set aside funds for Economic Growth Center Development Highways, for the purpose of stimulating growth in the rural areas. State governors were asked to recommend areas as growth centers, and the federal government's share for highway construction in these areas was upped to 95 percent of costs.

The culminating federal entry into the field of urban transportation was the Urban Mass Transportation Assistance Act of 1970. The meager appropriations that characterized previous legislation were replaced by a federal aid program of some $10 billion over a twelve-year period. The act also provided for long-term assistance and advance contract authority. Paralleling the 1970 Federal Aid Highway Act[42] is a provision requiring public hearings on projects to consider the economic, social, and environmental impact of urban transit projects.

THE TRUSTBUSTERS

The controversy concerning the highway program raged on in the early 1970's with the Highway Trust Fund under assault. The trustbusters considered the fund to be the arch-enemy in the revitalization of urban transportation. The fund provided for continuing support of the highway program without the need for dipping into general revenue (as is the case with mass transportation projects). Furthermore, the funding provisions for highways with the 90/10 formula made it politically difficult for hard-pressed urban governments to opt for an extension of mass transportation facilities in which a higher proportionate share of local funds was required. Finally, there was concern that the urban transportation question was not so much a "more-or-less" question but rather an "either-or" question, and if urban centers wanted to devote their full share of federal money regardless of whether it is derived from the trust fund or general revenues for transportation, they should have the choice. Although one might think that the "home rule" argument parallels the "states' rights" arguments of many Southerners and rural congressmen, Congress failed to see the similarity.

The first major assault on the Highway Trust Fund came in early 1972 when the Nixon administration and Secretary of Transportation Volpe came out strongly in favor of using trust fund monies for mass transportation. On September 8, 1972, the Senate Committee on Banking, Housing, and Urban Affairs issued a favorable report, recommending that the law

be amended to provide that funds authorized for the Federal-aid urban system be available for the acquisition and construction of rail transit facilities and equipment. This approach, the so-called "Cooper-Muskie Amendment," would allow metropolitan transportation agencies in urbanized areas to use their share of the $800 million authorization for the Federal-aid urban highway system for whatever urban transportation capital projects they deem necessary to meet the needs of their communities.[43]

The Cooper-Muskie Amendment passed the Senate on September 19, 1972, by a vote of 48 to 26. Because of differences between the Senate and the House versions, the bill was referred to a conference committee. Although the Senate conferees stuck to their position, the House conferees failed to budge, and no agreement was reached.

In early 1973, newly appointed Secretary of Transportation Claude Brinegar reaffirmed the Nixon administration's position on using the Highway Trust Fund for mass transportation. The proposed highway bill, which emerged from the Senate Public Works Committee, authorized the expenditure of some $18 billion, including some $850 million for buses. The Muskie-Baker Amendment proposed that funding be authorized for rail transportation in addition to bus transportation. The amendment carried by a vote of 49 to 44. A proposed amendment by Senators Weicker and Kennedy sought to broaden the scope of funding, providing $2.3 billion out of the $6.1 billion yearly outlay for public transportation; but this amendment was defeated by a vote of 70 to 23.

The House followed the same pattern that it had in 1972. In addition to increasing the expenditure level to $25 billion for the three-year period, the House bill contained no provision for public transportation. The House Public Works Committee, which has served as the bastion of highway interests, beat down an attempt to include funding for public transportation by a vote of 28 to 9. With this defeat, efforts to amend the bill turned to the Rules Committee, which can grant or deny permission to bring amendments up on the floor. In contrast to 1972, the Rules Committee permitted the Anderson Amendment to be introduced on the floor. The Anderson Amendment paralleled the Muskie-Baker Amendment, but in the floor fight it was defeated by a vote of 215 to 190. The House passed the committee's bill, which provided no funding, on April 19, 1973.

Because of the substantial differences between the two bills, especially the inclusion of the Muskie-Baker provision in the Senate version, the bill was referred to a conference committee. On the Senate side, four of the seven members favored the Muskie-Baker provision, but only two of the nine House conferees had voted for the comparable Anderson Amendment. In early August, the conferees reached agreement, and retained the controversial Muskie-Baker Amendment, which for the first time opened up the Highway Trust Fund for mass transit purposes. The conference committee bill was approved by the Senate 91 to 5 and in the House 382 to 34.[44] Table 3-3 indicates the major points of contention in the House and Senate bills, and the final compromise bill.

Although the emergent energy crisis of 1973 renewed interest in mass transit, the federal government stumbled about without any clear-cut goal. Of critical importance for the development of mass transit was federal

funding for operating subsidies. The Senate, which had passed operating
subsidies legislation on several occasions, renewed its effort in late 1973
and by a vote of 53 to 33 reasserted its position. The House, on the other

TABLE 3-3

The 1973 Federal Aid Highway Act

Issue	Compromise Bill	Senate Bill	House Bill
Interstate transfer (of controversial urban links)	Reimbursement from General Treasury	Reimbursement from Trust Fund	Reimbursement from General Treasury
Transfer of $ for urban systems projects	From Trust Fund: $0 / 1974, $200 m 1975 (for buses) $800 m / 1976	From Trust Fund: $850 m / year	From General Treasury: $700 m / year
Funding levels from Trust Fund	$19 b / three years, including $1 b for transit	$18 b / three years, including $2.55 b for transit	$25 b / three years; none for transit
Priority primaries	No mileage specified; $100 m / 1974, $300 m / 1976	No provision	10,000 mile system; $300 m / year
Operating assistance	No provision	From General Treasury: $400 m / year	No provisions
Moratorium on removal of "directional signs"	No provision	No provision	Included
Brackenridge Park Fwy / San Antonio	Bypassing requirements for environmental protection	Bypassing requirements for environmental protection	No provision
Crosstown Expressway / Chicago	Bypassing requirements for environmental protection	No provision	No provision

Adapted from *The Concrete Opposition*, Aug. 1973, p. 8.

hand, had repeatedly opposed operating subsidies, and the Nixon administration threatened to veto any legislation that included operating subsidies.
But, during the energy crisis, the House reversed its long-standing opposition

and narrowly defeated an amendment to delete operating subsidies from a companion bill. A jurisdictional battle over the House bill developed. Traditionally the Banking and Currency Committee had responsibility for mass transit legislation, but the Public Works Committee, which was also considering a similar bill, asked the Rules Committee to defer any action on a conference committee report. The House voted to shelve the Banking and Currency Committee's bill by a vote of 221 to 181. It took almost five months for the Public Works Committee to ready its bill, but on August 20, 1974, the House of Representatives passed a six-year mass transit bill developed by the Public Works Committee. House members cut the total amount of funds from $20 billion to $11 billion and the federal share of operating subsidies from 50 percent to one-third. A proposed amendment by Representative Dale Milford to eliminate operating subsidies altogether was defeated by a vote of 202 to 197—based, to a large extent, on President Ford's eleventh-hour endorsement of the subsidy provision.

Again, because of the differences between the Senate and House versions of the bill, a conference committee was established to work out the differences. Reacting to Ford's threat to veto any inflationary bill, Senator Williams made a last-ditch effort to save the two-year emergency legislation passed by the Senate by offering to scale down the authorization from $800 million to $600 million for fiscal year 1975–76; but President Ford held out for the long-term bill passed by the House. Finally, almost a year and a half after the Senate's original passage of the subsidy bill, the House-Senate conferees reached agreement on a six-year, $11.9 billion, mass transit bill, and in late November both the Senate and the House passed the compromise version.

Until the passage of the 1973 Highway Act and the Federal Mass Transportation Act of 1974, federal policy largely devoted its efforts to highway construction. Even with the passage of these two acts there actually has been no abatement in highway construction, except for Nixon's impoundment of funds, which was reversed by President Ford in early 1975. There is, however, some hope that these two acts will redirect transportation efforts in our cities. For example, eighteen months after the passage of the Highway Act, which gave cities the option of using funds for transit facilities rather than interstate roads, several cities have taken steps to exercise this option. Both Boston and Philadelphia have canceled costly and controversial highway projects. In Philadelphia, a controversial segment of Interstate 695 was junked, and the Southeastern Pennsylvania Transportation Authority received $51 million for capital projects. At least six other cities, including New York, Washington, Chicago, Los Angeles, Seattle, and Portland, considered the cancellation of interstate projects in early 1975. Before the passage of these two acts, Smerk contended, "there was little incentive to change the situation that has been developing for the past 50 years"[45] in regard to the federal government's preference for highways. These two acts might provide some incentive for change, but it seems doubtful whether the incremental transportation policies evolved through federal legislation and the fiscal disparities between mass transit and highways will have some meaningful impact on urban transportation.

CONCLUSION

In this chapter we have attempted to show how the political values of highway-oriented interests are embodied in both fiscal and legislative policies. But for those who seek change in transportation policies, it is insufficient merely to understand the policies. The institutional framework for developing these policies is also of great importance, and the implication of our next two chapters is that institutional change may have to precede policy change. In the following chapter, the power of economic institutions that foster highway-oriented policies will be examined. Then, in the subsequent chapter, the political structure, and its linkage with economic interest groups, will be explored. With an understanding of the institutions which undergird these policies, one can more clearly understand the "urban transportation problem."

4

THE ECONOMIC SYSTEM
AND URBAN
TRANSPORTATION PRIORITIES

If politics can be defined as the "authoritative allocation of values," then economics can be defined in a parallel manner as the allocation of resources. Because the political and economic sectors are so closely intertwined, the economic system wields great influence over the allocation of values while the political system intervenes in the allocation of resources. Public authority and private power go hand in hand in shaping transportation policy in the modern mixed economy.

If urban transportation is in serious difficulty, as numerous critics of the urban scene attest, it got that way through policies shaped by economic interests in concert with the political system. Our current policy emphasis is on still further development of the automotive-highway transportation system, an emphasis supported by a very large scale commitment of the nation's resources. Mass transit is going nowhere, a fact assured by the automobile interests and their allies through the skillful use of a web of economic and political interests that extends across the length and breadth of the national economy. This great aggregation of power has been used to control our urban transportation policy and, in turn, to exert a powerful and detrimental influence on the quality of urban life.

The current economic crisis in the United States, which has pushed unemployment rates to thirty-year highs, has temporarily strengthened the position of automotive and highway interests. The shock waves which have spread throughout the economy as a result of the slump in auto sales have underscored dramatically the significance of the motor vehicle industry to the national economy. From the industry viewpoint, the economic crisis could not have occurred at a more propitious time. The auto-highway interests have been under heavy attack for several years from environmental and citizen interest groups. But of late everyone has been anxiously awaiting the revival of auto sales to help stimulate economic recovery. No one wants to be responsible for policies which might now be charged with creating further unemployment.

At the same time, inflation has contributed to rapidly spiraling costs for alternative urban transportation systems. The squeeze on public revenues occasioned by falling employment and earnings has caused numerous public transportation projects to be temporarily shelved or halted altogether. One such victim was the San Jose County dial-a-ride system, which was terminated in November 1975 (ironically) because it was too successful—i.e., generated too great a ridership. County officials determined that heavy demand was costing the county too much to operate the subsidized system.

THE AUTO-HIGHWAY LOBBY

The auto industry, as we will be emphasizing below, is protected and defended by scores of related industries and interests whose continued good fortune is believed to depend on the continuing dominance of the automobile in our economic life. Lost jobs and declining output, even if only temporary, serve as powerful disincentives to those who would tamper with the automobile. Its sphere of influence is further extended by the enormous profits and corresponding power that it derives from that favored position. The Highway Trust Fund, a vast subsidy for the automobile and a barrier to the development of a mass-transit alternative in urban transportation, is successfully defended by the auto-highway lobby; legislation favorable to the automobile society is continually insured through campaign contributions, strategic payoffs, and direct intervention in national and local political affairs. We explore below these various sources of the auto industry's economic and political power, the costs that power imposes on our cities, and the need for a change in urban transportation priorities, a change we believe can be attained only through the development of a comparable political force to counter the influence of the auto lobby.

DENSITY, LOVE, AND CONSUMER SOVEREIGNTY

Two major themes characterize the current public defense of our present urban transit policy. The more sophisticated of these arguments, one usually aimed at academic critics, is the density argument. Cities such as Los Angeles and Dallas are said to be too spread-out to support mass transit on an economical (pay-for-itself-out-of-the-farebox) basis. The only form of mass transit that is at all possible for these cities, we are told, is bus service, one that makes use of the same facilities used by, and constructed for, the automobile.[1] The other theme we hear from the auto interests is the popular folklore position that Americans are in love with the automobile,[2] an idea that is worth exploring in greater detail because it leads directly into the major aspects of this group's control of both transportation policies and transportation consumers, two of the major characteristics of the present system.

The proponents of the love-affair thesis argue that an attempt to lure Americans away from the automobile is not only doomed to failure but is undemocratic as well. The auto is said to represent the demonstrated preference of consumers, and at least one major interested party has publicly declared that if an auto-highway lobby exists, it consists of the 103 million licensed drivers who want to keep their automobiles.[3] Elaborate surveys are undertaken in cities all over the nation to prove the obvious, that Americans prefer the familiar form of transportation, the automobile.[4] Although these surveys have about as much significance as a study demonstrating that the French prefer Camembert cheese to Kraft American slices, questioning their validity is not popular and indeed subjects one to the charge of seeking to substitute one's own values for those of the individuals making the choice in question. A related argument of comparable persuasive power is that because so many people continue to drive automobiles and because so many new roads are constantly being built without general armed revolt, the wisdom of the present policy is necessarily being repeatedly vindicated.[5]

ABSENCE OF SUBSTITUTES AND ECONOMIES OF SCALE

In truth, of course, the auto's continued place of privilege in the United States is attributable to the fact that alternatives to the car are virtually nonexistent; that some very powerful economic interest groups have labored hard and long to keep it that way; and that the structural characteristics of the nation's economy work to prevent the kind of changes needed to develop viable transit alternatives. In the classical version of the competitive free-enterprise economy, consumers are supposed to have convenient substitutes for each product offered and, in addition, to have effective knowledge of the existence and characteristics of those available alternatives. The consumer must also have, however, the power to call forth the development of substitute products—i.e., to determine the full array of what is to be produced in the first place. And this power can exist only when there are no effective barriers to the entry of new firms and new products to meet the consumer's demands for such alternative items. Given the tight control of the American transportation industry by a small number of price-setting firms, the transportation consumer in fact has only one other convenient substitute for the automobile: another automobile. He can choose one of the automobiles offered to him, or he can walk. The industry sees to it that would-be producers of mass-transit facilities never get a chance to do so on a mass—i.e., profitable—basis.

The principal technique used by the automobile industry to prevent the development of a viable mass-transit substitute is simplicity itself, one that effectively combines the carrot and the stick. It is, in effect, an indirect regulatory system, one that goes under the unassuming name of the Highway Trust Fund.[6] This fund has no direct mandate to regulate rates and routes, as in the case of the ICC and the CAB, but its operations produce an even more significant and favorable form of government regulation, one that, by regulating the demand for automotive transportation, assures the automobile and related industries a continuous and growing market for their products. The auto has thus attained that ultimate nirvana of business affairs, government regulation that assures a growing use of its products plus the exclusion of competitive substitute products, all without any corresponding regulation of its own activities.

The federal government, using the money collected by the trust fund's supporting taxes, heavily subsidizes roads, but not other forms of transit, a discriminatory policy that provides states and cities with a powerful incentive to opt for highways as the answer to their transportation needs. Other modes of transportation, being required to operate at a competitive disadvantage, are systematically strangled by this artificial diversion of consumers to the automobile alternative. Rapid transit systems will continue to face virtually insuperable barriers until it becomes reasonably certain that they will ultimately be widespread enough to permit the economies of scale needed to make their production profitable over the long term, not just as a short-run opportunity. Present transportation policy provides a negative assurance that no such thing will happen, and this, in turn, further encourages everyone even remotely connected with the gainful fallout from the present reliance on the automobile to resist change or, if not actively resist, at least to approve tacitly of the bigger fish who *are* active resisters.

PRICE LEADERSHIP

The automotive industry long ago achieved internal stability through the adoption of a system of relatively stable "administered" prices. Competition of the kind described in economic textbooks was abandoned early as an unbusinesslike way of doing things. Through a system of high-cost styling changes and exclusive-dealership arrangements, entry barriers were raised that have effectively closed the auto industry to new entrants for the past twenty years. Only four firms remain, and one of these, American Motors, with some 3 percent of the market and still losing ground, is probably not destined to be around much longer.[7] The three largest firms control 97 percent of domestic auto production, and the largest, General Motors, serves as the price leader. Its announcements of new prices for the current year are promptly matched by the other firms. And if those others have previously announced their own prices for the sake of appearances, they naturally make "adjustments" to make them conform to whatever prices General Motors might subsequently announce.

This self-regulation has been very profitable. According to profit data published by the Federal Trade Commission, the automobile industry has been the most profitable of our major industries in recent years. Its average rate of profit after taxes as a percentage of stockholders' equity for the four-year period 1962–65 was 19.4 percent, compared to 18.7 percent for the drug industry, 16.8 percent for computers, and 15.9 percent for industrial chemicals, the three next most profitable industries. "For other corporations engaged in manufacturing, average rates of return have been about 8% to 10% in recent years, which yield a margin of no more than 4% to 5% profit above the bedrock cost of capital (as shown by government bond rates). By contrast, the leading automobile firms have had net margins averaging about 15%—about three times the average for all industry."[8] General Motors had sales of more than $30 billion in 1972 and net profits of $2.16 billion. Profits rose to an all-time record of $2.4 billion in 1973. Adversely affected by the oil embargo of 1973 and the subsequent severe economic recession that slowed the economy throughout 1974 and early 1975, General Motors recently reported a return to normalcy with its second greatest fourth quarter profit in history for the final three months of 1975. Using this fourth quarter showing, analysts predicted 1975 profits of about $1.2 billion, up about 25 percent over 1974.[9]

15 MILLION JOBS DEPEND ON THE AUTO?

The power of the automobile industry is not measured, however, solely in terms of its internal structure and thus its ability to realize supercompetitive profits. Its power is grounded in a number of other dimensions, including its enormous size, its critical role in the entire transportation sector of the economy, and the vast network of related industries that depend on it for their livelihood in one way or another. The four auto companies had sales of $27 billion in 1969. Some 800,000 workers were employed in the manufacture of automotive vehicles and parts in that year, for a total payroll of $6.5 billion. It has been estimated, moreover, that no fewer than 15 million American jobs were directly or indirectly dependent on the automobile. Mr. L. A. Iacocca, then an executive vice president of the Ford Motor Company, in his 1970 testimony before the Senate Subcommittee on Air and Water Pollution, stressed the importance of the automotive industry to the committee members in the following vivid terms:

> The Senate Subcommittee on Air and Water Pollution chaired by Senator Muskie of Maine has just adopted an amended Clean Air Act. Some of the changes in this bill could prevent continued production of automobiles after January 1, 1975. Even if they do not stop production, they could lead to huge increases in the price of cars. They could have a tremendous impact on all of American industry and could do irreparable damage to the American economy. And yet, in return for all of this, they would lead to only small improvements in the quality of the air.

> The manufacture of motor vehicles and parts is the largest industry in America—first in sales, first in employment and first in payrolls. Automobile manufacturing and distribution and automotive transportation provide 15 million jobs—28 percent of private non-farm employment.

> Each car and truck manufactured and sold in the United States generates $1,200 in taxes—nearly 35 percent of the average retail price. And these taxes provide 5 percent of the total tax revenue of all units of government.

> That is why this bill is a threat to the entire American economy and to every person in America.[10]

THE TRANSPORTATION SECTOR

Transportation costs ranked third in 1972 in terms of expenditures by the American consumer, behind only food and housing and ahead of clothing, medical expenses, and recreation. Consumer spending in that year totaled $721 billion and 13.6 percent of that total—$98 billion—was allocated to transportation. The gross auto product, a special table in the official national income accounts of the Department of Commerce, totaled $43 billion in 1972. While the figure is slightly less than 4 percent of our overall GNP, it exceeds the national income generated by agriculture, forestry, and fishing combined; is almost as great as the entire mining and construction industries combined; is nearly a third of the value of all manufactured durable goods; and is almost a third of the national income generated by all government and government enterprises.[11]

ELEVEN KEY INDUSTRIES

The automobile industry is also the most important of a small group of key industries, those that have an importance beyond their actual percentage of the country's total economic activity.[12] This is the group of industries that forms the core of what Galbraith, for example, has referred to as the "Industrial System," the world of "the few hundred technically dynamic, massively capitalized and highly organized corporations."[13] Robert Averitt, calling this same network of giant firms the "Center Economy," identifies them as the ones that "participate in the innermost councils of government [and constitute] the backbone of American industrial strength in war and peace."[14] Averitt lists eleven such key industries, including the automobile industry itself and four others that are closely related to it, petroleum, rubber products, iron and steel, and machinery.[15] The membership roster of four of these industries reads like a Who's Who of American industrial power—General Motors, Ford, Chrysler, American Motors, Exxon, Mobil, Texaco, Gulf, Standard, Goodyear, Goodrich, Uniroyal, US Steel, Bethlehem, Inland Steel, Armco—and the four account for roughly 15 percent of the GNP. Of the hundred largest industrial corporations in the United States in 1973, thirty of them were in these four critical industries. Together, they were responsible for nearly half (49 percent) of the combined total sales of those hundred largest corporations in the nation.[16]

CORPORATE COLOSSUSES

The importance of the automobile and related industries is even more apparent in a list of the country's twenty largest corporations. As indicated in Table 4-1, no fewer than twelve of these twenty largest industrial firms are directly linked with the automotive industry, including four of the top five. Those twelve corporations accounted for 21 percent of the country's gross nonfinancial corporate product and their combined profits accounted for a similar percentage of total nonfinancial corporate profits. Each of the twelve also belongs to one of the key industries mentioned above. In short, the great corporations that have emerged to fill the transportation needs of American society have put together the most imposing concentration of private economic power the world has ever seen. They are corporate colossuses, industrial giants approached in economic power only by the giant firms in the electrical-equipment and computer–business machine industries. They are not just economic behemoths: they are the key organizations in our economic system, the ones that determine how well or how poorly our economy performs.

TABLE 4-1

The Twenty Largest Industrial Corporations, 1972

Rank	Firm	Sales	Assets	Net Income	Employees
		(Millions of Dollars)			
1	General Motors	$ 30,435	$ 18,273	$ 2,162	759,543
2	Exxon	20,309	21,558	1,531	141,000
3	Ford Motor	20,194	11,634	870	442,607
4	General Electric	10,239	7,401	530	369,000
5	Chrysler	9,759	5,497	220	244,844
6	IBM	9,532	10,792	1,279	262,152
7	Mobil Oil	9,166	9,216	574	75,400
8	Texaco	8,692	12,032	889	76,496
9	ITT	8,556	8,617	483	428,000
10	Western Electric	6,551	4,309	282	205,665
11	Gulf Oil	6,243	9,324	197	57,500
12	Standard Oil of California	5,829	8,084	547	41,497
13	US Steel	5,401	6,570	156	176,486
14	Westinghouse Electric	5,086	3,843	198	183,768
15	Standard Oil (Indiana)	4,503	6,186	374	46,627
16	E. I. Dupont de Nemours	4,365	4,283	414	11,052
17	Shell Oil	4,075	5,171	260	32,871
18	Goodyear Tire & Rubber	4,071	3,476	193	145,201
19	RCA	3,838	3,137	158	122,000
20	Proctor & Gamble	3,514	2,360	276	45,000
		$180,358	$161,993	$11,593	2,936,709
	Auto and auto-related total	$128,677	$117,021	$ 7,973	2,240,072
	Auto-related percentage of 20-firm total	71%	72%	68%	57%

Source: *Fortune 500: The Largest U.S. Industrial Corporations* (May 1973), p. 22.

THE RIPPLE EFFECT AND THE PRINCIPLE OF
COLLECTIVE ECONOMIC INACTION

But the automobile complex is not *just* a collection of giant industrial corporations. In a democratic society, numbers count, and the automobile industry affects literally millions of *small* firms and individual citizens, all of whom thereby acquire a vested interest in its continued prosperity. The ripple effect that flows from an increase or decrease in a particular industry's production is a matter of no small importance in assessing the power of that industry to resist legislative reform. The larger that ripple effect, and the greater the number of industries, business firms, and individuals it touches, the greater the sum total of the opposition there is likely to be to public policies that might reduce the accustomed flow of economic benefits.

It might well be, of course, that proposed reforms would produce, in the long run, gains to society that exceeded the sum of the individual losses involved in effecting those changes; but the gainers and the losers are not likely to be the same persons, firms, or industries. And even if it could be shown that the losers in the current reforms would also be the gainers in some new economic arrangement, it would be almost impossible for any one individual to perceive a personal advantage to him for the change *if* the new arrangement could only be reached by *collective* action. The immediate loss is a certainty, while the larger future benefits—unless one can be assured in advance that everyone else is going to cooperate—are a dubious contingency. Proposed reforms of this kind are not likely to sound like a good bet to those adversely affected in the first instance; thus they give rise to a resistance that might be called the principle of collective economic inaction. Until the widespread use of rapid transit systems has been assured, for example, it is not only possible but indeed highly probable that the benefits to be realized from the development of an alternative rapid-transit system cannot be obtained by an individual firm or person. *Collective* action is in fact required and, so long as the auto-highway lobby is able to guarantee that this is not going to happen, everyone even remotely connected with the profitability of our present reliance on the automobile has an incentive to resist any proposed change.

THE FABRIC INDUSTRY AN AUTO LOBBYIST?

The industries that sell a large portion of their total output to the auto manufacturers are of course especially beholden to the motor car. A study of the input-output matrix published in *Fortune* magazine, for example, reveals that thirty-two industries sold $100 million or more of goods or services to the automotive industry in 1966.[17] Of those thirty-two industries, seventeen of them count the automotive industry as one of their four largest customers. Nine of them count it as their *largest* single customer. Are these latter industries a part of the automotive lobby? Undoubtedly. But how about an industry like "Broad and Narrow Fabrics, Yarn, and Thread Mills," with 1966 sales to the car producers of "only" $104.9 million? Could a firm in this industry be classified as a member of the automotive lobby? Probably not in any strict definition of the term. But it is also not likely to be a supporter of measures that would adversely affect *any* of its customers, including the automobile producers. While the just over $100 million worth of fabrics bought by the auto industry in 1966 was of course a very small percentage of all fabric sales in that year, business firms can't afford to be attentive to the interests of large customers only. The sales represented by a particular customer might well represent the margin between a quite profitable operation and one that is just getting by. No matter how small the advantages of the present system might be to the individual businessman, they always exert some influence in favor of continuing the status quo until the likelihood of much larger benefits from a proposed change can be seen with some real assurance. It might well be, for example, that the fabrics and yarn industry will some day sell an even larger percentage of its output to the manufacturers of cars for mass-transit facilities than it sells to the auto producers today. But the incentive to pursue such a speculative future advantage is in no way comparable to the incentive to maintain the realized advantages of the present.

CONCRETE, CONSTRUCTION, AND HIGHWAYS

The previous example illustrates the interconnections between the industries which act as direct suppliers to the motor vehicle industry. While these are of great significance, there are other, even larger industries, which, while not acting as direct suppliers to the motor vehicle industry, are more or less dependent on the automotive industry for their continued success and, in a few instances, very existence. To complete the picture, these industries, in turn, have all the same set of interlocking relationships with their own suppliers as depicted for the automotive industry in the preceding set of thirty-two industries.

To take a "concrete" example, and also in the process to give some indication of just how deep into the economic system the built-in resistance may extend, imagine an individual firm in the ready-mix concrete industry. Again, even though such a firm sells concrete for numerous purposes and is not even a direct supplier to the automotive industry, the firm nevertheless sells some 5 percent of its total output to local highway contractors. And again, this marginal 5 percent of sales may provide the difference between a profitable operation based on volume, and business losses. Is this firm a member of the highway-automotive lobby? All of the same built-in incentives to favor the present reliance on automotive transportation are present, even though it does not sell directly to the automotive industry itself.

This hypothetical firm, however, has served an even more significant purpose: it has led us directly to a completely separate, huge industry which buys nothing from the automotive industry and sells it nothing, yet is totally dependent on the existence of the automotive industry for its own existence. The highway industry, which sells its products directly to the public through state and federal government agencies, is more than one-fourth the size of the motor vehicle industry itself. It provides millions of jobs and extends into every nook and cranny of the nation. Is this industry a member of the highway-automotive lobby? With a vengeance.

TACIT COLLUSION AT THE GROCERY STORES?

It is not just the industries that buy from or sell to the automotive industry that make up the auto complex we are talking about here. Each industry that does business with the auto makers has its own satellite industries, and these, in turn, have *their* sets of dependent industries. Figure 4-1 attempts to represent diagramatically the major features of this system. Consider the country's giant petroleum industry, for example. Very little of its product is sold directly to the auto manufacturers. But auto *consumers* spend an enormous amount of money for the fuel needed to run the auto industry's cars, and they support a vast network of gasoline service stations located in virtually every village and hamlet across the country, each operated by a small businessman with a very large stake indeed in the future of the automobile. And then there are the myriad industries that supply the petroleum industry itself, all the way from the wildcatters who bring the crude out of the ground to the financial institutions and even retail trade establishments that supply it with goods and services. Table 4-2, for example, lists some of the major input suppliers to the petroleum refining industry, each of whom supplies *it* with $100 million or more worth of goods and services per year. And of course a similar table can be constructed for each of the other industries either directly related or complementary in one way or another to the auto industry. Some of these industries are farther removed from the automotive hub than others, but all of them have a mutual interest here, and all are in some degree engaged in tacit collusion to protect the automotive manufacturers. Even grocery stores, movie theatres (particularly

FIGURE 4-1
The Great Web (Wheel) of Automotive Interests

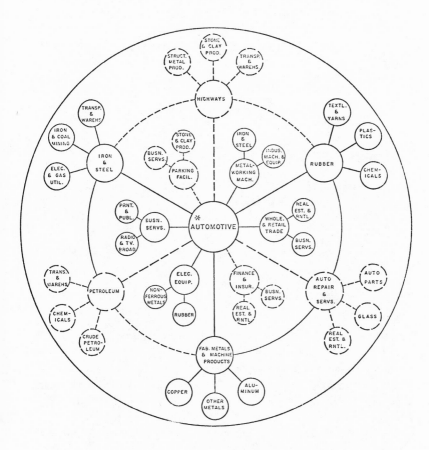

Note: Solid lines indicate direct input suppliers; broken lines indicate complementary industries and their input suppliers.

drive-ins), and housing reflect the hegemony of the private automobile, a product that enjoys a degree of significance and economic power that no single industry has ever attained before.

TABLE 4-2

Industries Supplying More than $100 Million of
Inputs to the Petroleum Refining Industry, 1966

Industry	Million $
Crude petroleum	$13,757.4
Chemicals	825.6
Petroleum	1,950.0
Fabricated metal products	299.0
Transportation and warehousing	1,439.0
Electric utilities	132.4
Gas utilities	273.6
Wholesale and retail trade	289.5
Finance and insurance	179.6
Real estate and rental	217.3
Business services	554.0

Source: "Input-Output Matrix of the United States Economy," *Fortune* (1966).

THE USES OF AUTO POWER—ELIMINATING THE COMPETITION

The history of the Big Three, and in particular General Motors's rise to economic prominence, is studded with direct actions to eliminate all viable alternatives to the automobile. This ability is directly related to the automotive industry's consolidation of power within its own industry and the ensuing system of administered prices. As noted earlier, this method allowed the auto sellers to earn great oligopolistic profits. These profits, in turn, enabled them to buy out and displace competitive means of transport or to force uneconomic policies on their rivals which eventually led to the latters' demise.

All these activities were perfectly consistent with the drive to maximize profits. A bus or trolley coach can put thirty-five automobiles off the road; a subway, streetcar, or rapid transit vehicle can supplant fifty passenger cars, and an interurban railway or railroad train can serve in the place of a thousand cars.[18] As long as these forms of transport continued as viable alternatives to the car, the auto industry could never grow to its present gargantuan size and have nearly total monopoly of United States ground transport.

The actual elimination of competition took place in three phases: the substitution of bus for rail passenger transportation; the acquisition and dismantling of local electric systems, to be replaced by buses; and the displacement of the uncomfortable and inefficient bus system with private passenger cars.

In 1925, General Motors acquired Yellow Coach, the country's largest producer of buses. It then assisted in the formation of the Greyhound Corporation one year later and became involved with that company's attempt to displace passenger rail with intercity bus service. Greyhound, in return, agreed to buy almost all its buses from GM, which also agreed not to sell any of its buses to Greyhound's competitors. By a system of pressure and agreements to coordinate intercity passenger service, Greyhound gradually began to replace the major railroads' commuter rail services. By 1950, about half as many intercity passengers were being transported by Greyhound as by all the railroads combined. GM remained instrumental in this operation throughout, lending money when Greyhound experienced temporary cash flow problems and continuing as the largest single shareholder in the Greyhound Corporation until 1948.

The next line of attack was to begin the systematic purchase of local electric transit systems, which were then literally scrapped and replaced by buses. GM thus formed a holding company, United Cities Motor Transit, whose sole function was to purchase electric streetcar companies, convert them to GM-built bus systems, and then resell them to local operators who entered agreements to purchase GM equipment. After several years this program was discontinued because of the censure of the American Transit Association.[19]

GM had at first intended to concentrate on the conversion of small city operations, gradually working up to the larger urban areas. But it now decided, in 1936, to undertake the conversion of the nation's largest city. Combining efforts with the Omnibus Corporation, in which GM had significant stock ownership and interlocking directorate influence, New York City's electric streetcar system was converted to GM buses in eighteen months. The demise of the world's largest electric streetcar system marked the turning point in the electric rail industry.

Emboldened by this success, GM set up a new holding company, National City Lines, Inc., which began operating along the same lines as the United Cities Motor Transit Co. But National City Lines was far more successful, buying up system after system in sixteen states, converting them to GM buses, reselling the properties to obtain cash to purchase and convert still another city, and taking pains to insure nonreconversion. How? By the simple expedient of demanding contracts from the new owners which forbade the use of "any new equipment using any fuel or means of propulsion other than gas."[20] The capstone to these operations was the purchase of the Los Angeles Railway local system by the GM- and Standard Oil–financed American City Lines. Its electric cars were scrapped, the transmission lines torn down, and the tracks ripped up. These were immediately replaced by noxious diesel-powered buses—provided by GM of course—and fueled by none other than Standard Oil.[21]

By the close of the 1940's, GM's devastating assault on the electric railways was virtually complete. GM had participated in the elimination of over a hundred electric transit systems in forty-five cities, including New York, Los Angeles, Philadelphia, St. Louis, and Baltimore. In 1949 GM was finally convicted, along with Standard Oil of California, the Firestone Tire Co., and others, of conspiring to eliminate electric transportation and monopolizing the sale of buses and parts. GM was fined $5,000 for its role, and one of its chief executives involved in these efforts was convicted and fined $1.[22] But the damage was already done, and the microscopic amount of the fines was only an additional insult added to injury.

The final phase of this decade-long operation was the replacement of the buses, which had been used to eliminate the electric rails, with passenger automobiles. Along the route to replacing inter- and intraurban electric rail transportation, GM had also monopolized the bus business. So effective was this monopoly that by 1973 only one other firm, the Flexible Co., which was controlled by a GM vice-president was still manufacturing city buses. The next move was, of course, predictable by now. GM allowed its buses to fall behind technologically and proceeded to charge monopoly prices. The sole alternative available to cities that wanted to lure people out of their cars and into public transit was now in the hands of its chief rival, the automobile. The diesel bus, as engineered by GM, has a shorter life expectancy, higher operating costs, and lower overall productivity than electric buses. GM has thus made the bus economically noncompetitive with the car also.

THE USES OF AUTO POWER—CAPTURING THE LEGISLATORS

Given the scope of the interlocking economic interests we have described above, it is hardly surprising that extensive means have been employed to protect and advance them, particularly the common device of attempting to gain systematic control of the various legislative bodies and governmental agencies that have the capacity to help or hurt the automobile and its friends.

While it is not easy to document the full extent of these activities, the weapons used here obviously include elaborate lobbying, campaign contributions to friendly legislators, and outright control of various regulatory agencies. One reason for all this is that many citizens are unwilling to believe that governmental agencies and legislatures *can* be controlled by private economic interests. Moreover, the notion persists that while the institutions of government might be *temporarily* sullied, they remain basically sound and well intentioned. More recently, however, the evidence has been accumulating that many powerful legislative committees, and particularly the government's regulatory agencies, are nothing more than extensions of the business interests of the economically powerful.[23] Legislation is either written for the express purpose of protecting special interests in the first place or it is subsequently distorted by the managing bureaucracy in a way that can cause even more harm to the public interest. The automotive industry, together with its chain of supporting interest groups and complementary industries, is one of the prime modern examples of this phenomenon.

THE BLESSINGS OF "REGULATION"

Legislative favoritism of economic interests should not be regarded as the result of either accident or faulty planning in the drafting of our laws or their subsequent enforcement. On the contrary, those in charge of these chores generally know quite well what they are doing and intend the full consequences of it. An early piece of evidence on this point is a letter written in 1894 by Richard Olney, Attorney General of the United States under Grover Cleveland. The president of a railroad, unhappy with certain activities of the recently created Interstate Commerce Commission (ICC), was considering whether the railroad industry should begin a lobbying campaign to get that agency abolished. Mr. Olney wrote to the gentleman and advised him *not* to pursue that course. He explained that first of all, the effort would probably be unsuccessful and would, if the attack centered on "the inefficiency and uselessness of the Commission," probably result in Congress's giving it the power it then lacked.

But Mr. Olney had an even more persuasive reason for wanting to keep the ICC. As he explained it:

The Commission, *as its functions have now been limited by courts, is, or can be made, of great use to the railroads.* It satisfies the popular clamor for a government supervision of railroads, at the same time that the supervision is almost entirely nominal. Furthermore, the older such a Commission gets to be, the more inclined it will be to take the business and railroad view of things. It becomes a sort of barrier between the business corporations and the people and a sort of protection against hasty and crude legislation hostile to railroad interests . . . *The part of wisdom is not to destroy the Commission but to utilize it.*"[24]

Succeeding events have done little to tarnish Mr. Olney's reputation as a prophet.[25]

SELF-REGULATION AS A BARRIER TO ENTRY

The auto industry has done better than any other industry that wanted "regulation"—i.e., subsidization of its interests and protection from competition—but without the burdens regulation might impose. The subsidy to and the competitive protection of the auto industry comes, as noted, from the operation of the Highway Trust Fund, a device that pours federal tax money into the construction of roads and thus discourages cities and states from turning to competing forms of transportation like rapid transit. Intraindustry competition is taken care of by the various competitive devices mentioned previously: frequent style changes, exclusive dealership arrangements, price leadership, and the like. In short, the industry has acquired and successfully retained the right to regulate itself, a right it has exercised with such prudence as to make the auto business the most profitable industry in the country.

A SURROGATE LOBBYIST WITH MANY FRIENDS

One of the more important advantages that the auto industry derives from its governmental protector, the Highway Trust Fund, is freedom from the necessity of having to lobby *directly* for special favors in its own behalf. The fund operates as a *surrogate* lobby for the automobile, thus shifting the focus of that lobbying effort away from the auto industry itself and onto the supporters of highway construction. And of course it picks up another and very important side benefit here, namely, the legislative support of traffic engineers, highway engineers, the construction industry, and the trucking industry.

THE GOVERNMENT–BUSINESS BROTHERHOOD

The lobbying efforts of the automotive-highway interests are reflected in three major areas: (1) the frequency with which major executives and industry personnel move between government and industry; (2) political contributions on behalf of strategically placed legislators; and (3) the constant barrage of publicity and public-relations work designed to influence—or confuse—the public in general and government agencies concerning the preferences of the American people and the values of the automotive society. On the first point, corporate administrators and technicians, particularly those of the auto industry, have long moved freely in and out of the federal government, thus blurring the line between government interests and those of private business concerns. Nowhere is this mutuality of interests more clearly understood or more staunchly promoted than among the leaders of the auto corporations themselves. James Roche, Chairman of the Board of General Motors, put it succinctly in a 1968 speech:

Business and government can ill afford to be adversaries. So mutual are our interests, so formidable are our challenges, that times demand our strengthened alliance. . . . Today, business and government are each becoming more involved in the affairs of the other.[26]

As still another commentator, this time not connected with the auto industry, put it:

The bonds which tie government and big business are in many ways closer than those which tie big business and small business. Seekers of jobs and favors move easily from Washington to Detroit, and vice versa, bringing with them lasting friendships and loyalties. A president of General Motors, Charles Wilson, becomes secretary of defense. He brings with him his vice president, Roger Kyes, to be deputy secretary; later Kyes returns to GM as vice president and director. A president of Ford, Robert McNamara, becomes *another* secretary of defense. A ranking member of the State Department, Thomas Mann, becomes president of the Automobile Manufacturers Association. A president of American Motors, George Romney, becomes secretary of Housing and Urban Development. A former secretary of commerce, John T. Conner, becomes a director of General Motors. Walter Mote, the brother of Lynn Mote, becomes an administrative assistant to Vice President Spiro Agnew.[27]

While these ties with government in the upper echelons are singularly important, they do not end there. As Ayres and many others have pointed out, young corporation lawyers interchange freely between the legal offices of the automotive corporations and such law enforcement agencies as the Antitrust Division of the Justice Department, the Securities and Exchange Commission (SEC), and the Federal Trade Commission (FTC). These young men are frequently placed there on loan for "public service" and subsequently return to work for their original employer. The failure to apply the antitrust laws to General Motors or any other automotive corporation is not difficult to understand when one remembers that the would-be prosecutors are, in effect, employees of the potential prosecutees.

CAMPAIGN CONTRIBUTIONS

Many Americans prefer to believe that favors from the federal government are not bought and sold. The confidence of others in their government and its officials has been seriously eroded, however, by recent disclosures in such matters as the infamous ITT and Milk cases, in which campaign contributions were apparently made with certain expectations of subsequent performance by the recipient or, from time to time, as a reward for services already rendered.[28] The highway lobby, for example, reportedly spends some $500 million a year on its various activities, including contributions ranging from $500 to $3,000 in campaign money for thirteen members of the House Public Works Committee, one of the most important congressional committees dealing with highway affairs.[29] Trade associations and other organizations associated with the Highway Users Conference reportedly pay key members of this committee speaking fees running as high as $5,000 per speech. This is of course not quite as much as a good rock performer can get at a college concert, but the music subsequently sung by the congressmen in question is no doubt far sweeter to the highway interests than the lilting lyrics of a Leon Russell. The latter, after all, do not mean millions of dollars in new contracts and sales opportunities or insure the continued flow of resources into the automotive transport mode, a flow that locks the nation ever more solidly in the grip of heavy fixed capital investment and binds it to a system that will be extremely difficult to junk at a later date.

GREASING THE WHEELS AT THE LOCAL LEVELS

The campaign contributions received directly by senators and congressmen from the automotive interests are not the full measure, however, of the financial influence exerted by those interests on the members of the national legislature. While the latter are supposed to represent national policy and national interests, they come from individual states and are elected to their national office by the residents of their respective home districts. And since even the most extensive support at the national level can seldom get a senator or congressman elected back home over the opposition of his home-state political machinery, contributions put into the proper political channels at the local level can generate intense pressure on the federal politician through his own local political machine. While this is an indirect method of lobbying for national policies, it has the advantage of being not only very effective but of reducing the risks for both the contributors themselves and the federal legislators to be influenced. Interest groups that share the same policy goals but are geographically dispersed—as are the automotive-highway industries—are ideally situated to carry out this kind of local lobbying effort.

THE MAYOR AN AUTO DEALER?

The automobile and its complementary industries are deeply involved in local politics in almost every state in the nation. A local automobile assembly plant, for example, with thousands of employees and hundreds of thousands of dollars of local property tax revenues at stake, can strike fear in the hearts of almost any state or local official. State highway departments are among the most important dispensers of political largesse in every state. Local government officials (mayors and councilmen, for example) tend to be drawn from the ranks of the local business leadership, especially where they are not remunerated for their services or receive only minimal compensation. Auto dealers, gasoline service station operators, parking-lot owners, and local construction firms virtually run many local governments. A disproportionately large number of mayors, for example, appear to be proprietors of automobile dealerships. From the upper reaches of the federal government to the bottom of the local political hierarchy, then, the tentacles of the automotive interest groups are pervasive. Indeed, they are so deeply embedded in the heart of the American economy and in the councils of government that those interests and government are virtually synonymous.

"SERVANTS OF THE SYSTEM"

Faced with the massive array of interlocking interests and well-orchestrated influence which characterize the political economy of the auto, what are the possibilities for the development of meaningful transportation alternatives? Probably not very great at the present time. A handful of cities have initiated well-publicized attempts to provide some improvement in mass transit facilities. But these will not accomplish very much because they are in all cases seen primarily as subsidiary efforts which will supplement the continuing main means of transport, the car. And even in these instances, the mass transit facilities turn out to be little more than highly subsidized commuter lines for affluent suburbanites. The federal government meanwhile has largely defined mass transit as the bus. This solves nothing, since buses need the same facilities to operate on as autos and thus facilitate continued auto domination.

The automobile is more than an economic problem. It is a *political* problem, one that, if it is to be solved at all, will have to be solved by political means. And that will not be an easy task. As Sam Bowles has recently noted,[30] the real range of policy alternatives is always severely circumscribed by the fact that policy makers working for change within "the system" cannot avoid becoming, albeit unwillingly, servants of the very power structure they are trying to change.

5

THE POLITICAL ESTABLISHMENT

A landed interest, a manufacturing interest, a mercantile interest, a moneyed interest, with many lesser interests, grow up of necessity in civilized nations, and divide them into different classes, actuated by different sentiments and views. The regulation of these various and interfering interests forms the principle task of modern legislation, and involves the spirit of party and faction in the necessary and ordinary operations of the government.

No man is allowed to be a judge in his own cause, because his interest would certainly bias his judgment, and not improbably corrupt his integrity.
    —James Madison, *The Federalist*, No. 39.

In American society economic institutions play an active and powerful role in public affairs. In view of the magnitude of those economic institutions just discussed, one would expect their influence to be of considerable importance in the formulation of transportation policy; hence a major concern of this chapter will be to explore the relationships between economic and political structures. Although economic power cannot always be translated directly into political gain, we will see that the economic power of the highway lobby is reinforced by several other characteristics that give it tremendous leverage in determining political policy. In addition, we will also examine those governmental agencies most directly involved with the development of transportation policy. Who actually decides what American transportation policy will be? What agencies are involved in support of the highway program and what—if any—counteragencies exist? Finally, we will examine the governmental structure at the state and local level. How do state and local political organizations affect transportation policy? Who actually determines transportation policy in our cities? How do variations in state and local political structures affect the kinds of decisions that are made?

INTERFACE: THE HIGHWAY LOBBY AND GOVERNMENT

Although the interest group is viewed by many as a corrupting influence in the political process, others, including several political scientists, conceive of these groups as a salutary component of the American political system.[1] The "group theory of politics" holds that in a complex society, individuals with shared interest band together in groups in order to press their demands and claims upon government. Politics, then, is nothing more than a struggle among groups who seek to gain governmental sanction for their objectives. Government is viewed as an arbitrator: it establishes the "rules of the game." Within the existing rules, the government's task is to arrange compromises among the contending groups, ratify those compromises, and then enforce them.

Lobbyists, of course, are the ubiquitous representatives of interest groups. Although the lobbyist of the past was often viewed as a dispenser of bribes, the modern lobbyist is much more sophisticated and, indeed, serves some useful purposes, such as providing legislators with information and research on pending bills.[2] The highway lobby, of course, is recognized as one of the most powerful lobbies in Washington, even though its members vociferously deny its existence and dislike being identified with it.[3] Their denials are understandable, since a great deal of derisive criticism has been aimed at the highway lobby, a conglomerate of private organizations seeking to perpetuate governmental policies in favor of the private automobile and highway construction. The criticism is not the work of the radical fringe groups, either. Even one of middle America's staunchest supporters, the *Reader's Digest,* took the lobby to task and depicted it as a "pressure packed alliance of all who promote highways for profit—from truckers and construction unions to billboard firms . . . riding roughshod over the development of a sane transportation system in the United States."[4]

Even when its members are forced to acknowledge its existence, they characterize it as truly democratic and people-oriented. Beginning with candor and ending with euphoria, Frank Ikard, president of the American Petroleum Institute, admitted: "There *is* a highway lobby in the United States—It is an active and powerful lobby—nationwide in scope and vast in membership. The card-carrying members consist of some 103 million licensed drivers."[5] Although the average driver might be quite surprised to find himself in such elite company, there is little that he can do to terminate his membership—except possibly burn his license. One critic of this claim suggested that "in the same vein, cigarette smokers can be called the cigarette lobby."[6]

The highway lobby also provides generous financial contributions to political friends. *Forbes* magazine, not known for its radical inclinations, reported that highway interest groups shelled out some $500 million a year in lobbying and campaign expenditures.[7] But financial support for candidates is not the only way that high-ranking officials of industry influence governmental policy. In many cases, there is an interlocking arrangement between industry and government, and many governmental officials, as noted in the previous chapter, are "on loan" from various industries.[8] In this way, the industry's influence is entrenched directly in various governmental departments. Charles Wilson headed General Motors at the time of his appointment as secretary of defense and brought along his vice-president, Roger Kyes, who subsequently returned to GM. Robert McNamara, another GM president, also became secretary of defense. George Romney, president of American Motors, became secretary of housing and urban development. Thomas Mann, a former official in the State Department, assumed the presidency of the Automobile Manufacturers Association after leaving his government job. Although these cases represent the links between industry and government at the highest levels, the lower levels of government also draw heavily on industry to fill other positions. The Antitrust Division of the Justice Department, for example, is staffed by many of GM's corporate lawyers.

The power of interest groups in American politics is of considerable concern; and, aside from the economic resources which can be brought to bear on political decision makers, there are several other reasons why one interest group is stronger than another. For example, cohesiveness is frequently listed as a key attribute in explaining the influence of an interest group. If the members of the group are unified in purpose, the group is more likely to succeed in attaining its objectives than a fragmented group. For example, the American Medical Association, although small in size, is an extremely cohesive interest group.[9] Size is also another factor accounting for the power of an interest group.[10] If an interest group with a large membership can translate its numbers into votes on election day, it can exert considerable influence in government. If the highway lobby actually consisted of the 103 million drivers as claimed by Mr. Ikard, it would be a large interest group indeed.

Although the highway lobby is characterized by both cohesiveness and large membership, there are two other characteristics that give the highway lobby significant leverage in the political process. Not only does the highway lobby consist of a wide variety of interlocking organizations on a horizontal basis, but its members are active at every level in our governmental structure, which provides the lobby with highly effective *vertical* pressure. The horizontal power of the highway lobby is a consequence of the diversified organizations with a shared interest in motorized transport and highways. To illustrate this diversity, one author identifies some fifty petroleum companies as members of the highway lobby, about fifteen from the trucking industry, and a like number representing automotive manufacturers. In addition, several major unions speak on behalf of highways as well as the pressure groups created by the bureaucrats who administer the highway program, such as the American Association of State Highway Officials.[11]

It is one thing for a single economic organization to pursue some political advantage, as the oil industry did to retain the oil depletion allowance, but it is a different ball game when the political decision makers face an array of powerful groups, groups representing every major spectrum of American society. The highway lobby represents more than several different types of business organizations: the labor unions and the auto associations[12] sit right alongside the industrial giants in demanding a strong highway policy. Few other political programs receive this kind of diversified support. For example, in the field of health, the AMA cannot call upon any labor unions to buttress its case, and the consumer, in fact, is likely to be openly hostile to political measures proposed by the AMA. Yet, even more significant is the vertical pressure which can be applied by the highway lobby. In many ways, the structure of the highway lobby parallels the political structure of American government. Our political structure is superbly tailored to facilitate and maximize the goals of the highway lobby. What this means is that the highway lobby is effectively and forcefully represented at each level of government, not just the national level. The parallel between the highway lobby structure and the political structure is illustrated in Table 5-1. This table clearly illustrates the extensive pressure the highway lobby can bring to bear on different levels of government policy. If we compare this kind of arrangement with the urban mass transit lobby, we find notable differences. Although mass transit is represented by a lobbying association at the national level,[13] its influence is virtually nil at the state level and is confined to only a dozen or so major cities at the local level. Obviously, the highway lobby enjoys a preponderant advantage in any confrontation with the miniscule proponents of mass transportation.

The vertical power of the highway lobby in American politics is reinforced in several other ways. In the first place, the business organizations depicted in the table represent significant economic activities at each level. But even at the state level, the lobby operating under guise of assorted names has demonstrated remarkable political sophistication. In Texas, for example, not only are business organizations with a direct economic stake in highways members of the "Good Roads Association," but a wide variety of other organizations and individuals have been recruited for the cause. Some 2,335 individuals, associations, firms, chambers of commerce, cities, and counties are listed as members of the association. Although most lobbies depend upon the goodwill of the press and seek out sympathetic editors, the Texas lobby can count on almost automatic support in the media since some twenty-three newspapers and publishing companies are members of the association, including newspapers in Dallas, Houston, Midland, and San Antonio.[14]

TABLE 5-1

Political Pressure Points and the Highway Lobby

Pressure Points	Representatives of Highway Lobby
Federal government	Auto producer associations; petroleum associations; national auto unions (e.g., UAW), auto consumer associations (e.g., AAA)
State government	State construction associations; regional and state labor unions, both construction and industrial; state auto consumer associations
Local government	Auto dealers; petroleum distributors; construction companies; local construction unions; automobile commuters; local auto associations

Nevertheless, it is the business organizations with a direct stake in the construction of highways, especially the contractors, who serve as the key political mobilizers of the lobby. As Daniel Moynihan points out:

In most states a symbiotic relationship has been established between the contracting firms and the local political organizations which obviates the usual forms of corruption. The contractors pay an honest tithe to the political parties' exchequers out of fair profits, which are large, mostly because the sums involved are vast . . . To the extent that this system works, it provides an excellent, if informal means of financing our parties out of tax funds. Contractors are normally apolitical, asking only that there be just a little more than enough work to go around. The politicians usually do their best.[15]

This same point is made by David Hapgood, who argues:

Money is the lifeblood of politics, and the richest blood that flows in the veins of state and local political organizations is derived from highways and their economic side effects. Nothing generates more financial return, legal or otherwise, to those in office than highway construction . . . State and local officeholders have everything to gain from highway construction, on which they can get more bang from the taxpayer's buck than from any other kind of spending.[16]

At the local level, the interest groups with a stake in the continuation of our present highway policies represent a sizable segment of the economic system. For example, the auto dealers, service station owners, and local construction firms constitute a significant economic coalition. This coalition is further buttressed by other powerful economic units, such as large-scale shopping centers and parking lot owners. But the prime beneficiaries of highways at the local level are the land developers and speculators. Building the highways is not nearly so lucrative as owning the adjacent land. Consequently, every new road and improvement greatly enhances the value of land. Even though the developers pay not one cent into the till, they are able to reap enormous profits from highway construction.[17]

Thus the highway lobby is represented at every level of government, at every access point in the political system, by powerful and diversified groups. These are the circumstances that make the lobby a strong influence on government policies.

DECISION-MAKERS AND FEDERAL TRANSPORTATION POLICY: THE CORDIAL ENTENTE

Every civics textbook on American government talks about democracy in some idealistic fashion. The political process begins with the people, who make their needs known. The political parties articulate these needs in their platforms, and the president and Congress ratify and legitimate these needs. An understanding of transportation policy suggests the inadequacies of this view of the democratic process. Transportation policy is developed by a rather narrow and semi-autonomous group of "subgovernments."[18] These subgovernments consist primarily of three sets of actors—the congressional committees, the administrative bureaus, and the interest groups.

Both the president and the Congress are ill equipped to participate in the policy process: Congress because of its archaic organization and the president because of his many responsibilities. Even though the president may appoint a cabinet officer over the administrative bureau, the cabinet officer at best serves as a presidential liaison and at worst a captive of the bureaucracy he symbolically heads:

Thus, except in the case of issues which become escalated to the level of compelling national concern, the resolution of most policy questions tends more often to be left to secondary levels of the political setting . . . the subordinate units of the Administrator and Congress.[19]

The major actors involved in federal transportation policy can be plotted on a triangle as in Figure 5-1.

The role of the highway lobby, the major interest group in the development of transportation policy, has already been examined. Although the congressional committee is theoretically a subordinate unit of Congress, it is not really subordinate. Indeed, the committee is the prime vehicle through which its chairman dominates the legislative process:

The power of the chairman is manifest in the legislative process wherever one looks. When hearings are held, he controls the time made available to both witnesses and members of Congress. When his committee recommends enactment of a bill, the report it submits has ordinarily been drafted by a staff subject to his will. When a committee bill is being debated on the floor of the House, he may be its "manager," controlling half the time that is made available for speakers and doling it out as he pleases. And when an effort is made to reconcile a committee bill passed by his house with a different version approved on the other side of the Capitol, he usually heads the "conferees" from his chamber.[20]

Figure 5-1. Federal Transportation Policy Actors

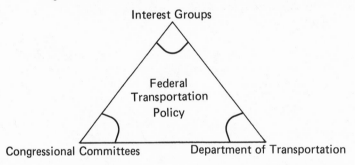

The two major committees in Congress that oversee the highway program are the Senate and House Public Works committees. Senator Jennings Randolph, former treasurer of the American Road Builder's Association, heads up the Senate Committee, and Congressman Robert E. Jones recently assumed the chairmanship in the House. Within each committee there are two subcommittees on roads. Congressman John C. Klucynski, a vociferous highway backer, chaired the House Subcommittee on Roads until 1975 and was replaced by Congressman James Howard. Senator Lloyd Bentsen is chairman of the Senate subcommittee. The two subcommittees represent the congressional guardians of the highway program.

Congressmen, of course, have some voice in their committee assignments, and their choice is often predicated on some political gain. Thus, congressmen from agricultural states totally dominate the agriculture committees in both houses, and their constituency is the farmer rather than the public at large. In addition, some committee assignments reap great benefits for the members in their home states. For example, although most military installations are located in southern states, it is hardly because of southern hospitality or the climate; the chairmen of both committees in Congress for a long time came from the South. So it is with the Public Works Committees which have jurisdiction over the construction of many federal projects, including highways. It is to the political advantage of a congressman to have these projects constructed in his own district or state, and membership on the committee is of considerable importance.

Disagreement among congressmen on transportation policy results to a large extent from their urban or rural orientation. Rural congressmen tend to favor the highway interests; urban congressmen tend to support mass transportation. For instance, Senator Robert T. Stafford, a Vermont Republican, switched his vote on a provision providing for the use of federal highway money for subways and other rapid rail systems in urban areas. "Overnight, on reflection, I realized that my original view was right," Mr. Stafford said, adding, "I come from a rural state, you know."[21] The same viewpoint is expressed by mass transit supporters. In explaining the failure of an important amendment that would have provided funding for mass transit, the Highway Action Coalition blamed the peculiar composition of the House of Representatives:

Over 50 percent of the congressmen represent districts which have less than 30 percent of their population living in urbanized areas of 50,000 or more. And half of them don't have any urbanized areas at all. In those areas, there are relatively few highway controversies and virtually no demand for mass transit. It became difficult, if not impossible, to convince the large number of congressmen without significant urban populations to vote for the amendment.[22]

The urban-rural split on transportation policy is illustrated in a study of key votes in the House of Representatives. On the question of authorizing funds for mass transit operating subsidies, 79 percent of urban congressmen voted in favor of the measure, in comparison with only 24 percent of congressmen representing rural districts. Suburban congressmen were much more divided on the issue, with 49 percent voting in favor of the measure. On the issue of diverting highway trust funds for mass transit projects, however, the suburban congressmen lined up with central city congressmen in favoring the proposal, with 77 percent of all urban members in favor and 72 percent of suburban members in favor. On the other hand, 93 percent of all rural congressmen opposed the move.[23]

Pro-highway congressmen are not all from rural districts and states, however. Since many of the industrial enterprises, such as the auto compa-nies of Detroit, are located in urban areas, one might expect that congressmen from these areas would also support highway legislation. This was demon-strated in a debate over a bill that would have required the auto industry to develop antipollution devices. A Michigan congressman, who describes himself as "one who represents a district in which the automobile industry is very important," cited the significant economic impact of the auto indus-try on the American economy. "You can know it all you want to," he argued, "and say that it is not doing a good enough job in getting rid of air pollution. But this industry means an awful lot to an awful lot of people in America, and I would consider that very careful before we tamper with writing standards that would affect it."[24]

Yet, responsibility for transportation policy in Congress is so fragmented that any cohesive and integrated system is difficult to attain.[25] While the House and Senate Public Works committees write the road building legisla-tion, the House Ways and Means Committee and the Senate Finance Commit-tee exercise jurisdiction over revenue bills and thus are responsible for mone-tary mechanisms, such as the Highway Trust Fund. Urban mass transportation legislation falls within the jurisdiction of the Committee on Banking and Currency in the House. The regulation of transportation is the responsibility of the Senate Commerce Committee and the House's Interstate and Foreign Commerce Committee. These latter two committees established an Airport and Airways Trust Fund and AMTRAK, the national railroad corporation for passenger service. There are still other committees, concerned with safety and environmental matters, that play a peripheral role in the development of transportation policy.

Nevertheless, the Public Works committees exercise the critical weapon in fashioning transport policy—namely, the power to authorize funds de-rived from the Highway Trust Fund. Because the fund is so well-heeled and because general revenue funds are a risky source for funding mass transpor-tation projects, the Public Works committees maintain a veto power over any major transportation legislation. While either the House or the Senate may amend legislation reported out by a committee, it is usually the chair-men of these committees who name members to the conference committee, and it is rare that bills passed by both the Senate and the House will not differ in several aspects. Therefore, these two committees and their chair-men still retain effective control over transportation legislation. The House committee is especially defensive with regard to the Highway Trust Fund, and in the legislative battle in 1972 it clearly wielded a veto power over all attempts to incorporate spending for mass transit.[26]

The third major partner in this coalition is the Department of Transpor-tation. Established in 1966, DOT pulled together disparate agencies and bureaus with the objective of rationalizing federal transportation policy. Within the department there are seven "line" agencies, including the Federal Highway Administration, the Urban Mass Transportation Administration, the Federal Railroad Administration, and others. As originally proposed, the department was to have major control over establishing priorities for the expenditure of federal funds; but Congress strenuously objected to any invasion of its prerogative.

The congressional debate that surrounded this issue illustrated how firmly entrenched are the forces that benefited from piecemeal federal planning. Obviously the change that this provision would have made posed a major threat to the long-established system of congressional control over transportation projects. But even more, it would have intensified competition among modal interests for allocation of funds from a single "transportation pot" for which the Secretary of Transportation would establish the priorities.[27]

The first secretary of this "umbrella" department faced the awesome task of realigning the orientations of various agencies into a cohesive whole.[28] For example, the Bureau of Public Roads was formerly lodged in the Department of Commerce, and its interest was to develop roads primarily for commercial purposes. In addition, the Urban Mass Transportation Administration, formerly housed in the Department of Housing and Urban Development, became part of DOT in 1968.

Although the Bureau of Public Roads occupied a secondary position in the departmental hierarchy, its organizational placement is misleading, for it was the Bureau of Public Roads which, in financial terms, was the largest agency in the Department of Transportation.[29] Created in 1918, the bureau was originally housed in the Department of Agriculture, transferred to the Federal Works Agency in 1939, transferred to the General Services Administration ten years later, and then to the Department of Commerce before becoming a bureau with DOT. The bureau has been the prime governmental spokesman for the highway lobby, and with the $4 to $5 billion budgeted annually for roads, it gained considerable power in recent decades as more and more federal funds went into road building:

While this has tended to develop a strong engineering hierarchy, it also has attracted some very fine men who have remained more flexible than might be expected. Still, the federal engineers are not infallible and at times are prone to get caught in the trap-thinking of purely engineering approach.[30]

This engineering bias is illustrated by this rather heavy-handed description of the interstate system:

The pavement of the system, if put into one huge parking lot, would be 20 1/2 miles square and over half of the motor vehicles in the U.S. could be parked on it. New right-of-way needed amounts of 1/8 million acres. Total excavation will move enough dirt and rock to blanket Connecticut knee-deep. Sand, gravel, and crushed stone for the construction would build a mound 50 feet wide and 9 feet high completely around the world. The concrete used would build driveways for 35 million homes. The steel will take 30 million tons of iron ore, 18 million tons of coal, and 6 1/2 million tons of limestone. The culvert and drain pipe required equals the quantity used in the combined water and sewermain systems in six cities the size of Chicago.[31]

It is not infrequent for administrative bureaus to "function to a considerable extent as freewheeling interest groups, and in their use of propaganda activities they are not exception.[32] In its early history, the bureau enjoyed a rather favorable image, but this was mainly due to the fact that the highway engineer could be contrasted with those who ran the railroads, a group of men who were rich, remote, and insensitive to the public. One has only to remember Andrew Carnegie's infamous "the public be damned" to understand why the highway engineer was viewed as a savior who eschewed profit goals and served the "common man."

But with new values emerging in an urbanized society, the highway engineers—like the railroad barons of yesteryear—faced an increasing number of adversaries. The response by the bureau has been to mount an intensive public relations program. In a speech before a Pennsylvania highway lobby, bureau director Ralph Bartelsmeyer recognized the deteriorating position of the highway engineers when he said:

I have been in the highway field long enough to remember when the highway engineers were heroes to the American people. They wore the white hats. Today, I am afraid some people are trying to make us the black-hatted villains. We must enlist public support for our program. This can be obtained only if the American people are aware of the contributions we can make to improve the quality of American life . . . There is no doubt in my mind that the time is long overdue for beefing up our public relations program so that the public is kept informed.[33]

The linkage between the bureau, state highway officials, and other interest groups facilitates lobbying efforts. In many ways, the bureau can enlist the support of other groups to speak in its behalf without involving the bureau directly. In sum, even though the bureau is technically under the secretary of transportation, it is a highly autonomous bureau that enjoys the same kind of supportive relationship and bureaucratic immunity as the Corps of Engineers in relation to the rivers and harbor lobby and the U.S. Army.

The Urban Mass Transportation Administration is the other major agency affecting urban transportation. The chief responsibility of UMTA is to administer the Urban Mass Transportation Act of 1964. In two respects, UMTA is the major competitor of the Bureau of Public Roads within the Department of Transportation. First, its funding level has increased markedly, and it is "currently the government agency with the brightest financial prospects."[34] The efforts of the anti-highway forces to raid the Highway Trust Fund also will redound to the benefit of UMTA; Carlos Villarreal, the former administrator of UMTA, has predicted that American cities will spend more than $30 billion on mass transit in the next decade. A second and more interesting aspect of UMTA's competition with the bureau centers on interest group realignment. In contrast to the industrial giants supporting the Highway Administration, it might be suspected that UMTA would be supported by the urban mayors, the urban poor, the harried commuter, the environmentalists, and those other groups opposed to the highway programs. But this hardly seems to be the case. At an exposition in 1972, the main attraction was a display of four experimental mass transit systems developed under contracts from UMTA by four different corporations. Two of the corporations were well-known aerospace contractors; one was developed by the Ford Motor Company, and one by a company described by UMTA as a spin-off from General Motors. Officials in the Bureau of Public Roads might well find the interest-group base developed by UMTA quite unsettling. UMTA is not only attempting to steal money from the Highway Administration's budgetary pot; it is drawing off some of the big corporate supporters.

If UMTA's money is designed for the hard-pressed urban areas in America, it is rarely evident in the way this agency has distributed funds. As one observer notes, "UMTA's 269 grants have the unmistakable smell of a space-age boondoggle, featuring a familiar corporate cast."[35] This space age boondoggle also is represented in the type of hardware that appeals to UMTA. Much of the research and design money has been expended on futuristic models that propel the commuter across the landscape at enormous speeds. Yet, Colin Buchanan urges that "transport technology be studied in the context of urban areas and the life and movement that goes on inside them."[36] He contends that the urban transportation problem "would be helped but little by the perfection of a tracked movement system offering speeds of 500 m.p.h., but would be greatly assisted by some better method whereby mothers with children could reach the shopping center."[37] Therefore, the kind of hardware and engineering orientation that pervades the Bureau of Public Roads is even more ensconced in UMTA. "Public transportation could be used to redistribute wealth and opportunity, and to redesign cities," observed Emma Rothschild, "but the suburban tram lines [that were on display at the transportation exposition] would not likely have this effect."[38]

It may well be that UMTA will shape an urban transportation system that simply parallels the deleterious kind of system envisioned by highway builders.

In conclusion, it appears doubtful that the creation of the Department of Transportation will result in innovative thrusts, for as one scholar puts it, "the legislative and administrative barriers to major change are very high and are continually reinforced by well financed lobbies which work diligently to preserve existing advantages."[39]

STATE AND LOCAL GOVERNMENT: THE FAITHFUL PARTNERS

If major changes are to be made in urban transportation policy, the prospects seem somewhat gloomy at the federal level. The technological perspective and the interlocking relationship between interest groups and governmental decision makers seem to insure that urban social values will be given short shrift in policy-making circles.

Yet, if we expect to find state government more sympathetic to the urban transportation problem, we will be greatly disappointed. Robert S. Friedman, for example, notes that "state politics in recent years has witnessed consistent victories by supporters of expanded expressways and freeways at the expense of the advocates of other modes of transportation."[40] Furthermore, the highway interests are even more thoroughly entrenched at the state level, and the highway forces have become so institutionalized and immune to any political control that major changes seem doubtful. "Regardless of the structure and staff capability," Alan Lupo notes, "state highway agencies have tended to be a power unto themselves."[41] One reason for this autonomous role, of course, is that highway financing is frequently accomplished through a trust fund. The Federal Highway Trust Fund is embedded in statutory law, and many state constitutions also include ironclad guarantees for the use of gasoline taxes for highways. In Texas, for instance, a Constitutional Revision Commission recently undertook the job of proposing a new constitution. Fearful that the commission might exclude the trust fund from constitutional protection, all three of the Texas highway commissioners sent a letter to each of the thirty-seven members on the commission arguing that the preservation of "the income for highways provides substantial benefit for the people of Texas."[42] In the United States, almost half of the states have constitutional provisions, called "good roads" amendments, that require highway-related revenues to be used for highway purposes only. In 1972, only one state—Maryland—had a *transportation* trust fund that allowed the state to expend revenues on various modes of transportation. In only six states are highway funds mandated through

statutes,[43] though in the past few years there have been concerted drives
to dismantle highway trust funds in various states, including California,
Massachusetts, Oregon, Connecticut, Michigan, and Virginia.

Highway expenditures, of course, constitute a sizable portion of a state's
budget, and in some cases they comprise one-third of all expenditures. In
no state do highway expenditures constitute less than one-eighth of the
total budget. In 1972, for example, almost $22 billion was spent in the
United States on road construction, and most of the funds were derived
from the federal and state highway trust funds, with more than $11 billion
coming from the state highway trust funds alone.[44] What are the major
reasons accounting for the expenditure level of state highway departments?
Although Friedman investigated several variables, including the organization
of the highway department and the party system, his study showed that
urbanization has been the major factor influencing highway expenditures.
In other words, he demonstrated that expenditures for highways declined
in proportion to other expenditures as urbanization increased. He explained
this finding by pointing out that in the more populous states "highway
expenditures must compete with state expenditure for education, welfare,
health, etc."[45] As a consequence of this competition, proportionately less
money is available for highway construction.

One reason for the rigidity of transportation policy at the state level is
the prevalent use of independent highway commissions. Ironically, independent commissions, once thought by reformers to be the enemies of vested
interests, have now become the spokesmen for the vested interest. An
independent commission at the state level is usually given jurisdiction over
some governmental activity. In many cases, it has executive power, including
the appointment of staff personnel, and in some cases, especially in regard
to highway commissions, a budget derived from earmarked funds.

Interest groups have found that independent commissions are much
easier to control than departments directly under the governor's control.
In many cases the commissioners are drawn directly from the ranks of
the interest groups, and any change in the structure of commissions is viewed
as a threat. To illustrate, during the 1961–62 constitutional convention in
Michigan the highway interest groups were quite explicit on this point:

Michigan's economy depends on highways, and highway construction and
maintenance are something apart from other functions. The governor's
view might control elsewhere but not with respect to highways. Michigan
has an outstanding system and this is due to two factors, a highway commissioner separately elected and a system ear-marking revenues for highway
needs.[46]

In 1965 almost half the states had independent highway departments, and in thirteen other states the department was partially dependent on the governor.[47] What difference does it make what kind of relationships highway departments have with the governor? Friedman argues that

the extent to which the governor can exercise control over highway policy determines, to a degree at least, the competitive position of highway building and maintenance vis-a-vis other programs. This proposition is based on the assumption that if the highway department is under the wing of the governor, it will have to compete with other functions for support. Where the department is independent its supporters and staff are freer to plead their own cause. Because of the visibility of highways and their tangible quality, only vigorous action by a governor is likely to restrain legislatures from pouring money into highways, rather than mental health and similar programs.[48]

In another study, which investigated transportation policy in two major metropolitan areas, Frank Colcord comes to a similar conclusion. In trying to assess the forces that accounted for a radical shift in transportation policy, he notes that "there is considerable evidence that the governor's office is becoming a more important source of initiative for innovations in transportation planning and programming."[49]

Obviously, the first task for altering transportation policy making in urban states is to place highway departments back in the mainstream of state politics or to establish state *transportation* departments. In the absence of any state-wide transportation agency, it is small wonder that mass transportation alternatives are seldom discussed. Only in a few states are there state-wide agencies responsible for mass transit—such as New York and New Jersey. Other states, such as California and Wisconsin, have likewise developed departments of transportation, but they have no jurisdiction over mass transit.

Transportation policy making at the municipal level has been much more flexible than at the state level. In the first place, street construction in cities is budgeted out of general funds, bonds, or individual assessments. The kind of "horn-of-plenty" provided by earmarked funds at the federal and state level has been absent in the cities, and every dollar spent on streets has been appropriated through a competitive political process.

Second, the organizational structure in cities is much more flexible. Even though the public works department is responsible for city streets, it has many other responsibilities. Furthermore, almost all cities have some type of planning department that influences the development of street networks and transportation systems. Hence, in contrast to the monolithic, autonomous structure at the state level, transportation decision making in city government is much fragmented.[50]

Transportation politics at the local level can best be understood by looking at the roles of the various participants. Alan Lupo and his colleagues identify three different orientations, including the technician, the planner, and the politician.[51] The technician sees transportation planning from a consumer-oriented, free-enterprise approach. The task of transportation planning for him is to determine the needs of the consumer and then plan accordingly. This viewpoint is most frequently adopted by highway engineers, state and federal highway officials, city public works departments, and traditional city planners. In many cases the philosophy of the transit engineer seems to be quite similar to that of his highway colleagues, and most of the debates concerning urban transportation systems have been based on this type of philosophical approach. Even non-engineers frequently espouse the technician's philosophy, and economists especially have adopted this philosophy, since their models can cope with the variables that are introduced.

The second role is that of the planner, whose task is to develop comprehensive plans to achieve broad community objectives. The planner is continually frustrated, since there are no such objectives. Whether goals are articulated or not, however, they are manifested in what the city does. Without a plan, there is no way to evaluate these manifestations. Although the planner is frequently at odds with the technician, the technician has a singular advantage in any confrontation: he can ignore the planner without any great risk.[52]

The third participant in transportation decision making is the politician. Although the days of the big city machine are gone, there is still a propensity for mayors to opt for pragmatic, short-term solutions. Although the politician would like to be viewed as a statesman and thus shares some of the values of the planner, the technician's simplistic solutions offer great appeal.

Although the actors in any transportation dispute in a city will closely resemble one of these three types, the power configuration will differ markedly. In Lupo's study of eight metropolitan areas in the United States, the influence of key actors in metropolitan transportation decisions has been evaluated. Using a composite score of the actors in each of these metropolitan areas, one can express the relative influence and assumed role orientation of the actors as in Table 5-2. The technician and the politician tend to dominate transportation decision making in these metropolitan communities. The role orientation of certain groups, however, tends to be ambivalent. For example, businessmen normally tend to subscribe to the technician's role. There is some diversity in their perspectives, however, and businessmen sometimes adopt the planner's orientation. Colcord, for instance, concludes that "the local stimulus for a rethinking of existing policy and for innovative action in the field of transportation has come almost entirely from central city actors."[53] Included in this group of central city actors would be businessmen from the central business district. Neighborhood groups also play different roles, depending on the issue. When neighborhood groups emerge to oppose highways, they frequently adopt the planner orientation and specifically reject the "consumer-is-king" argument of the highway engineers. They often argue that there are various values that must be protected in the city and that transportation values should not be given sole consideration in the decision-making process. Yet, even neighborhood groups can succumb to the technician's role. When the city plans to build a thoroughfare through a given neighborhood, it is not unusual for the citizens to argue that the thoroughfare should be routed through some other neighborhood because of the heavier traffic volume there.

TABLE 5-2

Distribution of Power by Role

Actor	Role Orientation	Influence Score
Highway department	Technician	29
Business groups	Technician/planner	27
Neighborhood groups	Planner/technician	24
Governor	Politician	23
Mayor	Politician	22
Transit authority	Technician/planner	18
Planning agency	Planner	15

Adapted from Lupo et al., *Rites of Way*, p. 205. Influence score was scaled as follows: high, 4; medium, 3; low, 2; and very low or none, 1.

Influence is one measure of the kind of configuration that emerges in transportation policy making. But in any metropolitan area, there are various governments that have a stake in the process; these include the state government, metropolitan-wide agencies, the central city, suburbs, and county governments. To what extent do these governments participate in transportation decision making? Based on an analysis of eight metropolitan areas, Table 5-3 reflects the extent of participation by various governmental actors.

State government dominated the development of highways, even in major metropolitan areas, and the other three levels of government play only peripheral roles. "Unless a major controversy develops over a new highway,"

Lupo notes, "local political officials have generally stayed out of highway planning except to give perfunctory formal approval."[54] In the two transit areas, metropolitan and central city governments play a moderate role; but because of the inadequacy of funds, their impact is minimal.

TABLE 5-3

Participation, Governmental Actor, and Transportation Areas

Transportation Areas	Participation Rate			
			Central	Suburbs/
	State	Metropolitan	City	County
Highways	32	1	18	15
Bus transit	4	20	20	9
Rapid transit	6	24	18	16
Commuter railroad	7	4	3	2

Adapted from Lupo et al., *Rites of Way*, p. 207. Scoring was based on following scale: decision-making power, 4; veto power, 3; strong tradition of participation, 2; political influence only, 1.

In conclusion, there are several forces at work that attenuate efforts to achieve some kind of "balanced" transportation system. In the first place, there are no funding mechanisms for alternate modes of transportation that compare to the federal and the state trust funds that bolster highway systems. Second, the major interest groups, even those with an interest in mass transit, are hardware oriented. Providing alternate modes of transportation, as we will see in subsequent chapters, is not the sole issue—and possibly not the most important. Third, state government is locked into a unidimensional approach. Road building and highways provide a tangible political reward for legislators; they can be dispensed with great equality to various regions in the state, and providing for rapid transit in one or two large metropolitan areas is not nearly as appealing as doling out highway construction funds throughout the state.

In characterizing the nature of American politics, it is frequently pointed out that the federal government has the resources, state government the authority, and city government the problems. The characterization may help us to understand how difficult it is to develop a viable transportation system for our cities. With regard to resources, cities are already strapped for funds. Establishing a mass transportation system places huge strains on already limited resources, and few city politicians are willing to ask their constituents to pay the cost. Even when cities make the effort, they usually have only one device, the bond election.[55] Furthermore, the orientation of most American cities squares with the technician's philosophy. With the advent of the reform government, city officials see government primarily as a distributor of services.[56] As a consequence, they tend to look at the transportation problem simply as a problem of mobility. If the city provides the streets and if congestion is minimized, what more could or should the city do? The political establishment is, therefore, immobilized and unable to mount any serious attack on the transportation problem in American cities.

6

THE OUTSIDERS

In his study of urbanism, Louis Wirth posits three concepts which characterize the modern city.[1] Density and size are two of the prime characteristics of urbanism. "Heterogeneity," the third major characteristic according to Wirth, "is a consequence of the social interaction among . . . a variety of personality types . . . which induces a more ramified and differentiated framework of social stratification than is found in more integrated societies."[2] Yet, it is striking that in the American city with its heterogeneous population, we have a homogeneous transportation system, one which caters basically to only one group of people. One should recognize, of course, that the urban transportation system is not neutral in this impact. It meets the needs of some groups, but at the same time restricts the mobility of others. The poor, the elderly, the handicapped, and especially those from minority groups can be classified as "the outsiders" in regard to our auto-oriented transportation system. They either are not permitted or are unable to drive the auto (as in the case of the elderly and the handicapped) or they are too poor to own a car. In Chicago, for example, 73 percent of all bus riders and 50 percent of all transit riders indicated that they could not have made their trips by auto. In another study in Pittsburgh, 85 percent of the mass transit riders could not drive or had no access to cars.[3]

Even though car ownership has increased markedly and although predictions abounded in the past that the time was not far off when the number of cars would equal the number of people, these claims are highly suspect for two reasons. First, the energy crisis, the spiraling costs of fuel, and the rapidly increasing costs of buying and operating a car seem to cast doubt on such a prediction. Indeed, the number of people who simply cannot afford the private auto will likely rise. Second, car ownership is not equally distributed among the urban population. In many affluent families, the number of cars may exceed the size of the family, whereas especially among the poor there is no car, or if there is one it is seldom in proper condition for use on high-speed urban expressways. Furthermore, even if there were two cars in every garage—the great hope of the Detroit auto makers—they would be useless to many either because of physical handicaps or because of legal restrictions which make it impossible for some to obtain a driver's license. Even if a family has a car, not all members of the family can use it. If it is used for the journey to work, it frequently sits idle for the better part of the day, and other members of the family must fend for themselves.

In this study we will briefly examine the travel characteristics of the outsiders. What is the magnitude of the problems for each group, and how are their mobility needs being met? Furthermore, we will examine some of the major proposals which have been offered to deal with the problems of the outsiders. Finally, we will offer an evaluation of the ways in which public transportation is meeting the needs of the outsiders.

THE OUTSIDE GROUPS

Throughout history, there have been certain groups in society which have been denied the full range of opportunities that are available to others. The "caste" system in some societies clearly differentiates and stratifies the individual members of that society. Within the United States, a similar system prevails. Although there is a wide range of activities in which this caste system operates, the transportation system in our cities offers a clear illustration.

For the purposes of our discussion, we have identified three major groups: minority groups, the elderly, and the handicapped. It should be recognized that certain factors which hinder the mobility of these groups are overlapping. For example, medical problems which impede mobility cut across all these groups, not just those we designate handicapped. Furthermore, poverty is a characteristic of all three groups. The incidence of poverty, of course, has a direct bearing on car ownership. For example, although almost 80 percent of all American families owned a car in 1972, only 68 percent of families with incomes between $3,000 and $4,999 owned cars. For those with incomes under $3,000, only 40 percent owned cars. In sum, the 20 percent of American families without cars is largely accounted for by the poor.[4]

In addition, there may well be other groups who stand outside of our transportation system. Certainly, the problems of transportation for the young could be appropriately included within this study. Even the transportation problems of the housewife might deserve some discussion. However, we have attempted to identify only those groups on which the impact is more severe.

MINORITY GROUPS

In the 1960s, a series of ghetto riots rocked many American cities. In 1967 alone, for example, more than 164 cities experienced one or more riots.[5] As a consequence of these riots, dozens of governmental commissions were established to examine the roots of the riots and to offer solutions. After the Watts riot in Los Angeles, for example, the governor established a commission to investigate the causes. Although the McCone Commission identified a wide range of causes, one of its major points concerned the transportation problems of the Watts residents. "Our investigation," the Commission asserted

has brought into clear focus the fact that this inadequate and costly public transportation currently existing throughout the Los Angeles area seriously restricts the residents of the disadvantaged areas such as south central Los Angeles. This lack of adequate transportation handicaps them in seeking and holding jobs, attending schools, shopping, and in fulfilling other needs. It has had a major influence in creating a sense of isolation. . . .[6]

The Kerner Commission echoed this viewpoint and argued that there is a major requirement for "better transportation between ghetto neighborhoods and new job locations."[7] It further recommended that "aid to local public transportation . . . should be expanded . . . with subsidies for routes serving ghetto areas."[8]

Although the riots generated a great deal of concern, it is not clear whether the concern stems from the fear of violence or the issue of social equity.

If the public concern is due to social equity considerations and the realization of existing urban inequities, then there appears to be some real hope for positive commentary and worthwhile programs. On the other hand, if the concern has been generated by fear of violence, then it is likely that solutions or programs will resemble palliatives rather than cures.[9]

The evidence, which will be discussed more fully later, indicates that the solutions offered in many American cities are mere palliatives. Even though the riots have largely subsided, the minority population of American cities is increasing at a rapid rate. Between 1960 and 1970, for example, the black population in the central cities increased by 58.2 percent while the white population declined by 0.2 percent.[10]

Although poverty is a phenomenon which cuts across ethnic lines, the impact of being poor is much greater for minorities. In the first place, minorities tend to live in the central cities rather than in the suburban areas, and it is apparent that transportation opportunities are limited. Also, residential segregation further aggravates the transportation problems for minorities. Even if they want to move to a location closer to their place of employment, they are frequently precluded from doing so by housing practices.

Although the population of minorities in the central city is increasing at a rapid rate, employment growth has been concentrated in the suburban areas. The rate of employment growth in various categories is five to six times greater in the suburbs than in the central cities.[11] In only a few areas, such as government and finance, have central cities shown an increase in employment.

The configuration of employment opportunities further aggravates the problem for minorities. What opportunities for employment in the central city do exist are largely reserved for the managerial class that lives in the suburbs. It is in the suburban areas where the semi-skilled and skilled jobs are opening.

David Greytak, for example, shows that the work trips for minorities differ markedly from those of whites. The average work trip for minorities takes 31.17 minutes to travel 9.01 miles. In contrast, the white work trip covers only 8.24 miles and takes only 25.87 minutes.[12] Furthermore, he notes that for those work trips originating in the central city, the work trip for minorities takes 20 percent longer and covers a distance which is 29 percent greater than for whites. "This would seem to indicate," he says,

that while on the average, the work trip originating in the central city tends to be shorter and less time consuming than those of the suburbs, it is the whites in the central city who reap the benefits associated with a central location as nonwhite work trips are on the average longer and more time consuming than those of all central city residents, suburbanites or all whites.[13]

A related study examined the work trip patterns of residents living in a poverty area of twenty square miles within Houston's central city.[14] Almost half of the white men worked in the area, but only a third of the black and Mexican-American men worked in the area. The same pattern existed for women, except for the fact that a higher percentage of Mexican-American women were employed in the area.

The survey revealed that minority women are much more highly dependent on public transportation than minority men. Indeed, more than 50 percent of black women used the bus, whereas only slightly more than 10 percent of black men used the bus for the journey to work. On the whole, the proportion of all employed women who used public transportation was four times greater than the proportion of men.

As one might expect, travel time for minority women far exceeded that of minority men. For example, only 7.2 percent of black men took more than 60 minutes for the journey to work, in comparison with 21.6 percent for black women. The same proportion was true of Mexican-American men and women. On the whole, however, the proportion of blacks who took more than 60 minutes to get to work was almost five times greater than for whites. Furthermore, the costs of transportation were also much higher for the blacks. Almost 25 percent of blacks paid 50 cents or more for a one-way trip in comparison with approximately 10 percent of whites.

Although most studies of minorities have focused on the journey to work, the work trip constitutes only a relatively small portion of their travel needs. In a survey of two low-income housing sections in Pittsburgh, the work trip accounted for only about 18 percent of all trips. Shopping trips, for example, accounted for almost 60 percent of the weekly trips.[15]

Even when it comes to shopping trips, however, minorities are at a disadvantage. Most of the large-scale shopping centers with lower prices are located on the fringe of the city. Not only is the distance factor considerably higher for minorities, but transportation access to these suburban shopping centers is almost totally restricted to the auto. As a consequence, their shopping needs are most frequently met by small local merchants, and the prices they pay are considerably higher.

The adequacy of public transit as perceived by low income and minority ghetto residents in Brooklyn was analyzed recently in a survey completed by the Central Brooklyn Model Cities Committee.[16] A generally high level of dissatisfaction or indifference was found for all four major transportation modes examined (social-recreational, shopping, employment, and medical needs) among blacks and Puerto Ricans. While there was considerable variation in the transportation needs of various subgroups, e.g., whites, elderly, and low versus moderate income,

the larger and younger families, which are primarily Puerto Rican and black, are highly dissatisfied with public transit for their social-recreational needs. The reasons given are first transportation inflexibility, since many recreation trips involve transfers and double fares and second the poorer scheduling on weekends, which causes peak overloads and discomfort for traveling with children.[17]

Also of special significance to the ghetto residents in general and especially to the Puerto Rican population was the adequacy of public transit for employment purposes. But blacks tended more to adopt a "don't know" or

indifferent position with respect to improved transit for employment purposes, probably reflecting the ingrained unemployment condition of this
group of ghetto dwellers.[18] Many do not believe improved transit can
materially alter their employment conditions.

In sum, the urban transportation system has failed to meet the needs of
minorities in our cities. Although there are several other factors which
account for their being trapped in the ghetto, the absence of any viable
transportation system remains one of the most critical causes.

THE ELDERLY

The elderly constitute a second major group in American society which
is disadvantaged by the current transportation system in American cities.
In general, there are three major factors which account for their plight. In
the first place, the income level of the elderly is generally greatly reduced,
and the financial problems of owning a private car are thus aggravated.
Second, the elderly are particularly beset by certain physical handicaps and
medical problems. Although only about 3 or 4 percent of the elderly are
hospitalized or in nursing homes, there are less severe handicaps, such as
failing sight or loss of hearing, which reduce their ability to drive. Finally,
retirement brings dramatic life-style changes for the elderly. The journey
to work is now of minimal importance, but other types of trips, such as
medical, shopping, and social, become quite important. Yet, our transportation system, especially the public transportation system component, is
geared to the journey to work.

It is now well recognized that the elderly population is increasing at
a more rapid rate than other age groups. Table 6-1 reflects the population
of the elderly in 1960 and 1970.

As one can see, these three age groups constituted 19 percent of the total
population of the United States in 1970, an increase of 6.5 million over
1960. In terms of total numbers, the population of these three elderly
groups increased by 20 percent during the ten-year period. In the age group
of 75 and over, the population increased by an astounding 37 percent.

For the elderly with substantial retirement incomes, there are some
opportunities to move to the booming retirement communities in which
transportation problems are minimal. Regardless of the social and psychological damage which may occur as a consequence of this segregated life style,
their immediate transportation needs are usually met. But for many others
and especially for those who cannot escape from the urban community,
the transportation system is a crucial problem. In one study in Pittsburgh,[19]
almost 90 percent of the elderly in two public housing communities had
family incomes of less than $3,000 per year and, as one might expect, 85

percent were without cars. Shopping trips accounted for the great majority of travel trips for the residents, and 70 percent of the trips were made by bus. But for the elderly, especially those with low income, there were major complaints about the bus system, especially the cost and the service level.

In another survey among the elderly in Baltimore, fully 75 percent of the elderly women were without a driver's license, in comparison with only 41 percent of the elderly men. Furthermore, more than 60 percent of the men were unwilling to drive a car downtown, and 50 percent indicated that they were unwilling to drive to work in the suburbs. If these elderly people were given an alternative of bus transportation—even if it required transfers—

TABLE 6-1

Elderly Population in the United States

Elderly Age Group	Population 1960	Percentage of population 1960	Population 1970	Percentage of population 1970
55–64	15,627,000	8.6	18,651,000	9.1
65–74	11,055,000	6.1	12,482,000	6.1
75 and over	5,624,000	3.1	7,695,000	3.8
TOTAL	32,306,000	17.8	38,828,000	19.0

Source: U.S. Department of Commerce, *Statistical Abstract of the United States, 1973* (Washington, D.C.: U.S. Government Printing Office, 1973), p. 6.

more than 70 percent of both elderly men and women indicated that they would be willing to take it to work.

The correlation between age and auto driving is dramatically illustrated in one study. Almost 90 percent of those between 20 and 34 years of age drive a car. For those between 35 and 54, some 15.2 percent are non-drivers, as are 30.0 percent of those between 55 and 64 years of age. For those over 65, fully 42 percent are nondrivers.

Trip purposes also differ greatly among age groups. Whereas the work trip accounts for anywhere from 23 to 28 percent for various age groups, it accounts for only 15.6 percent of the trips made by the elderly. On the other hand, shopping trips by the elderly account for 13.7 percent of their trips while they only account for slightly more than 8 percent for the other age groups.

For those who live in the core area of the city, the mere task of shopping is difficult. The range of other activities is also limited.

Because of the difficulty in arranging transportation, the oldster puts off the trip to the doctor, the dentist, or to stores to shop around for items to suit his taste or meet the stringency of his purse. Social life is increasingly given up because getting to a club or visiting a friend becomes unmanageable. There is a consequent withdrawal of personality which can go from discouragement to depression.[20]

In a Brooklyn survey which analyzed, among other dimensions, the transit needs of the elderly, it was concluded that the public transit system was largely "irrelevant and alien" to the social-recreational needs of this group. The elderly, while expressing indifference to public transit for shopping needs, did significantly voice dissatisfaction with public transit in meeting their medical needs.[21]

But even though these surveys tell us something about the travel characteristics of the elderly, they cannot tell us what trips the elderly might take if they had greater options. We cannot really determine what trips were not made because of limited mobility, nor can we assess adequately the degree of social isolation which our transportation system has created for the elderly.

THE HANDICAPPED

The transportation problems faced by the elderly are similar to those faced by the handicapped, except that in many cases where the elderly may have some meager retirement income, the handicapped are often faced with the task of earning a living. Whereas isolation and the lack of mobility may generate serious psychological and social problems for the elderly, the lack of mobility further compounds the physical limitations of the handicapped in securing a job.

The urban area is a difficult enough setting for the nonhandicapped to move about in, but the vertical characteristics of urban areas—stairways and steps—provide serious impediments for the handicapped. Horizontal mobility, on the other hand, is relatively easy for the individuals in wheelchairs and even the blind. Yet, most of our transportation systems are unsuited for the ambulatory individual. Buses, subways, and elevated systems usually provide no easy access for the physically handicapped. Some, of course, have specially-equipped automobiles, but for most, these automobiles are too expensive.

Recently, some attention has been given to the needs of the handicapped public transit user. In hearings before the House Committee on Public Works in 1972, Washington Metro Authority officials estimated that there were 9,600 disabled persons who would be unable to use the escalators in the new Washington Metro. Elevators would be needed to accommodate these handicapped persons. It was further estimated that by 1970 this group of handicapped persons would number 14,000 and would make approximately 4,900 daily rail trips on the Metro system if elevators were installed. The cost of installing the elevators in 85 stations was estimated to be $65 million. Because of the cost, however, there was reticence on the part of the Metro board to proceed with this installation without special additional funding by Congress. These halting steps, though encouraging, are still hopelessly inadequate in the face of the great need. In the vast majority of our cities, the special transit needs of the handicapped continue to be cruelly ignored.[22]

The size of the handicapped population in our cities is much greater than one might think. The National Health Survey, conducted by the Department of Health, Education, and Welfare, indicated the extent of chronic handicaps, except for the institutionalized population, as of 1966. Based on this survey and excluding certain categories (such as those confined to bed), one study estimates that there are some 3,203,000 chronically handicapped residents in the metropolitan areas in the United States.[23] Approximately half of this group is under 65 and thus would be high potential users of the transportation system. Furthermore, it is estimated that there are approximately 1,580,000 persons in the metropolitan areas at any one time with acute handicaps of short duration.

Even though this population is rather extensive, the handicapped also suffer from economic disabilities. It is estimated that 45 percent have family incomes of less than $3,000, and only 10 percent have incomes of more than $10,000 per year.[24]

In sum, the transportation system in our cities ill serves the needs of the handicapped person. The physical handicap in itself may well be the least serious impediment she or he faces. The real impediments may be social rather than medical.

PANOPLY OF SOLUTIONS

The problems of minorities, the elderly, and the handicapped, of course, have received considerable attention, and several remedial approaches have been offered.

One possible solution which has received widespread attention is to furnish cars directly to the "carless." At present, of course, the government is a partner in the transportation system since it provides the highways and in some areas transit services. Why should not the government also supply the cars themselves, at least on a selective basis?

Sumner Myers, the most notable proponent of this solution, argues that for better or worse the car is an essential feature of survival in urban America.[25] Yet, some 60 percent of households with incomes of less than $3,000 per year are without cars, and the cars that the poor do own are generally unsuitable for longer trips. For example, almost 20 percent of the cars owned by the Watts residents were deemed to be unsafe for use on the Los Angeles freeways.

Although part of the problem may be attributed to the spatial design of the city and the segregation patterns, the poor cannot wait until some future date when planners rectify this situation, he argues. Furthermore, providing the poor with cars would be a productive investment. Myers shows that through wholesale purchases of cars the outlays might be minimal compared with the benefits, that is, the increased employment opportunities for the poor.

His "new volks for poor folks" proposal seems quite appealing on the surface. It has an egalitarian flare, but it is the kind of proposal which further exacerbates the transportation problem in our cities. There are three major criticisms one can make. First, this kind of solution may merely perpetuate the single-mode system that we now have and further aggravate the other problems associated with the auto, including urban design, housing segregation, pollution, and the waste of resources. The fact that new industries are located on the fringe of the city and in suburban areas is hardly accidental, and the extension of the auto system may result in a further dispersal of job locations. Even with improved transportation, the job opportunities of minorities may not be enhanced. One study, for example, makes the point that the transportation barrier for minorities may only have served as a convenient excuse for racial discrimination. "When the improved transportation services were provided, the jobs still did not materialize."[26] Second, this solution merely resolves the problem for one group of "outsiders" but fails to aid other groups, primarily the handicapped. By instituting a system of free cars for the poor, urban government may be tempted to abandon its responsibility for providing alternate modes of transportation and salve its conscience by pointing out its "generous" program of providing cars for the poor. As a consequence, such a solution may well end any hope of a multiple system of urban transportation.[27] Finally, if the problem of the poor is being poor, and if society commits itself to subsidization, a far preferable solution would be merely to give the poor the money. Some may use it for cars, but others may use it for purchases on which they place a higher value. Some simply may not want an automobile.

Another major proposal is the expansion of taxi and jitney service. Taxis and jitneys, of course, have advantages over buses operating on fixed routes.

They are more flexible in their routing and furthermore do not depend on a large volume of passengers. Because of the rigid licensing practices followed in many American cities, the taxi system is inadequate in providing more than limited service at a fairly substantial cost. In addition to suggesting personal transportation for the poor, Myers also advocates a demand-actuated taxi-bus system which "would use a vehicle like a minibus to pick up passengers at their doors or at any one of a very large number of street pick-up points shortly after they had called for services."[28]

Sandra Rosenbloom also advocates an expansion of jitney and taxi service. Even though there would be several serious obstacles in its implementation, "deregulation of the taxi industry and expansion of the jitney industry would bring real and significant employment opportunities to the urban poor. In addition such deregulation would bring a social interaction as well as physical mobility to the ghetto as drivers would bring their vehicles home to the ghetto community...."[29]

With some modifications, jitneys could also provide service to the elderly and the handicapped. Cordelle Ballard argues that public bus transportation cannot meet the needs of the elderly, but that jitneys could be provided to meet the special requirements of this growing segment of our population. "To meet the needs of aging persons," Ballard suggests, "vehicles should be designed with the entrance in the rear like a 'paddy wagon' to make steps easier for arthritic limbs."[30]

Although these proposals move us out of the "privatized" transportation systems implicit in Myers's personal transportation for the poor, there are still several major problems associated with these proposals. First, deregulation of the taxi industry would be a major political undertaking. Taxi licenses in some cities are worth as much as $27,000 to individual operators. Second, commercial jitneys and taxis both compete for the same clients. Given a limited market, the expansion of one would be at the expense of the other. Third, many of the deleterious effects of the private auto, including pollution, are inherent in such a system. If jitneys and taxis were expanded without any commensurate reduction in the use of the private automobile, this "solution" would merely aggravate other urban problems.

Free urban transit service is a third proposal for remedying the problems of the outsiders.[31] Since poverty is a common and pervasive characteristic of the outsiders, free transit service would at least eliminate the financial burden. The advocates of free urban transit service frequently present several goals which would be achieved, including:

Improved accessibility of job opportunities to the poor;
Revitalization of central business districts;
Reduction of auto congestion, pollution, and parking facilities;
Reduction of *total* transportation costs.[32]

In analyzing this proposal, two scholars conclude that "while free transit does, in general, contribute to the goals that its supporters seek to achieve, improved transit service is generally a more efficient means of promoting these objectives."[33]

The problem of public transit is frequently not its cost but its poor level of service, particularly its routing. As we noted previously, job opportunities in the metropolitan area are largely found on the fringes of the city. Yet, most transit systems merely link the ghetto to the central business district, where jobs are virtually unavailable.

In rejecting the idea of free transit, these same scholars note that a larger percentage of transit users are not poor, and the provision of free transit would subsidize not only the poor but the affluent as well. One must realize, of course, that most subsidy programs which operate in various sectors of American life do not even have this affect, but more frequently subsidize the affluent at the expense of the poor. Indeed, these same authors show this to be the case. The profit-making routes, they note, operate in low-income neighborhoods with dense populations and indirectly subsidize the other routes which operate in less densely populated neighborhoods in which higher income groups live.

CONCLUSION

Although transportation planners readily acknowledge the transportation problems of the outsiders, they frequently try to pass these problems on to someone else. At a recent conference at the Department of Transportation in Washington two officials of mass transit agencies explained the problem in making provisions for transportation for the handicapped. The costs, they asserted, would be way out of proportion to the benefits. Furthermore, even if modifications were made in rapid transit facilities, the handicapped person still could not get to the rapid transit station, since other modes of transportation, such as buses, were not set up to accommodate handicapped riders. Some form of personalized transportation system was their "solution" to the problem, but unfortunately they never identified the agency responsible for implementing their solution.

The means of transportation—the autos, the buses, the trains—have no intrinsic value in themselves. They merely have an instrumental value, and that value is to provide access to activities. Yet, the city is becoming more dispersed, and it is because of our auto-oriented system that the instrumental value of transportation and the city have been undermined. If millions of suburban Americans find comfort in this process, if because of circumstances they still have access to a great variety of activities in the urban community, millions of other urban residents are effectively cut off from the activities of the city. Although they are "outsiders" especially in regard to the transportation system, the impact extends to many areas. Because of their limited access, they frequently live in areas with poor educational facilities. They have limited opportunities on the job market. And as a net result, they have little access to the political system. It is the political system which could serve as the catalyst for improving their lot. But because of their limited access, their needs are ignored, as attested to in the previous example as to why public transit facilities could not cope with the problems of the handicapped.

But, surely, it will be argued, public transportation will serve the needs of other groups—the poor and the minorities. Yet, the plight of the poor and the minorities can be no better illustrated than in the development of recent rapid transit projects.[34] While the proponents of mass transportation frequently point to the needs of the poor and minorities as the rationale of developing public transit systems, one may well wonder who is being served by rapid transit systems that are actually built. The Bay Area Rapid Transit system (BART) is often viewed as a model for other cities to emulate, but if so, it will only assure that the poor and the minorities remain effectively shut out. BART is really not an intracity system, but rather serves as a transportation link between the suburbs and the central city. In the first phase of development, thirty-four stations were constructed, and only a handful are located in the inner city.

It might well be, of course, that the BART system would provide a transportation link for the poor to work in the suburban areas. Yet, all of the suburban stations provide for auto parking. It is one thing for the suburban resident to drive his car to the station, and take BART to the central city, whence he can walk to his job; it is quite another thing for the inner-city dweller to walk to a BART station (there are no parking lots), and take it to a suburban station. Once he gets there, his means of transportation is at an end.

A proposed transit system in Fort Worth and Dallas also illustrates that rapid transit will be of little use to the outsiders. These two cities would provide a rapid rail link from each downtown area to the new regional airport. It could be that some poor and minorities might be able to use such a system if they happened to work at the airport. However, poor people are not employed in large numbers by the airline industry. Rather, the rapid transit link would merely provide additional alternatives to those who are already served by the urban transportation system.

In conclusion, the directions in which we are heading leave one with little hope that the urban transportation system is beginning the task of serving all people in the city. In one sense, the deprivation of mobility for the outsider is merely another manifestation and reflection of our insensitivity to many other needs of the outsiders. If one examines other aspects of the outsiders' lives—housing, education, medical care, or employment— one will find the same neglect. Although transportation is a critical point for improving the lot of the outsider, it will be of little value if other functional needs are neglected.

7

URBAN DESIGN AND
THE ENVIRONMENT

And God said unto them, Be fruitful, and multiply, and fill the earth and
subdue it; and have dominion over the fish of the sea and over the birds of
the air and over every living thing that moves upon the earth.

Genesis, *1:28*

The ecologist Ian McHarg has noted that the ethos of Western civiliza-
tion has been characterized by an all-compelling urge to dominate and
conquer the earth and nature. The values of Western man, unlike those of
such societies as the Oriental, encourage him to seek not unity with nature
but conquest.[1] As the biblical injunction suggests, the role of man under
Western religions was to proliferate and dominate the earth and everything
thereon. Perhaps never had the biblical command been so fully realized until
the advent of the auto age. If obedience is the mark of righteousness, then
suburbia might be characterized as the twentieth-century Garden of Eden.
Without question man and his auto have subdued the urban earth.

The word *subdue* has several meanings. One is to "conquer" or "van-
quish." Synonyms include "defeat," "annihilate," and "destroy." When
it comes to the auto-dominated urban world in which most of us live, the
latter term seems more descriptive of the impact of the road and car on the
environment. The urban landscape has been cut up and sectioned off by
massive freeways, wide boulevards, and suburban streets. A grid has been
imposed on the urban landscape. Nature has been scarred and altered by
man's roads and storage facilities for the car. Rivers have been spanned
and smaller waterways drained or covered with concrete. If the urban
environment has not been destroyed, it is certainly not for want of human
effort.

In this chapter we will examine the impact of the auto transportation system on three dimensions of the urban environment: spatial characteristics and design, the physical environment, and the use of natural resources. The first refers to the land use features of the transportation system as well as its effects on the location of industry, housing, commercial activities, and open space. Design implications in regard to neighborhood integrity and community identification will also be evaluated. Other problems include the effects on the physical environment, especially the now-familiar litany of ills attributed to the automobile: air, visual, noise, water, and solid waste pollution. The first form of pollution is more familiar to most of us because of federal regulations on emissions, but the other effects (especially on water) may be more devastating in the long run.

Lastly, all transportation systems use resources—a simple fact that has become a critical issue during the last decade. The auto's role as a resource user, both in its production and consumption, will be explored later in this chapter. Particular emphasis will be placed on the energy-efficiency characteristics of the auto. The recent energy crisis has made us more acutely aware of the potential for breakdown in our transportation system based on oil. But the energy impact of the auto society is much wider than the use of petroleum. It extends backward through the entire production process and forward through the service and consumer related characteristics of the urban society the auto helps to create.

URBAN SPATIAL CHARACTERISTICS AND DESIGN

The news media have made *urban sprawl* a familiar term—almost a cliché. Sprawl implies no overall unity of design or plan in the spatial characteristics of our cities. The urban area grows ever outward, leapfrogging entire sections, as it spills over into the countryside in an uncoordinated maze of random and haphazard development. City officials seem powerless or even uninterested when confronted by this sprawl. Master plans for land use are made, but these are often circumvented, while fragmented suburban political units vie for development and special interest groups force variances in proposed land uses.

Hence present land use patterns are random—or at least it is safe to say that they are rarely the results of comprehensive plans for urban development. This does not mean, however, that urban growth is not shaped by some significant forces that are responsible for the chaos.

Transportation has always been influential in shaping our cities. The earliest cities were shaped by pedestrians and work animals. Even the location of cities was influenced by transportation factors such as deep water harbors, the confluence of rivers, and the juncture of important overland trails with waterways. By 1950, of the nineteen cities in the United States with populations of more than half a million, all were located along sea or lake coasts or along navigable rivers.[2] Over the years cities have evolved and adapted to changes brought about by wagons, river barges, and railroads. In the past, transportation terminals were located in or near the central business district. Access to transportation terminals fostered the development of industry and commerce in the central business district, creating higher densities and encouraging close-in living by the urban populace.[3] But all of these changes have been relatively mild when compared to the changes wrought by the complex forces of the automobile.

In the early 1900's the car was greeted almost as a new plaything. The streets along which these new machines cavorted were public places for meetings and marketing and for visiting with friends. At first the car was just another element in this busy, bustling scene. But its ever-increasing speed spelled danger for pedestrians. And the ever-multiplying cars began to replace other means of transportation. The car was already on its way to establishing one of its main characteristics: its inordinate ability to consume land, to crowd out other land uses. Soon urban roads became congested, choked, noisy, and ugly; they covered over one-third of all urban land and effectively denied pedestrians access to the city.[4] An urban geographer has noted that even the one-third figure for land use is ridiculously low when one considers that a great deal of land ordinarily classified as commercial, for instance parking lots, is so dependent on transportation as to make differentiated classification meaningless.[5]

An idea of the quantity of central business district land which is used for streets and parking is suggested in Table 7-1. It is not surprising that the highest proportions of such land used to accommodate the auto are found in Los Angeles and Dallas, younger cities that have experienced their major growth along with the development of the auto society.

Even though transportation systems have had enormous impact on the design and growth of cities, they have seldom been developed consciously as tools to bring about broader community goals. Transportation facilities in the past and even those currently being planned are usually viewed almost exclusively in relation to transportation needs.[6] Transportation planning in this sense is reactive rather than creative. It makes no conscious effort to determine the character or design of the environment it shapes. The resultant pattern is urban sprawl, with its attendant social and environmental problems.

SCALE

Though much of this book is concerned with the problems created by the auto-oriented society, one particular problem directly concerned with auto transportation and urban design is that of scale or proportion. Scale, like form, is a quality or condition that is difficult to define and equally difficult to see or conceptualize. It almost has to be experienced.

TABLE 7-1

Proportion of Central Business District Land
Devoted to Streets and Parking

| City | Year | Total acres | Percentage devoted to | | |
			Streets	Parking	Streets and Parking
Los Angeles	1960	400.7	35.0	24.0	59.0
Chicago	1956	677.6	31.0	9.7	40.7
Detroit	1953	690.0	38.5	11.0	49.5
Pittsburgh	1958	321.3	38.2		
Minneapolis	1958	580.2	34.6	13.7	48.3
St. Paul	1958	482.0	33.2	11.4	44.6
Cincinnati	1955	330.0			40.0
Dallas	1961	344.3	34.5	18.1	52.6
Sacramento	1960	340.0	34.9	6.6	41.5
Columbus	1955	502.6	40.0	7.9	47.9
Nashville	1959	370.5	30.8	8.2	39.0

Source: John B. Rae, *The Road and the Car in American Life* (Cambridge, Mass.: MIT Press, 1971), p. 220.

A properly scaled environment is almost unnoticeable until one comes into contact with an environment suffering serious distortions of scale. Such distortions can make one feel out of place, uncomfortable, lost, or dissociated. They may also foster dysfunctionality as the out-of-scale environment poses obstacles to users and impedes the normal conduct of affairs. For example, a small person (a child perhaps) finds furniture, bathroom facilities, and virtually every feature of the environment planned for larger persons. Experiments have been conducted with adults in which oversize chairs, tables, and other ordinary household furnishings were created. One's appreciation of scale is greatly sharpened if one has to climb into the seat of a chair five feet off the floor or bring a small step stool to get something from the refrigerator. Less dramatic, but nonetheless illustrative, are the problems tall Americans have in parts of the world where their heads are easily and frequently bumped on low door arches, or where some must sleep in boomerang positions in hotel beds.

This disparity in scale is one of the design attributes of the automotive society. Both the speed of the car and its own bulk contribute to the development of a larger-than-human scale for the urban environment. The space required to house, feed, and tend the car is larger than human, and its speed creates drastic alterations in our perceptions of distance.

The scale of the urban area has been determined by the needs of the auto rather than the needs of humans. This is one of the key aspects of sprawl, for much of the urban environment is out of proportion. "Sprawl city" puts a premium on the ease of movement and storage of autos and these are the values imposed on urban design.[7]

IMPACT OF SPRAWL ON NEIGHBORHOODS

In the last thirty years low density sprawl has been the most common form of metropolitan growth. Several factors contributed to this development. The number of passenger cars registered increased from 3,717,000 in 1940 to 9,658,000 in 1973, while the number of trucks and buses registered grew from 755,000 to 2,980,000. Between 1950 and 1972, municipal highway mileage increased from 323,000 to 614,000 miles. This massive mobility caused a demand for roads that penetrated the farthest reaches of cities. These roads made feasible the development of less expensive tracts of land on the urban fringe. The desire to develop land on the outskirts of the city had always been present, but in the past developers had been forced to provide transportation systems (usually electric trolleys) to spur land sales. Many of these either went bankrupt or had to be taken over by the municipality when the land developer's interest in the project had ended.[8] But the happy convergence of the automobile and public road building changed all that. The initial call for more new roads to relieve the congestion on the way to the suburbs became a roar in the 1950's and 1960's.

Another significant contributing factor was the general prosperity following

World War II and the birth of low interest rate, low down payment, and government-backed mortgage lending. It appeared possible to escape the increasingly congested (by autos) conditions of the inner city for less expensive, roomier, and quieter housing in the suburbs. Seemingly the only cost was a thirty-minute trip to work: once one owned the car, the roads were there, free for everyone, and it made economic sense to maximize the car's use. The automobile was the key to the suburban boom.

As the original suburbs became congested, the logical solution was to move even further out into the country. As developments leapfrogged ahead, they went beyond the city's boundaries, either landing in small, outlying communities' backyards or opening unincorporated areas, which imposed little or no restrictions or demands on the developers. This allowed the developer to cut costs even more, costs subsequently borne by the cities as their boundaries expanded. In some instances development of unincorporated areas led to the birth of new communities. These newly created municipalities, as well as the existing outlying communities, sought ways to bolster their tax base; naturally they encouraged the developers. They hastened the bulldozing and the building and helped to get the roads and highways needed for these new developments. What was referred to almost everywhere as "progress" was in reality developmental chaos. Soon problems associated with this style of residential development were too obvious to ignore.

One of the earliest identifiable problems was what was to become of the houses and people left behind in the flight to the fringe. Another question was what would happen to the concept of neighborhood or community in old central cities and in suburban communities? As the suburbs expanded, the need for newer and wider transportation arteries to get the suburban dweller back into the city or to another part of it became paramount in the eyes of transportation planners. But the only way to accomplish this was to cut through existing older neighborhoods with ever-widening strips of concrete.

By now the history of the destruction of American neighborhoods by the urban highway is familiar to almost everyone. Small businesses were lost; entire communities uprooted. Even if residents were fortunate enough to relocate quickly, they often suffered the psychological side effects of the loss of a sense of community.

That neighborhoods, social interaction, and transportation and communication networks are interrelated is a firmly established tenet among urban sociologists and urban planners. In his book *The Image of the City*,[9] Kevin Lynch describes the access routes or "paths" as "the network of habitual or potential lines of movement through the urban complex and . . . the most potent means by which the whole can be ordered."[10] The circulation elements or "paths may be streets, walkways, transit lines, canals, or rail-roads. For many people, these are the predominant elements in their image. People observe the city while moving through it, and along these paths the other environmental elements are arranged and related."[11]

The impact of our present system of roads on neighborhoods is readily apparent. The automobile takes up more space than any other form of urban transportation, and, as we have seen, distorts space. A nine- by eighteen-foot storage space is needed at both the origin and destination of every trip. Moreover, a typical residential street's right-of-way is fifty feet wide, a typical four-lane secondary street's right-of-way is eighty feet wide, a major six-lane divided thoroughfare can use up to 150 feet of right-of-way, and a freeway might require from 200 to 300 feet of right-of-way.[12] These space requirements have their greatest impact on the inner-city neighborhoods. Many of these have been crisscrossed by road "improvements" primarily designed to increase traffic capacity so that those living in the outlying subur-ban neighborhoods can travel through the city.[13] The increased space consump-tion as well as the increase in traffic have multiple negative effects on these neighborhoods. Important subjective values such as neighborhood unity and sense of form and design are lost. Safety, mobility, and communication are adversely affected. The effects on social interaction as a function of traffic have been aptly depicted by Appleyard and Lintell (see Figure 7-1). These auto-imposed restrictions have even entered the popular folklore: "To survive in Manhattan, so goes the advice, make no crosstown trips at lunch-time, no appointments before 11 or after 3, no subway trips except in off-peak hours and no friendships beyond walking distance."[14]

Crisscrossed by ribbons of concrete, with businesses destroyed and families uprooted, these neighborhoods were left to deteriorate as the more affluent sped away to the suburbs. The undesirable, ugly, noisy, and fragmented inner city neighborhoods soon became the repositories for the urban poor as the cores of America's cities rotted.

While the impact on the inner city neighborhoods is greatest, suburban dwellers suffer their own particular brands of design and space utilization dysfunctionality. There is the ugliness of unplanned commercial strips on the way to the suburbs, featuring used car dealers, the ubiquitous burger stand, and drive-in pawn shops. There are rows of look-alike houses where the trees have been bulldozed, in part to make room for the access arteries, and there are, of course, traffic jams in suburbia. The mixed blessings of life on the urban fringe are summed up in these lines from "L. A. Freeway," a pop song of the seventies:

> If I can just get off that L. A. freeway
> Without getting killed or caught,
> Down the road in a cloud of smoke
> For some land that I ain't bought.[15]

Figure 7-1. Social Interaction as a Function of Traffic

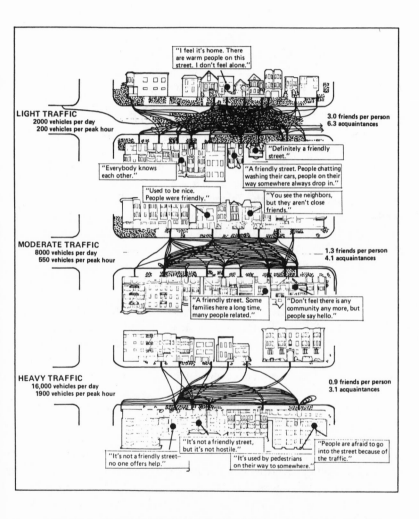

Source: Donald Appleyard and Mark Lintell, "Social Interaction as a Function of Traffic," in Peter Wolf, *The Future of the City: New Directions in Urban Planning* (New York: Whitney Library of Design, 1974), p. 44.

INDUSTRIAL AND COMMERCIAL EFFECTS

The impact of the auto society on the residential and neighborhood characteristics of cities was accompanied by alterations in industrial and commercial developments. Industry has two critical variables affecting its location: access to markets and access to labor. The growing networks of roads not only crisscrossed and encircled the cities, they also provided major intercity transportation link-ups; hence they affected the location of industry in several ways. Industries were no longer tied to the railroad terminals and the wharves of a central city. The growth rate of truck sales surpassed even the rate of car sales, and trucking soon dominated freight transportation.[16] This meant that terminals could be located on the urban fringe for easy access to pick-ups and deliveries via interstate loops and interstate highway systems. In addition, the other critical variable for modern industry, a skilled labor supply, was now located in suburbia.[17] There are, to be sure, other variables affecting urban industrial location on the periphery, such as the enlarged requirements for assembly line production techniques and the lower cost of land. But the point is that the automotive-truck-highway oriented transportation system was what made the realization of these other advantages possible.

The growth of suburban shopping centers and the decline of central city commercial centers have likewise followed logically from the population and residential shifts occasioned by the automotive society. The central marketing district, which used to serve as the focal point for the commercial activity of the city, has given way to the neighborhood shopping center with its large branch department stores offering goods and services formerly available only in the center. These centers have followed the shoppers to the suburbs, for those who remained in the older, central city are generally lower income groups.

Strip commercial developments along the main thoroughfares leading to the suburbs have been another feature of the commercial development of the city. The walk-in store gave way to the drive-in, or the shopping center provided massive expanses of macadam, dotted in the middle with the familiar mall of department stores and specialty shops. The space needed for the shoppers' vehicles was several times greater than the space needed for the shoppers themselves; this ratio was a crucial factor for the new urban landscape.

Banking and finance likewise took its cue from transportation developments and residential, industrial, and commercial shifts. The branch bank (complete with drive-in windows) became a familiar neighborhood fixture. In some instances the neighborhood branches were more active than the downtown banks.

URBAN ARCHITECTURE

It is clear that the design of the city was affected by the auto through land consumption and the reconfiguration of residential, industrial, and commercial activities. Similarly, urban buildings were shaped by the dominant mode of transportation, though this effect of the auto never achieved the exaggerated impact suggested by some.

We have already noted the ubiquitous drive-in everything, from movie theaters and groceries to banks and pawn shops. Another significant addition to urban architecture was the highly visible high-rise parking garage. These pigeonhole structures, with their hundreds of pairs of chrome-rimmed eyes peering out over the city, were rivaled only by the soaring, magisterial shapes of the crisscrossing concrete ribbons, which increasingly encircled and strangled the central city. High density apartments gave way to one-story, detached residences linked to the ever-present carport or garage. Industrial buildings were spread out to accommodate new assembly-line production processes; they were also surrounded by acres of parking lots. The buildings were open, well ventilated, and well lighted; they were also flat and spacious.

Between 1900 and 1950 there were many "progressive" architects who hoped to accommodate the city to the car. Their designs for urban buildings included multilevel streets to give cities room for both cars and people and traffic overpasses, which would later evolve into cloverleaves. In Algiers, there was even a suggestion to suspend buildings underneath a wide roadway.[18] The first regional plan for New York (1931) included using the lower two floors of buildings for traffic lanes.[19] "The Metropolis of Tomorrow," a design by Hugh Ferris, featured skyscrapers with stepped sides that would be made into automobile highways at the fifth, tenth, fifteenth, and twentieth floors.[20] By the 1950's however, there was a reaction against the auto; a few architects designed cities without cars. For example, Louis Kahn's proposed center city for Philadelphia was patterned after the medieval walled city. People could pass freely through the gateway, but autos were kept outside the city walls.[21]

On the whole, however, the buildings constructed during the last fifty years reflect the expansiveness and the clutter of the spread-out city. Most cities are places to drive through, or to drive into in the morning and out of in the afternoon. Their architecture is that of a way station, not of a place to live.[22]

THE NATURAL ENVIRONMENT

The impact of the automotive system on the natural environment is one of the best-documented but most complex areas of urban transportation analysis. The ecology of the natural environment is delicately balanced. Changes in one area can spread quickly throughout the entire system and synergistic effects can be produced.[23] The auto has contributed heavily to our assault on the urban environment by introducing various pollutants of its own into the atmosphere and by contributing to urban developmental forms that produce still other adverse environmental effects.

We have already referred to one general environmental problem of the auto: the use of great quantities of land. But what kind of land? In the past few decades much of the prime agricultural land that ringed the cities has been withdrawn from agricultural use, subdivided, and turned into tract developments. Often, this land is easy to develop because it is flat and cleared. At the present time, it is estimated that some four thousand acres of prime agricultural lands are being converted daily to other uses. The extent to which this withdrawal of land from agriculture is reversible is at present unknown. But in a world threatened by mass starvation due to the population explosion, soil depletion, and the irreversible loss of fertile land, such policies for urban development pose serious environmental questions.

Another critical area of land use—or misuse—directly related to the auto transportation system is encroachment on parklands, open space, and flood plains. These pristine lands are "free"; they already belong to the public. Furthermore, the red tape of condemnation, assembly of parcels, and hearings involving citizen reactions, all the bane of highway planners, could, at least in the past, be more quickly dispensed with. The costs to the public may be immense in the long run and big enough in the short, but they are less immediately apparent than a bond election or an increase in the tax rate.

In Memphis, for instance, a six-lane interstate was run through the middle of a 340-acre park; in Philadelphia expressways go through and bound Fairmount Park, the largest park in the world, and rip through a public golf course; in Wilmington, Delaware, an interstate highway scars a beautiful, quiet park along the Brandywine Creek; and in Milwaukee, a six-lane freeway will cut through the lovely Juneau Park and Lagoon along the shore of Lake Michigan. Citizens of San Antonio, which seems to have more than its share of auto-related ills, have been fighting for years to prevent the completion of Interstate 35 through the heart of the city. As described by a San Antonio city planner, the expressway

curves and winds its way through virtually every element of a system of park lands and recreation areas. It crosses an Audubon bird sanctuary and Olmos Creek, a tributary in its natural state to be converted into a concrete ditch; it moves through a picnic ground and recreation area obliterating a Girl Scout Day Camp and a nature trail; it stretches across the Olmos Basin and rises to enormous height, roller coaster fashion, to go over Olmos Dam; it severs the campus of Incarnate Word College, forcing the closing of an elementary school; it cuts through the lands of the San Antonio Zoo; it blocks off the half-built public school gymnasium, slides along the rim of the famous Sunken Garden, hovering over in cantilever the edge of the outdoor theater, squeezes itself between this and the municipal school stadium, blocking a major entrance; it slashes through residential areas, shaves a municipal golf course, and then brutally cuts across a wooded portion of the San Antonio River's natural water course, one of the few remaining wilderness touches left within the city.[24]

The loss of agricultural lands and parks to transportation-related developments are only two problems of environmental land use. Others involve such dimensions as the suitability of different soils for building purposes and the appropriateness of development in certain critical ecological zones. Soil subsidence, dangers from mud slides, the destruction of wild life refuges in the city, development on aquifer underground water supply recharge areas[25] and ecologically delicate ecotones[26] are all critical environmental problems affected by the urban development associated with the automotive life-style.

AIR QUALITY

The internal combustion engine is responsible for more than half the nation's air pollution. In areas such as Los Angeles and New York City the amount of automotive-related air pollution is close to 75 or 80 percent. But even areas relatively "free" of air pollution, Southwestern cities for example, do not meet minimum air quality standards and frequently experience moderate to heavy air pollution. In these cities the auto is the dominant form of transportation and the major cause of air pollution.

Each year cars deposit as much as 180 billion pounds of contaminants in the air.[27] Major pollutants related to automobile use (but not limited to auto sources) are:

1. Carbon Monoxide (CO)—a poisonous gas which is both tasteless and odorless, produced by incomplete combustion of carbon in fuels.
2. Particulate Matter—particles of solids or liquids in a wide range of sizes from microscopic to visible smoke or soot. Lead is one toxic particulate associated with gasoline burning engines.
3. Hydrocarbons (HC)—as with carbon monoxide, these represent an incomplete combustion process. They are not directly toxic like carbon monoxide. They combine with other pollutants to form photochemical smog.

4. Nitrogen Oxides (NO_x)—are formed when fuels are burned at very high temperatures. In sunlight, nitrogen oxides combine with hydrocarbons to become photochemical oxidants.[28]

Meteorological factors influence the impact of pollution on cities. The amount of air pollution present at a particular place and time depends to a great extent upon wind and other climatic conditions. Emergencies can arise when pollution becomes trapped over a city by a temperature inversion. An inversion occurs when cool air near the ground is sealed off by a layer of warmer air. Air at ground level cannot rise, and pollutants are trapped. Pollutants continue to accumulate until the inversion is broken. Several serious air pollution disasters have resulted from inversions.

Although air pollution emergencies are rare, they demonstrate the effects of air pollution on the body. Deaths during these disasters are caused by the aggravating effects of pollution on previously existing conditions. Numerous recent studies show a definite correspondence between increases in pollution ratings and the rise in respiratory disease deaths, cardiovascular disease, infant mortality rates, and death rates of persons over sixty-five. Both emphysema and lung cancer may be closely linked to air pollution. For many years there has been considerable debate over the long-term effects of pollutants on health because it has been difficult to isolate the pollutants or combinations of pollutants that contribute to disease. We can see dramatically the effects of carbon monoxide poisoning from accidental leaks in car exhaust systems and from suicides. But what are the effects of smaller doses of carbon monoxide? Carbon monoxide can cause drowsiness and alter driver response, possibly contributing to traffic accidents and fatalities. Hydrocarbons from automobiles (and other sources) have been identified as being carcinogenic. One hydrocarbon, benzo-a-pyrene, has been most closely associated with cancer. A nonsmoker in a polluted area takes in more of this chemical daily than he would get from a pack of cigarettes. Perhaps the admonition "Warning: [This area] may be hazardous to your health" should be posted around urban streets and sidewalks.[29]

Since the early seventies, attempts have been made to curb air pollution from automobiles. In 1970, the Clean Air Act set up emissions standards for automobiles, which car makers were to reach by 1975. In 1975, Congress gave the automakers an extension through 1976 and allowed a one-year extension of 1977 standards for hydrocarbons and carbon monoxide subject to approval by the Environmental Protection Agency and establishment of new interim standards for 1977. Nitrogen oxide emissions standards were also set for 1977.[30]

There is little evidence, however, that the auto manufacturers are making really serious efforts to reduce air pollution. The auto industry, which seeks to retain the internal combustion engine, continues to make largely cosmetic efforts to reduce emissions. The industry's "advanced" pollution control system, called the Chrysler Clean Air Package, amounts, according to Nader's Task Force, to a fine tune of the engine which must be repeated frequently. As Nader's group points out, what the auto industry is doing in pollution control was technologically possible ten years ago. Crankcase emission controls use a fifty-year old method, while carbon monoxide and hydrocarbon emissions are "controlled" by simple adjustments to the carburetor and ignition system.

There is mounting evidence that the steam-driven motor car is a feasible alternative to the internal combustion engine,[31] even though the automotive industry has taken great pains to demonstrate that it is not. General Motors's example of a steam-powered car at the 1969 Power of Progress Show was notable for its failures. It was noisier than the conventional steam engine, which is notably quiet. It spewed smoke and soot; the normal steam engine is clean. It weighed five hundred pounds more than the conventional steam engine. L. William Grouse, Jr., an authority on steam engines, says that most investigators conclude that the steam engine is both feasible and safe —*if* the investigator is not associated with the auto industry.

Many of the environmental problems of the auto society would remain, even with steam-driven cars. But the technology is no doubt available to make a significant impact on auto-related air pollution. That no more has been accomplished merely serves to reinforce the conclusion that the economic interests involved have little concern for the development of policies that regard the public.

Finally, it should be noted that regardless of the efficiency of emission controls or the pollution characteristics of the steam engine, air quality can be dramatically improved by the nature of urban development. Recent research has suggested that the pounds per day of carbon monoxides, hydrocarbons, and nitrogen oxides in high-density planned development may be only half the levels in low-density sprawl development.[32] Planned communities, with well-coordinated land use plans, may significantly reduce air pollution.

WATER POLLUTION

Possible contamination of underground water supplies through sprawl development along aquifer recharge zones has already been noted as one form of water pollution related to the automotive society. There are, in addition, more direct contributions to water pollution associated with cars, buses, and trucks. Though difficult to isolate as a separate source, runoff from urban streets and highways contains oil residues and other chemicals associated with motor transport. Petroleum refineries and mining and steel, all critically associated with the automotive industry, are major sources of water pollution. Oil spills from tankers and blown wells in the ocean represent other sources of water contamination. All of these, of course, cannot be totally attributed to the automotive society; there are many other uses of steel and oil. But autos are major users of these products and their facilities; hence they play an important role.

In still another related fashion the car contributes to water pollution through atmospheric chemical reactions and the subsequent contamination of rainfall. An illustrative case of attempts to control air pollution that created another problem is described by Barry Commoner: The present smog control technique—reduction of waste fuel emission—by diminishing the interaction of nitrogen oxides with hydrocarbon waste, enhances the level of airborne nitrogen oxides, which are themselves toxic. In the air, nitrogen oxides are readily converted to nitrates, which are then brought down by rain and snow to the land and surface waters. There they add to the growing burden of nitrogen fertilizer. What is surprising is the amount of nitrogen oxides that are generated by automotive traffic: it accounts for more than one-third of the nitrogen contained in fertilizer currently employed on United States farms.[33]

NOISE POLLUTION

"Noise is a classic example of an 'externality,' the side effect of a private action, imposing an unwanted cost upon third parties who aren't partners to the action and who receive no benefit from it."[34] Noise has increased steadily as a by-product of urban living. Since the industrial revolution, but especially during the last half century, there has been a constant acceleration in urban noise; the loudest noises to which mankind is exposed have increased at the rate of about one decibel per year over a period of three decades. All of us contribute to noise, but the effects of our noise are unfortunately not limited to ourselves.

Noise levels are increasingly a source of dissatisfaction and irritation to urban residents. Motor vehicles are the major source of urban noise pollution, and while cars are not as noisy as buses or trucks, they exist in such large numbers that their combined impact may be greater. The "roar" of an urban freeway provides corridors of background noise over and above the ambient sound level.

Some analysts have concluded that noise levels produced by traffic are not sufficiently high to pose a direct and immediate threat to health.[35] Nonetheless, recent "scientific study has extended our knowledge of the physical effects of noise to include chemical and physiological reactions involving blood, heart, eyes, skin, stomach and esophagus. It is now well established that noise above 75 dB (A) [decibels] produces temporary changes in the physiological state of man."[36] Urban traffic noise is usually measured in units called decibels. A car horn three feet away produces approximately 115 decibels; a heavy truck fifty feet away about 90 decibels, enough to cause hearing damage to anyone exposed to it for extended lengths of time. From Table 7-2, which depicts specified noise levels associated with urban transportation, it would appear that many forms of urban traffic generate sufficient noise to be harmful.

TABLE 7-2

Urban Transportation Sound Levels

Noise source and distance		Decibels
(Threshold of pain)		140
Overhead jet aircraft (500′)	just below	120
Unmuffled motorcycle	above	110
Subway train (20′)	just below	100
Heavy trucks (20′)	just below	100
Train whistle (500′)		95
Small truck accelerating (30′)		85
Heavy traffic (25′ to 50′)	above	80
Light trucks (20′)	above	80
Autos (20′)		75

Source: G. M. Stevenson, Jr., "Noise and the Urban Environment," in Thomas Detwyler and M. G. Marcus, *Urbanization and Environment* (Belmont, Calif.: Duxbury Press, 1972), p. 197.

The psychological effects of noise are more difficult to define. Apparently, humans are able and willing to adapt to a wide range of noise conditions. But psychological principles suggest that this very adaptation takes its toll in the unconscious realm of the mental-nervous system. Researchers studying sleeping patterns are attempting to determine the disruptive effects of noise upon the unconscious. Both psychologists and psychiatrists agree that noise affects the unconcious mind and the central nervous system as an irritant or in some other disruptive manner.[37]

A noise survey conducted in central London in 1961–62 found that traffic noise was an important source of annoyance to people, whether they were outdoors, at work, at school, or at home. For average exposure levels of greater than 55 decibels in a 24-hour period, which encompasses typical urban traffic noise, over 20 percent of the individuals surveyed considered themselves to be "considerably" disturbed. Thirty-six percent of those surveyed were disturbed by traffic noise.[38]

The same survey recorded peaks of 90 decibels at the curbside of arterial roads with many heavy vehicles. "For 80 percent of the time (excluding the lowest and highest), the noise levels ranged from 68 to 80 dB/A by day and 50 to 70 dB/A by night."[39]

NATURAL RESOURCES AND ENERGY

The motor vehicle industry is one of our greatest consumers of natural resources. When combined with the highway construction industry, the petroleum industry, and related, ancillary industries, it has a truly formidable resource impact. The impact of the motor vehicle industry alone on selected resources is shown in Table 7-3.

Current EPA estimates of identified resource availability reveal that the motor vehicle industry does not pose a serious threat to natural resource depletion.[40] The identified resources, which in most cases are classified as large, appear to be sufficient to meet future needs. This does not imply, however, that the present wasteful system of resource use for transportation should be condoned. Reserves, at present rates of consumption, are adequate only through the year 2000 in several critical materials. New resources will be available only through costlier extraction processes, the use of lower grade ores, and the development of expensive new technologies. The maintenance of the present transportation system can be accomplished only at escalating costs.

One of the most critical areas is that of energy consumption. The transportation sector in the United States currently accounts for 25 percent of all domestic energy consumption and is the largest petroleum user, consuming 60 percent of all petroleum used in the United States.[41] Transportation is heavily dependent on oil-based fuels; 96 percent of all transportation energy is supplied by liquid hydrocarbons.[42]

Table 7-4 reveals that over half of the energy used by the transportation sector was used by automobiles. If trucks are included, this figure was well over three-fourths of the total transportation sector energy use. Of some 5.75 million barrels of crude oil consumed in the United States in 1975, almost 3.5 million barrels were used by cars, trucks, and buses, with the overwhelming share going to automobiles. By the year 2000, based on present projections, total crude oil consumption will amount to over 10 million barrels annually, with the auto-highway system using 6 million barrels. The rising demand for oil in the industrialized world is being driven

TABLE 7-3

Resource Consumption by U.S. Motor Vehicle Industry, 1974

Resource	Total U.S. Consumption	Automotive Consumption	Automotive Percentage
All steel (million tons)	111.4	23.2	20.8
Sheet steel	37.2	15.5	41.8
Bar steel	12.9	3.3	25.4
Aluminum (million lbs.)	14,555	1,719	11.8
Copper and Copper alloys (million lbs.)	7,384	650	8.8
Lead (short tons)	1,541,209	970,962	63.0
Malleable iron (000 of tons)	1,030	482	46.8
Natural rubber (long tons)	685,000	507,000	74.0
Synthetic rubber (long tons)	2,400,000	1,483,000	61.8
Zinc (000 of tons)	1,504	501	33.3

Source: Motor Vehicle Manufacturers Association, *Automobile Facts and Figures* (1975), p. 59.

to a great extent by the rapid growth of car ownership. At present, only 17 percent of crude oil consumption in Europe goes into fuels for road vehicles (as compared with 60 percent for the United States), but this figure will be grossly inflated if the world car population grows at current "official" projection rates. Unless some very shaky estimates of ultimate world oil reserves prove correct, then the demands for fuel for road transportation are likely to provoke a severe shortage of oil by the end of the century.[43]

TABLE 7-4

Distribution of Energy within the Transportation Sector

	Percentage of Total Energy	
	1960	1970
1. Automobiles		
urban	25.2	28.9
intercity	27.6	26.4
	(52.8)	(55.3)
2. Aircraft		
freight	0.3	0.8
passenger	3.8	6.7
	(4.1)	(7.5)
3. Railroads		
freight	3.7	3.2
passenger	0.3	0.1
	(4.0)	(3.3)
4. Trucks		
intercity freight	6.1	5.8
other uses[a]	13.8	15.3
	(19.9)	(21.1)
5. Waterways, freight	1.1	1.0
6. Pipelines	0.9	1.2
7. Buses	0.2	0.2
8. Other[b]	17.0	10.4
Total	100.0%	100.0%
Total transportation energy consumption (10^{15})	10.9	16.5 Btu

[a]Data from Federal Highway Administration, highway statistics.

[b]Includes passenger traffic by boat, general aviation, pleasure boating, and nonbus urban mass transit, as well as the effects of historical variations in modal energy efficiencies.

Source: Eric Hurst, *Energy Consumption for Transportation in the United States,* Oak Ridge National Laboratory. ORNL-NSF-EP-15 (Mar. 1972), p. 27.

Mass transit has the greatest potential for energy efficiency, as is illustrated in Table 7-5. It is interesting to note that the large American passenger car with only one occupant has a worse fuel efficiency ratio than does the supersonic transport. Some analysts have pointed out, however, that even given this energy efficiency potential of mass transit, it will not be possible to shift sufficient ridership to mass transit to effect significant energy savings.[44] This argument is probably correct in the short run, given the current fixed options in urban mobility. But this position is similar to the density argument used to criticize mass transit in the cases of low density cities such as

TABLE 7-5

Energy Efficiency of Various Passenger Transport Systems
in the United States

Transport Type	Passenger miles / U.S. gallon fuel (or 130,000 Btu)
Helicopter	7.5
Large car (1)	8.0
U.S. SST plane	10.0
B707 and DC8 jet plane	20.0
Most cars (2)	30.9

Small car (2)
  Non–5th Avenue bus
  European wagon lits
  Noncity metro
	60.0

Small car (4), 2-level city bus	100.0
Suburban bus	250.0
2-level electric train	300.0
Microbus (7)	350.0
Broad gauge train	375.0
Bicycle	1,000.0

Numbers in parentheses=occupants

Source: Gerald Leach, *The Motor Car and Natural Resources* (Paris: Organization for Economic Co-Operation and Development, 1973), p. 32.

Los Angeles. The effort to concentrate on achieving energy savings through improving the efficiency of the passenger automobile may serve to divert attention from the long-run need to significantly increase ridership of more efficient types of transportation. And the combined development of the highway-auto mode, even given the ultimate maximum energy savings of

20 percent, will not avert critical energy depletion for much longer than the presently forecasted quarter of a century.

PROSPECTS FOR THE FUTURE

As an influence upon the urban scene, possibly the only factor that can compare with the car is population growth itself. Urban areas have grown because so many Americans have moved to them. Moreover, if present trends continue, in the next twenty-four years we can expect to add some forty-five million more to our numbers. And probably 80 to 85 percent of these will be living in urban places by the year 2000. This means that over the next quarter of a century approximately half again as many new houses, industrial and commercial buildings, and transport facilities will have to be built as have been built in the entire history of our cities. At present rates, this also means that we will gobble up as much additional land as is presently urbanized.

Most of this growth will be on the metropolitan fringes, filling in the gaps between existing metropolises in several cases and giving birth to megalopolises along the Eastern seaboard and along the California coast. Vast areas are likely to become almost continuous urbanized places.

But this type of growth can take place only at great costs. As Robert C. Weaver, writing in 1965, noted:

The previous 40 years of metropolitan growth has produced a phenomenon variously known as "Spread City," "urban sprawl" and "slurbs." In other words, much of our suburban development heretofore has been a mess. Not only has it resulted in ugliness and botched land uses, but it has also been tremendously wasteful. Community facilities, such as sewer systems and water supply, have been built on a piecemeal, too-little too-late basis. Roads and highways have been developed with little thought to repercussions on future land-use patterns, and commercial and industrial buildings have gone up, willy-nilly, wherever a local zoning ordinance could be obligingly bent.[45]

More recently, in an exhaustive study conducted by the Real Estate Research Corporation for the Council on Environmental Quality, the Department of Housing and Urban Development, and the Environmental Protection Agency,[46] it was concluded that:

a. Total capital costs for the high density planned community are 56 percent of those for the conventional low density sprawl development, resulting in a cost savings of $227.5 million for communities with 10,000 housing units.

b. Savings in land costs amount to 54 percent ($12,725,000), with savings of 40 percent for streets ($15,103,000), and 63 percent for utilities ($39,542,000).

c. Operating and maintenance costs in the high density planned community are estimated to be approximately $2 million (11 percent) less per year then the low density sprawl development after completion of the total development. Savings are largely due to less road and utility pipe lengths and reduced gas and electric consumption in the high density community.

d. Compared to low density sprawl, the amount of total capital costs borne by local government may decrease by almost 50 percent for high density planned communities. Operating and maintenance costs borne by local government may decrease by 13 percent.

e. Total air and water pollution and other forms of environmental degradation are similarly reduced. Air pollutants from automobiles are reduced 50 percent and those from space heating and other natural gas uses are reduced 40 percent. Sediment is reduced 30 percent and total storm water runoff 20 percent.

f. Energy consumption is reduced 44 percent and water consumption 35 percent in high density planned communities as compared to low density sprawl communities.

This means that if the low density sprawl fostered by the motorcar society continues, the price of urban development will be nearly double what it would be in almost every category noted above compared with its costs with higher density planned development.

Much of this high-cost urban development can be attributed to the dominant force of the auto-highway system. Many additional elements have intervened and have contributed to the problems of design and environmental deterioration discussed in this chapter. But the special kind of mobility afforded by the automobile made it all possible, and the car bears a particularly heavy responsibility.

Perhaps it will be possible for us to plan with more care in the future and to make our cities livable for people, plants, and wildlife. Hindsight is always easy. The real question is whether we will be able to anticipate better the consequences of today's actions. Changing from an auto transportation system to one based on mass transit will not solve all the city's environmental problems. It will not solve industrial pollution or pesticide contamination. It will not instantly remove urban ugliness, nor will it immediately restructure already sprawling cities into organized communities. Nevertheless, changing to a mass transit system will force examination of various alternatives and their possible impacts on all sectors of the city *before* decisions are made. Such careful consideration should lead to planned city development. A mass transit system will leave more land for parks and open spaces, allow blocks to be reclaimed for pedestrian use, and provide urban dwellers with the monumental challenge of rebuilding cities to meet the needs of people.

Various new forms have been envisioned for cities of the future—compact cities, arcologies, new towns of many shapes. Most of these designs attempt to integrate the man-made world into the world of nature. Whether we are building a new city or rebuilding old ones, an awareness of environmental constraints is essential.

First, in designing new urban transit systems, one must consider the constraints imposed by the man-made environment. We cannot simply destroy all the buildings of the past and start over. How can we make a transit system fit into the present structure of the city and still use it as a tool for reshaping the city?

Second, and more important, the constraints imposed by the natural environment must be respected. The transportation system must be planned with desire for the minimum waste of resources and the least possible damage to the environment. As Ian McHarg has observed: "Let us accept the proposition that nature is process, that it is interacting, that it responds to laws, representing values and opportunities for human use with certain limitations and even prohibitions to certain of these."[47] We must consider the aquifers and floodplains, the geology, the plant life, and the form of the urban area, not just the dollar costs or political feasibility of a proposed system. Our automotive cities are products of our tendency to ignore nature or to attempt to conquer it with machines and concrete. Our hope for the future may be in McHarg's philosophy of man as steward for nature—"enhancing the creative fit of man-environment, realizing man's design with nature."[48]

8

CITIZEN REACTION

As you drive through downtown Dallas, a rather peculiar-looking object meets your eye—an unused six-lane elevated highway that extends through part of the city and then abruptly stops. It just sits there, enduring in a rather grotesque way as a monument to the efforts of various citizen groups who successfully forestalled the disruption of a major urban neighborhood. The American landscape, especially in the cities, is dotted with many such monuments.

Since the 1960's, activist citizen groups have rocked the American political system, and citizen groups have since demanded a stronger voice in a wide range of public policies, including the environment, poverty programs, zoning, and land use. Citizen groups have also been increasingly active in the area of transportation policy, especially in their opposition to highway programs.

In Chicago, for example, people in a South Side neighborhood learned that their homes lay along the route of a proposed eight-lane crosstown expressway that would displace some 10,400 people in its 22-mile course.[1] A few neighbors gathered at a church to discuss what they could do. Although only eight persons attended this first meeting, several hundred residents showed up at a neighborhood hearing a short time later, and the Anti-Crosstown Action Committee was born. Shortly thereafter, the Anti-Crosstown Action Committee joined with other groups in a loose coalition to oppose the Cross-town expressway. Most of their efforts were directed at elected officials. Since both city and state elections were at hand, the citizens elicited the support of various candidates seeking elective office, including incumbent Senator Charles Percy. As a result of this full-fledged campaign, Secretary of Transportation Volpe agreed to intercede in the matter, and the Illinois governor cut off funds for further land acquisition for this highway project. The Crosstown controversy is only one of the battles raging in dozens of American cities over the construction of highways. *Business Week* reported that "in 20 or more cities various groups are waging bitter fights against expressways that disrupt homes and businesses, bulldoze historic sites, or block scenic views."[2] In eleven cities, there were sections of the interstate highway system which the Department of Transportation considered "completely essential to an integrated national system," but which it also conceded faced serious problems because of local opposition.[3] The extent of citizen reaction to proposed highways is so great that *The Concrete Opposition*, published by the Highway Action Coalition, carries a separate column in each issue entitled "Bulldozer Blocking," which summarizes the efforts of citizens to halt highway projects.[4]

The pattern of development for these citizen groups is quite similar. Usually a small group of citizens meets to oppose some highway project, primarily because of its adverse impact on a neighborhood or the environment.[5] Other groups and citizens are attracted to their cause, and a political strategy is developed. But not all these groups enjoy the same degree of success. In many cities, citizen groups are badly beaten and emerge from the fray disappointed and frustrated. Why are some political strategies successful in changing policy while others are not? What are the crucial factors which underlie this political process? These questions will serve as the basis of this chapter.

STRATEGIES OF CITIZEN INTEREST GROUPS

For conducting a citizen campaign against a highway project, several strategies have been suggested. In this section, we will briefly summarize the strategies offered by Ben Kelley and Daniel Zwerdling.[6] Obviously, a strategy depends to a large extent on the actual situation. What works in one community may be inappropriate for another. But the basic components of the strategy may be drawn from these suggestions:

1. ORGANIZE EARLY

As soon as information indicates that a proposed highway will be routed through a neighborhood or community, it is important for citizens to organize themselves. In most cases, the organization will evolve in a single neighborhood, but there are usually other existing organizations in the community that may be of assistance. These include schools, environmental organizations, recreational departments, and even civic organizations. Organizing also implies some type of action, and the "quickest way for a fledgling anti-freeway movement to nip itself in the bud is through inaction."[7] Control of information is, of course, a crucial advantage for the proponents of highways. In his study of the Crosstown freeway, Elliott Pavlos argues that the city of Chicago deliberately withheld proposed plans from the community until the plan was adopted by the official governmental decision makers. The reason for this is obvious: "The more advance information given out, the more ammunition for those who may be in opposition."[8]

2. APPLY POLITICAL PRESSURE

A standard political maxim is that government will respond only to pressure. Some pressure points are better than others, however, and the limited resources of citizen groups should be judiciously applied. In most cases it is fruitless to direct appeals to the highway agencies proposing the project. Kelley also argues against lobbying Congress to halt a highway project.[9] In one controversy where Congress intervened, it ordered the city of Washington to construct the Three Sisters expressway bridge against the city's will. Still, in some cases individual members of Congress may be sympathetic and intercede in the dispute.[10] Nevertheless, in many situations, it may be more productive to appeal to local or state officials.

What kind of pressures should be applied? Threatening an unsympathetic office holder with defeat at the next election is probably the least useful tactic. You must remember that citizen groups are transitory; office holders may have the advantage of time on their side. Letter-writing campaigns and personal visits by members of the groups to their elected officials, are more promising tactics. Picketing governmental offices and marching require considerable work, although they may be successful.

3. FIND OUT WHAT THE LAWS ARE

In many cases, lobbying efforts may be doomed to failure, since the highway lobby exerts tremendous influence. Knowing what the laws require provides citizen groups with some significant advantages, especially if the group intends to take its case to court. Since 1969, hearings have been required for federal aid highway projects. These requirements, although frequently honored in the breach, can force administrative agencies to consider citizen demands. Moreover, if the project will adversely affect a park, wildlife area, or historic site, the Transportation Act of 1966 provides additional protection. Finally, one should find out the legal powers of local government. In some states local government can exercise a degree of veto power over proposed projects.

4. PREPARE FOR HEARINGS

Under the 1969 procedures, state highway departments must hold two public hearings before they can receive federal funds for a highway project: the first on the location of the route and the second on its design.[11] Notice of the hearing must be given thirty days in advance; frequently hearings are "staged" to counter adverse presentations. In Seattle, for example, state officials scheduled a hearing on a project that would go through a black community; but the meeting was held at an all-white country club at 10 o'clock in the morning.[12]

In order to have a significant impact at the hearings, citizen groups must do their homework. Citizen groups should organize their presentations by assigning specific problems to individuals. For example, one member might discuss environment, another safety, another neighborhood impact, and so forth. If citizens merely show up on the day of the hearing, unarmed and unprepared, they will quickly be outflanked by the experts. What should probably not be discussed, however, are alternative routes to the proposed highway plan. Although the law now provides that states can substitute highway trust fund monies for other types of transportation projects, it is usually self-defeating to suggest an alternative highway route. Too frequently the alternative routes will damage some other part of the city, frequently low-income and minority neighborhoods: " 'Through the park or the ghetto' is the urban highway planner's slogan."[13] Moreover, if a citizen group offers an alternative route, highway departments can claim that the requirement for citizen participation in route selection was satisfied.

5. PREPARE ALTERNATIVE STRATEGIES

If the state highway officials decide against a citizen group at the hearings, there are at least two alternative strategies. First, one can appeal to the secretary of transportation, though no formal procedure has been adopted. In several instances, including the Crosstown controversy in Chicago and the Belt Line controversy in Boston, the secretary of transportation has intervened. Second, citizen groups can seek injunctive relief through the courts. If procedural requirements were not followed or if the planned project conflicts with other laws, citizens can ask the courts to stop the project. In Kanawha County, West Virginia, the City Council of Neighborhoods filed a suit to halt the conversion of the West Virginia Turnpike to interstate standards.[14] Indeed, the number of court cases filed by anti-highway groups is increasing so rapidly that the American Association of State Highway Officials has advocated that highway programs be protected from legal actions "by requiring the plaintiff in such injunctive proceedings to post a bond of sufficient amount to show sincerity of purpose and to discourage any irresponsible harassment and delaying tactics."[15]

THE POLITICAL MILIEU AND CITIZEN REACTION

Even though these strategies have been used widely by citizen groups, they have not met with unqualified success. Indeed, if some pat formula could be devised, there would be little value in continuing this discussion. There are several reasons why these strategies have not been uniformly successful. To a large extent, they are based on assumptions which over-simplify the political world. For example, applying political pressure on our elected officials assumes that they are responsive solely to citizens in the community. Yet, elected officials face constant pressure from all sides. Moreover, citizen groups tend to take a moralistic view of their own position and find it difficult to believe that others do not share their values. If you battle with the highway builders to protect the environment or save a neighborhood, who could be against you?

Citizen action groups, then, must understand the political milieu in order to adapt their strategies to different situations. There are several basic and crucial characteristics of our political system, and it is important to understand the linkages between these characteristics and the types of strategy which will aid citizen action groups in their efforts. For the purpose of exploring these linkages, five basic characteristics of our political system can be defined, including legitimacy, the scope of conflict, the span of attention, technocratism, and immobilization.

1. LEGITIMACY

When issues arise in the political arena, the antagonists either implicitly or explicitly stand for certain kinds of values. For example, in the debate over the Vietnam War, debate revolved around an array of conflicting values, and each side appealed to the values it believed had the highest degree of legitimacy for the public. As for highway construction, advocates of more roads frequently argue for increasing the mobility of automobile owners, enhancing economic prosperity, and increasing personal freedom. In selling the Interstate Highway Program in 1956, the advocates went so far as to claim that such a system was necessary for the national defense; indeed, the full name of the act was the "National System of Interstate and Defense Highways." Citizen groups who oppose highway construction have seldom appealed to such grandiose values. Most of the opposition in the 1950's and early 1960's was based on a belief in neighborhood integrity or, negatively, on the decline of property values. The environmental movement, which started in the mid-1960's, however has given the opponents of highways a new and more acceptable value to which they can appeal—namely, the protection of the environment.[16]

Each side in the conflict attempts to discredit the legitimacy of the opposition, either by trying to persuade the public that the values of their opponents are a facade and that baser and selfish motives are at work, or by marshalling "scientific data" to support their position. Factual support helps buttress the case of one or both contending forces, but another major ingredient in establishing legitimacy is the source of support. For example, a common practice of interest groups is to seek the support of highly respected leaders who will endorse their efforts. Usually, a long list of prominent names is printed on the letterheads of various organizations seeking public support. Thus, the "who" becomes as important as the "what" in creating legitimacy. At the same time, there are strenuous efforts to discredit the opposition. It is almost axiomatic that citizen groups who challenge a highway project will be castigated by highway builders as a "small, vociferous minority" or "a band of discontented obstructionists."

The appeal to legitimacy serves as the beginning point in a political conflict. It is a highly visible factor in the policy process but rarely is it the deciding factor.

2. SCOPE OF CONFLICT

The appeal to legitimacy normally provides only the "climate" for the resolution of political conflict. But how do such conflicts emerge in the first place? Although the precise roots of political conflict are difficult to trace, E. E. Schattschneider argues that

private conflicts are taken into the public arena precisely because someone wants to make certain that the power ratio among the private interests most immediately involved shall not prevail. . . . Conflicts become political only when an attempt is made to involve the wider public.[17]

Protagonists seek to enlarge the scope of conflict. A neighborhood group, for instance, faces overwhelming odds when it confronts a state highway department. Only by thrusting the issue into the public arena can the neighborhood group hope to achieve greater bargaining power. The more the protagonists are able to increase the scope of conflict, the more likely they will be successful in their efforts. Of course, the major problem for those seeking to alter policy is the generation of wider public support. For example, in any dispute, the highway department will argue that the neighborhood group is taking a parochial view, that the highway is needed to serve the public interest. The highway department will try to show how its program will benefit automobile owners in other parts of the city and in the suburban areas. If the highway department can isolate the efforts of the neighborhood groups, its chances of success in overcoming opposition are quite high. But if the neighborhood group can attain support from other neighborhoods and committees, the argument of the highway department is deflated.

The expansion of conflict also serves to increase the pressure points. As new groups and individuals become involved in the controversy, the opportunities for increased access to political decision makers are also enhanced. A small neighborhood group will have limited influence and limited access. But as others become involved, they will provide new access routes to political officials. In this expanded arena, then, the costs of ignoring the conflict become quite high for elected officials; in other words, when a citizen group expands the conflict to a point where a nondecision becomes more costly for elected officials than a decision on the problem, then the citizen group has achieved one of its major political goals.

3. SPAN OF ATTENTION

Related to "scope of conflict" is a third factor, namely, the "span of attention" factor. The span of attention factor is extremely important in American politics because of the way in which we have structured our governments. In general, American government—federal, state, or local— is a rather cumbersome vehicle for changing public policy. All kinds of obstacles, the so-called checks and balances, have been established to protect the public from rash and hasty decisions. Therefore, a considerable period of time is required for the political process to work its wonders. At the same time, the staying power of reformers and citizen groups is extremely short, and they are derisively referred to as "morning glories" by their opponents, since they tend to fade in the heat of a lengthy political battle. Citizen groups involved in transportation controversies operate in much the same fashion, since they "usually disappear as organizations after their own battles are lost or won."[18]

There is, of course, a wide range of political issues competing for public attention. Although a crisis may propel an issue into the political arena, there is no assurance that wide-spread public attention will immediately alter governmental policy. For example, time and again the American public has witnessed various mine disasters. Yet, after the body of the last miner is extracted from the caverns and buried, so is the question of mine safety. Similarly, Americans become highly agitated about highway safety at certain and by now predictable times throughout the year, yet highway accidents were not effectively reduced until recently with the advent of the energy crisis.

In addition, government agencies have a vast arsenal of strategies for blunting and diverting public attention. One of the oldest and most success-ful tactics for attenuating citizen agitation is to "study the problem." This can be achieved most effectively by appointing a blue-ribbon commission. The commission strategy is often predicated on the span of attention factor. For example, after the ghetto riots in the 1960s, President Johnson appointed the Kerner Commission. Although the report of the commission was praised for its thoroughness, only one of its minor recommendations became public policy in the first year after it was submitted to the president. Ignored were recommendations to deal with the transportation problems of the ghetto as pointed out by the previous McCone Commission, which studied the Watts riot.

A further advantage of the commission strategy is that it permits political officials the opportunity to make decisions after public pressure has dis-sipated. For a citizen group to maintain pressure during the extended life of a commission is quite difficult, since the appointment of the commission gives the illusion that something has been done. The commission, then, serves as a useful tool for the decision makers to avoid any decision, since commissions are rarely endowed with any substantive authority. President Nixon's use of commissions illustrates this point. In many cases, he not only ignored the recommendations of commissions but frequently repudiated recommendations even before they were made public.

The span of attention factor is of considerable importance even after citizens win some policy victory. To cite only one example, reformers in the late 1800's fought a bitter battle with the railroad industry over rates. With the establishment of the Interstate Commerce Commission, the re-formers won a significant—but short-lived—victory. The ICC and many other regulatory agencies of federal and state governments are prime examples of how the "protectors of the public interest" tend to be captured by the forces that they were supposed to control in the first place.[19] Even the environmentalists, who instigated the move to create the Environmental Protection Agency, have discovered to their dismay that many of the agency's decisions assist industry rather than protect the environment. Without some ongoing, institutional base, reformers will find that the objectives of some new policy can be subverted by the very governmental agency charged with responsibility for enforcing the policy.

4. THE TECHNOCRATIC FACTOR

A fourth characteristic of the policy process can be referred to as the technocratic factor. In a complex, technological society experts move to positions of preeminence in policy making.[20] Probably their most significant source of influence is their control of information.[21] Although citizen groups face severe handicaps at the hands of experts, even elected officials, including legislators and political executives, often are prisoners of the expert bureaucracy.

Experts have other advantages working in their favor. They frequently cloak themselves in the mantle of neutrality, thus stepping into the political arena with a high degree of legitimacy. In addition, there is a high degree of continuity within the expert bureaucracy. Most of its members are socialized into the profession and ascribe to the values of the profession. Many have the same kind of academic background. Although elected officials come and go, bureaucrats can wait out a recalcitrant elected official who is unsympathetic to the bureaucracy's goals. Compared to citizen groups, the bureaucratic experts are experienced in political battles.

In many cases, citizen groups launch their crusade on the false premise that bureaucratic officials are incompetent bunglers. Frequently, they will pool their funds to hire some respected local attorney with great forensic skill to oppose some proposed program. Because they underestimate their opposition, they enter the fray with great expectations. In such an ordeal the attorney for the citizen group is often outflanked and discredited, and the citizen challengers emerge in a state of disarray and shock. Thus when citizen groups have a better understanding of the advantages of the bureaucracy, they have taken a first step toward political maturity.

Another dimension of the bureaucracy, one that is often overlooked by citizen groups, is its increasing reliance on long-term planning. Almost all governmental agencies have now instituted what can be called research and planning divisions. Planners in certain fields are much more significant than those in others. In city government, for example, the planning department often plays a marginal role in effecting policy, and the "master plan" for most cities is given nothing more than lip service.[22] At the same time, planners in single-purpose agencies, such as highway departments, have considerable impact. It is important to realize that many activities of government require substantial lead time from conception to fruition. During the process of constructing a highway, route selection may occur a decade before the cement starts flowing. Land acquisition also occurs well before construction begins. Because the average citizen is uninformed about these preparatory steps, often the first full realization that a neighborhood is to be disrupted is when the bulldozer arrives.

Although many planning agencies have made great efforts to involve the "client," much of the planning process is still highly suspect.[23] For instance, the policy of most highway departments is to hold public hearings on projected highways. But most of these hearings receive little notice and are attended primarily by the highway administrators and construction industry spokesmen, who congratulate each other on the high degree of consensus reflected at the hearing. Even when government agencies try to generate grass-root attendance at meetings, many people believe that the meeting serves to present a sales pitch rather than generate meaningful and critical dialogue. Again, the net result of the planning process is to further remove the citizen from participation in the formulation of public policy.

5. THE IMMOBILIZATION FACTOR

The final underlying characteristic important in the policy process is "immobilization," a factor which consists of several dimensions. "Sunk costs" represents the first dimension of the immobilization factor. Sunk costs are the amounts of money, resources, and commitment the government has invested in any policy. Often the greater the sunk costs, the more difficult it is to alter a policy. Even when majority support is marshalled to change government policy, sunk costs are frequently cited for justifying governmental immobilization. American foreign policy in Vietnam epitomizes the extent to which sunk costs controlled policy. The transportation system in the United States further illustrates the corrosive effect of following a policy with huge sunk costs. Although arguments in favor of shifting our transportation priorities in urban areas are overwhelming, the arguments often flounder on the rock of sunk costs. Hence for citizen action groups, sunk costs represent the "catch 22" argument: "We can't really change our program because we've got too much invested, and even though the program isn't working too well, we've got to invest more to make it work better." For citizen groups who challenge the highway department, the sunk cost argument represents a major obstacle. After thousands of dollars are spent on surveys and route selection and millions of dollars invested in land acquisition, highway engineers are incredulous that "progress" on a highway should be halted. To stop the highway is a gigantic waste of money. Although citizens have equally high costs invested in their neighborhoods and their environment, the social costs seldom seem important to the engineer.

A second element contributing to immobilization in the policy process can be referred to as guildism. Policies that are very beneficial to one group alone and only marginally harmful to the public in general tend to be perpetuated. For example, proposed changes in policy to eliminate visual pollution, such as billboards, are staunchly resisted by the billboard industry, even though this industry is quite small. A change in policy to eliminate billboards from our highways, of course, would significantly reduce the profits of the sign industry. Guildism underlies a variety of public policies. Almost all of the regulatory activities carried on by government are supportive of guildism. Many cities, for example, have electrical boards or plumbing boards, and these, too, serve to foster the interests of a particular economic group. While the public may pay high total costs, the per capita costs may be quite low. The federal Highway Trust Fund is another manifestation of guildism.[24] Like the guild of the seventeenth century, the highway industry through governmental policy has been able to establish a perpetual revolving fund which can be drawn on exclusively by the highway guild. Although the fund subverts any meaningful balance in the urban transportation system, the guild has until recently effectively neutralized the efforts of others to "plunder" the fund and have thus made a public program private.

IMPLICATIONS FOR THE FUTURE

Five major factors have been identified that affect governmental policy, especially transportation policy. For citizen action groups, this catalog of factors might sound quite depressing. Most of the factors seem to work in favor of the status quo. For the average citizen, the odds appear to be stacked in favor of the large-scale government bureaucracies and interest groups that dominate American political life. The highway lobby might take comfort from such an interpretation since everything seems to be working in their favor. But there are trends that might alter the balance of power. To be more specific, let us reexamine these factors in light of these emergent trends.

In regard to legitimacy, it seems that in the future citizen groups can be assured of a more respectful hearing. No longer will the American citizen be victimized by the appeal to national defense and security. New national values, especially environmental values, are gaining strength. Furthermore, spokesmen for the highway system are on the defensive; they are rapidly losing support. At its peak, the highway lobby could claim the blessing of one of the most popular presidents in American history, Dwight D. Eisenhower. But in recent years, the defections have been many, and even former Secretary of Transportation Volpe, whose appointment was approved by the major highway interests, espoused a heretical position in regard to the highway trust fund by advocating its use for mass transit. In addition, the mayors of most American cities are joining forces with citizen action groups in opposition to further road building. It seems that at least in terms of legitimacy the anti-highway forces are winning wide public appeal.

With regard to the scope of conflict, the transportation crisis in urban America lends credence to and gains support for the anti-highway forces. For many years highway congestion served as a valuable ruse to argue for more highway construction. But "crying wolf" no longer generates the public support it did a decade age; it may even be counterproductive. Highway officials are less likely to suggest that more highways will serve the urban areas. Indeed, a Texas state highway official suggested that highways could more appropriately serve as links for the urban resident to recreational areas outside the city.[25] Highway transportation in the city is an increasingly risky business, as attested to by a recent advertisement advocating a massive "farm-to-market" road system.[26] In other words, even the highway builders foresee greener pastures in the rural areas of America.

Several factors are mitigating the ill effects of the "span of attention" and "technocratic" factors for citizen groups. In the first place, the ad hoc nature of citizen groups, so evident in the past, is changing, and many groups have developed ongoing organizations.[27] Furthermore, there are other groups which can assist citizen groups. Even though most of the Centers for Transportation at the major universities are nothing more than arms of the highway and automobile industry, there are countergroups developing in the university setting whose values are quite akin to those of citizen action groups. While engineers have generally considered transportation within their jurisdiction, social scientists, urban designers, and city planners have found that the transportation system is of vital concern, that transportation transcends technological problems. As a consequence, engineers no longer monopolize transportation expertise. After all, most of the important questions concerning transportation, especially by citizen action groups, seldom deal with purely technological problems.

Although there are some grounds for optimism in regard to the first four factors, the prospects are less hopeful for citizen action groups in regard to the final factor—immobilization. Sunk costs and guildism, the two components of immobilization, seem as strong as ever. If we closely examine the history of American political policies, we find that the system favors the status quo. Our entire system of government provides these forces with tremendous advantages. Indeed, most textbooks describing the legislative process recount the numerous barriers impeding the passage of new legislation. We have a bicameral legislative system, each chamber having a set of almost autonomous committees in which a small minority in the Senate through a filibuster can stop legislation. If legislation is successful there, the president can veto the measure. If a law is declared constitutional by the courts, Congress can underfund the program, or the president can impound funds, thus crippling the program. Finally, even if the policy is declared constitutional and is fully funded, the bureaucracy can nullify its effects or subvert its objectives.

As a result, success would seem quite difficult for those advocating a drastic change in our transportation policy. But immobilization is a two-edged sword. Because it gives advantages to those opposed to change, it can also be used by such groups for their purposes. While it might be difficult to change our transportation policies, it is less difficult to block specific highway programs. Given enough money and time, a citizen group can easily halt the construction of a proposed highway in any city in America. The fact remains, of course, that they seldom have either enough money or time.

Nevertheless, there seem to be serious dangers in this confrontation. Many struggles over highways have become paranoid crusades. Although the highway lobby now has the upper hand, its predominant position seems to be waning. It is possible that if citizen action groups replace highway proponents as masters of the situation, projects that have great benefit for the larger community may be blocked. If this occurs, those monuments in American cities—the unfinished bridges and the uncompleted highways—will testify not only to the success of citizen action groups to negate change but also to the inability of a political system to work out a viable transportation policy for urban America.

9

THE PROSPECTS AND
LIMITS OF MASS TRANSIT

Until a few years ago mass transit was virtually a forgotten issue in the United States. Transit systems built around the turn of the century were allowed to deteriorate, and no new systems were constructed. Ridership in all but a few major cities continuously declined on both rapid rail and bus systems. Bus systems throughout the nation either went into receivership or were taken over and operated at a loss by city governments. Without much thought and consideration, the private automobile roadway system became the overwhelmingly dominant transportation mode in the United States.

The automotive society did not come without some severe and very visible consequences. By 1970, for example, over 50 percent of the land area of central cities was reserved for automobile use. The impact of the automobile on urban design, the natural environment, and aesthetics was immensely detrimental.

The emergence of interest in mass transit, propelled in recent years by critics of the automobile and inconvenienced suburbanites, has been given a tremendous boost by the current energy crisis. With hundreds of motorists queued up in Tucson and other cities around the nation to obtain scarce supplies of gasoline at rapidly inflating prices, mass transit suddenly became more than a pipe dream of radical reformers. The automotive society, with its metal behemoths transporting one or two people dozens of miles across the city twice daily, is one of the prime causes—and victims—of the energy crisis. The United States automobile alone consumes 28 percent of the nation's petroleum. With shortfalls in petroleum supply estimated at anywhere from 15 to 25 percent, it is inevitable that motorists will be required to bear the brunt of restrictions on oil use.

If the energy crisis had never occurred, however, the problem of urban transportation would still be one of our paramount concerns. Indeed, the other ills created by our auto-oriented cities in many respects are far worse. The most obvious and far-reaching is the deleterious effect of the auto on the physical environment—especially on the quality of air and water. But the social costs—while the least visible and least understood—may in the long run be the most damaging.

In dozens of cities throughout the United States, massive highway projects have disrupted entire neighborhoods, upsetting social life, destroying small businesses, and bringing grief to many residents of the area. Many people in the city, especially the minorities, the aged, and the handicapped, find themselves completely isolated by the present transportation system. Finally, the city as a product of human creativity and as a place for optimizing human existence is undergoing a rapid transformation. The impact of the auto on urban design has disfigured and distorted the face and character of the city.

The impact of the auto on urban survival, of course, is recognized by many, and "mass transit" is frequently held out as a great panacea for resolving urban ills. Mass transit is seen by some as the savior of the city. Our purpose here is to examine these claims and to suggest what mass transit can do for the city while evaluating some of its limitations. Before undertaking this examination, it may be beneficial first to discuss what we mean when we use the term *mass transit*.

THE CONCEPT OF MASS TRANSIT

Discussions of mass transit in the past have suffered because of confusion surrounding the terms. For the most part, mass transit has been defined in technological terms, and when we talk about it we tend to think of the objects of transportation, such as buses or fixed-rail vehicles.

The technological characteristics of mass transit modes and systems are important insofar as they have differing impacts on the physical, environmental, and social characteristics of the city. Many innovative models have been developed in recent years, but the criteria for evaluating these models have been restricted primarily to their mobility function and their cost. For example, moving sidewalks, subway complexes, minibuses, and dial-a-bus systems all have their ardent advocates.

But mass transit is more than a mere physical object or a set of objects. The real meaning of mass transit can be discerned from the functions it fulfills for the community, and a teleological definition offers greater opportunity for analysis. Although many authors regard mobility as the sole function of any transportation system, there are several other functions which may be of even greater importance. One is to configure the shape of the city in desired ways, and in this regard a mass transit system is something quite different from an auto-oriented system.

Let us illustrate this point by examining bus systems. Bus systems operate in many cities throughout the United States, and if one accepts the standard definition, it can be said that mass transit systems operate in these cities. On one level, such a statement may seem to be satisfactory. But at another level these so-called mass transit systems have no impact in shaping the character of the city, because buses use the same rights-of-way as the private auto, and the road network and the major arterials are designed for the private auto, not the bus. As a consequence, it is the auto system which essentially determines the configuration of the city, with the bus system merely a "mass transit" appendage. Even in cities which provide separate lanes for buses, it is still the auto-oriented system which prevails. In sum, the mere fact that certain kinds of transport modes operate in a city is insufficient evidence that the city has a mass transit system.

There are several other functions of urban transportation which also deserve consideration. For example, transportation systems can function to integrate communities. They can also preserve natural beauty and minimize harmful impact on the natural environment. Finally, transportation systems can maximize the efficient use of land.

Based on these *multiple* functions, we would define urban mass transit as a technological and spatial system for moving large numbers of people rapidly and efficiently with a minimum use of land space in a manner designed to promote harmony with the natural environment, aesthetic urban design, and social and economic integration of the urban community.

WHAT MASS TRANSIT CANNOT DO

In the past, many claims have been made that mass transit would resolve a whole series or urban problems in one fell swoop. Especially among radical planners, the auto-oriented system epitomized what was wrong with American cities, and the institution of a mass transit system was viewed as a revolutionary mechanism, an essential key, in restructuring every facet of urban life. There are several direct effects of a mass transit system on urban life, especially the redesign of the city, which we will discuss shortly. For the moment, however, we might examine other urban ills which would remain largely unaffected.

THE ECONOMIC SYSTEM

The present urban transportation system has developed partly as a result of the impetus given automobile transit by federal and state governments. But by far the most important impetus has come from within the economic system itself, with its ideological commitment to private industry, particularly the automotive industry, to meet national and urban transportation needs. The results of this commitment also are not limited to urban transportation.

The effects of the present economic order in the city are manifest in other areas of critical concern as well. Environmental pollution in general, the inability of industry to internalize the large social costs or spillover diseconomies of production, and chronic inflation coupled with high levels of unemployment are all significant economic ills of the city. These are systemic and cannot be corrected by improving urban transportation alone. Urban transportation problems to some extent are merely another manifestation of the same social syndrome. Mass transit surely can play a role, but endemic economic problems of the city can be met only through more far-reaching changes.

Mass transit also cannot deal directly with two other important correlated ingredients of the existing urban transportation system. There is a huge existing investment in highways. These sunk costs cannot be recaptured and will continue to stand as important obstacles to the full development of urban mass transit. Nor can mass transit halt the built-in impetus to automotive transportation provided by the captive user-fee highway trust fund. Even though the trust fund may be "tapped" for mass transit, the real problem is the elimination of the subsidy to automobile transit. Such a change can come only from the Congress, and not too much can be expected from mass transit until that elected body is ready to act.

URBAN POLITICS

There are some claims that a mass transit system will alter the nature of politics within the city. For example, if mass transit facilitates more diversified neighborhoods, it may well result in more representative government and a greater degree of sensitivity to problems affecting certain groups. No longer would these problems be invisible to the decision makers as in the past when certain groups, such as the poor, lived in isolated sections of the city. Whether a mass transit system can ever achieve the "noble" city, however, is highly speculative.

Furthermore, the fragmentation of governments in metropolitan areas would remain largely unaffected, and it will take much more than mass transit to resolve various regional problems. Even here, however, the advocates of mass transit will argue that the explosive expansion of urban areas, with the concomitant establishment of hordes of suburban governments, will be partially stemmed, and indeed, might well reverse the trend because of the centripetal forces at work. But given our government's immobility in dealing with the regional issues and the tremendous economic forces at work to sustain the centrifugal character of metropolitan regions, it seems doubtful that such hopes will be realized for quite some time.

FISCAL PROBLEMS

The fiscal problems of cities are produced essentially by an outmoded revenue collection system and the huge growth of "public needs." The latter accumulate in cities because the city serves as a refuge for the needy, because many modern urban goods and services are provided publicly or not at all, and because many urban goods (parks and traffic police, for example) are required less in nonurban areas. Added to this is the fragmentation of governments via the creation of suburban municipalities and the resulting exodus from the city of important elements of the tax base. These problems will continue despite the advent of mass transit. Depending on the method of finance adopted, mass transit may even aggravate them, especially in the short term.

The extension of a mass transit network may deter the further fragmentation of the city by the creation of a more compact city with more efficient use of land, but the initiative for metro fiscal government through the integration of existing municipalities must come from other sources. In fact, depending on the method of financing adopted—i.e., the proportion of any regional system borne by the center city—mass transit may aggravate fiscal problems.

RACE RELATIONS

Many proposals for mass transit have been made on behalf of various minority groups, and indeed, the McCone Commission, which was established after the Watts riot, advocated public transportation for the purpose of getting black workers to jobs outside the Watts area. If improved race relations means a better shake for minorities, then mass transit may have some beneficial effect. But if it means the humanization of our relations, tolerance and even appreciation of ethnic identities, then it seems likely that a mass transit system will have little impact.

But will not mass transit create more diversified neighborhoods, as noted above? Will not segregated housing patterns be attenuated, resulting in a greater degree of integration? Even though the answer is obvious, the consequences are not. If they mean more intensive efforts at "wasping" minorities, if they further submerge cultural identities and create greater "rootlessness," then mass transit is certainly not the answer for improving race relations.

URBAN CRIME

Many opponents gleefully point out that the problem of crime is highly intensified as a consequence of mass transit facilities. News stories of muggings and assaults at bus stops and on the subways abound. The city traveler, safely ensconced in his automobile, is highly protected. Yet, if these types of crimes tend to occur at mass transit facilities, such illegal activities may be the consequence of other factors, such as the isolation of the facilities. In any event, the advocate of mass transit would quickly point out that one never heard of a bank robber using the bus as a get-away car. Indeed advocates might well argue that the number of crimes associated with the automobile is so much greater than those related to mass transit that any argument suggesting that mass transit "causes" crime is patently absurd.

Furthermore, the fact that our cities are designed for cars and not for people is the kind of thing which dulls the citizen's sensitivity to what's happening. Yet, the roots and causes of crime are the consequences of both psychological and social factors, and it is doubtful whether there is any direct linkage between crime and the type of transportation system in our cities.

INCOME

Class and income differences are the source of much social disruption in United States cities today. These differences are basically products of an economic and social system which divides the spoils on a power basis. As the present world-wide economic decline deepens, produced in part by the energy crisis, these conflicts are likely to become more acute. In the past, constantly rising income for almost everyone has served to divert attention from differences between groups. When everyone is forced to tighten his belt, these differences are not going to be readily accepted.

Mass transit can serve to lessen this strife only very indirectly, by providing the same kind of transportation for everyone in the city and by lessening the ability of suburbanites to insulate themselves from the central city's problems. If the effect of a more compact distribution of population is to make more apparent how the other half lives, then mass transit might even aggravate these conflicts.

URBAN EDUCATION

For many citizens today, transportation and education are intimately related problems. Indeed, the whole issue of busing is posited by some as the only problem with urban education. If as a result of mass transportation, neighborhoods become more diversified in terms of race and income level, then mass transit would serve to attenuate the problem and largely make the issue of busing a moot point. Yet, it seems unlikely that such an event will occur—at least for the immediate future—unless housing policies are also altered.

Yet, the problem of urban education extends far beyond the housing issue. The quality of education, inadequate facilities, finances, and the relevance of schools to the community are all significant issues, and it hardly seems likely that mass transit will have any immediate impact on these problems. Indeed, the most immediate impact of mass transit may well be to exacerbate problems for certain schools, especially those schools now located in white, middle-class enclaves. With the changing composition of neighborhoods, new demands will be placed on schools, and the capacity of schools in responding to these demands appears quite limited.

WHAT MASS TRANSIT CAN DO

URBAN DESIGN

Probably the single most important impact of mass transit on the city is in the areas of urban design, land use, housing patterns, and employment and commercial location. While these are principally physical effects, they have important impact on a wide variety of social characteristics of the city.

The present design of most United States cities is almost random. Developers can go almost anywhere and open new areas for housing or industrial or commercial use. Industrial plants, able to draw a labor force from any part of the city and to have trucks call at their door for shipments, may locate almost anywhere they choose. They increasingly choose to locate on the fringe where land is cheap and restrictions are likely to be less severe.

That the automotive system was creating huge, ugly, anonymous spread cities, gobbling up immense quantities of land covered with asphalt and concrete, and avoiding the internalization of the enormous costs in air and water pollution and inconvenience to the transportation-using public was and still is difficult to perceive. It is almost impossible to relate these costs specifically to any individual or firm. They are cumulative, the results of thousands of individual actions, much like the trampling of grass on public walkways by hundreds of feet. No one pair can be singled out, yet the barren ground is stark testimony to their cumulative effect. The ability of the automobile to follow development, rather than lead it, is both its genius and its nemesis. It puts the responsibility for urban design on everyone and hence on no one.

Mass transit is capable of affecting the design and layout of the city by forcing one to think through where and how the city *should* develop. Because of their great carrying capacity, rail lines will encourage high intensity land use along their corridors. They also require far less land themselves to move large numbers of people. In Toronto as well as in cities like Paris, commercial shopping and small business districts tend to cluster around subway or rail stations. Nearby, high rise apartments and more intensive residential land use in general develop to provide convenient access to the mass transit lines. Between major lines, less intensive development may occur because of a lesser convenience to access. Thus, greater variety and diversity in housing styles is encouraged within a single area of the city. There will be less leap-frogging of tracts, a practice which leaves unplanned, vacant, and often ugly sites in the midst of developed areas. Mass transit will also encourage greater density in the central city. Living in high density central areas can be both convenient and attractive, if one does not have to use a ton of steel to get everywhere and if one does not have to endure the noise of traffic or inhale exhaust fumes.

Mass transit may be used to encourage the development of order in industrial and hence employment location. Employers will have to become more responsive to the transportation needs and possibilities of potential employees. Rapid rail lines may also double for freight hauling to central distribution centers in off-peak hours and at night, thus further affecting industrial location. Moreover, an interconnecting series of mass transit lines may assure accessibility to almost all employment centers for everyone in the city.

THE ENVIRONMENT

The quality of life in cities is increasingly a function of the natural environment: air, water, plants, green spaces, and quiet. The potential for reducing noise, water, air, land, and visual pollution is undoubtedly one of the greatest attributes of mass transit. By encouraging more intensive land use near the center of the city and along mass transit corridors and by saving on the quantity of land necessary to support the transport system itself, mass transit can effectively increase the amount of land available for parks and open space, thereby shortening the access to the countryside. Merely halting highway departments from gobbling up existing green space for new highways would be a vast improvement.

The automobile, as is well known, is one of the major contributors to air and noise pollution. In certain areas of the city the roar of traffic can be deafening, and exhaust fumes literally choke the lives out of people and plants. Mass transit can almost completely eliminate these ills.

Land pollution (junk yards and concrete-surfaced wastelands) and water pollution, especially runoff from city streets covered with petroleum and other automotive residue, can be effectively reduced by mass transit.

Lastly, the environment is not strictly a matter of life support systems. The lack of pleasantness and aesthetic appeal is increasingly felt to be a shortcoming of the city. By creating a more orderly, creative, and less ugly place to live, mass transit can improve the quality of life in cities.

THE DEMOCRATIZATION OF URBAN TRANSPORTATION

A third major contribution of mass transit would be the democratization of the urban transportation system. By this we mean that the current auto-oriented system is highly stratified and caters to only one group of people. While providing for the needs of this group, it at the same time restricts the mobility of others. The poor, the elderly, the handicapped, and especially those from minority groups face serious problems. They are either not permitted or not able to drive the auto, or they are too poor to own a car.

Even though car ownership has increased markedly and although predictions abounded in the past that the time was not far off when the number of cars would equal the number of people, these claims are highly suspect for two reasons. First, the energy crisis, the spiraling costs of fuel and the tremendous expense of owning and operating a car would seem to cast doubt on such a prediction. Indeed, the number of people who simply cannot afford the private auto is likely to rise. Second, car ownership is not equally distributed among the urban population. In many affluent families, the number of cars may exceed the size of the family. Furthermore, even if there were two cars in every garage, they would be useless to many because of either physical handicaps or because of legal restrictions.

If democracy means something more than a mere set of *legal* rights, if it means that all citizens will be guaranteed equal opportunities and access to the vast array of activities in the city, then mass transit can well serve to democratize American cities.

THE ECONOMY OF TRANSPORTATION

Finally, mass transit, though at first seemingly expensive, can ultimately reduce the real out-of-pocket costs of transportation for the consumer. If only half the amount of real resources invested in automobiles, trucks, and roadways during the past two decades (assuming that to be 15 percent of the GNP) had been available for mass transit, more than five hundred complete BART systems could have been built at their 1970 cost. The direct costs of the automobile to the American consumer are staggering: approximately $800 per year for every man, woman, and child in the nation. If to these are added the indirect costs, such as social and environmental damage, costs of governmental services (including more extensive utility lines, police and fire protection, and traffic courts), they are incalculable but stupendous. Mass transit's biggest savings may come in the indirect category, but there is good reason to believe we can also save on direct costs.

CONCLUSION

The modes of transportation—the autos, the buses, the trains—have no intrinsic value in themselves. They merely have instrumental or functional values, and one value is to provide urban residents with access to activities. The city can be viewed from the same perspective. It is an organizational arrangement to facilitate access, and thus the city and the transportation network in combination can be considered as a communications system.

Yet, our metropolitan areas are becoming more segmented, and it is because of our auto-oriented system that there is dissonance between the instrumental values of transportation and the city. As an alternative, we have argued, a mass transit system would merge these instrumental or functional values.

In a number of cities, rapid transit systems have been developed or are being planned, and one might think that revolutionary changes are under way. What will be the effect of these developments? Will these rapid rail systems achieve those objectives discussed previously, including the reconfiguration of urban design, the amelioration of pollution, and the democratization of the transportation system?

Yet, our previous discussion of two rapid rail systems, one in operation in the San Francisco region and one planned for the Dallas–Fort Worth region, leaves considerable doubt. The most highly publicized venture in the past decade, the Bay Area Rapid Transit system, is viewed by many as a model for other cities. Yet, BART is not really an intracity system but a transportation link between the suburbs and the central city. A new rapid rail system in Dallas and Fort Worth is much the same except that it provides a rapid rail link from each of the downtown areas to the new international airport.

What are the prospects that mass transit, other than bus service, will come to a large number of American cities? And what are the prospects that these systems, if they come, will be something more than fast commuter lines for upper income groups?

There appear to be several major factors which will give impetus to the development of mass transit systems. The decay of the central city creates discomfort and financial loss for some very significant economic and financial interests. Reviving the central business district has become an important theme for many influential business and civic groups in the past few years. The realization that there is simply not enough space to accommodate the people with their automobiles has made mass transit an imperatively logical choice for these groups.

The threat of the automobile to the environment of cities will continue to provide additional impetus for mass transit. The logical end, an almost totally paved central city to accommodate traffic, is apparent to many now, and unacceptable.

Fuel costs themselves, even at a dollar per gallon of gasoline, will not deter many motorists. But gasoline rationing and a determined effort by the federal government to cut fuel consumption through such measures as pooling, no-driving days, and direct taxes on motorists, will. There is little reason to expect the oil situation to ease in the coming years, especially given the annual growth in the voracious American appetite for oil. As the United States becomes more and more dependent on foreign petroleum, the push to a less oil-intensive transport system should be greater.

Despite these very persuasive incentives to develop mass transit systems, there are some equally important obstacles. The automobile-highway complex is the most powerful single economic group in the United States, and the resultant pressures to maintain the automotive society are immense. With one out of every seven jobs indirectly related to the automobile and some 15 to 20 percent of the GNP originating therefrom, it is not likely that mass transit will be accepted enthusiastically by everyone.

Another obstacle is the difficulty of raising the same amount of revenue for public use (mass transit) via taxes as is presumably spent on automotive transport. A nationwide $40 billion bond election for mass transit construction for one year is not likely to be passed, even though Americans spend that much annually on their automobiles. Part of a railcar on a mass transit line just doesn't carry the same amount of psychological satisfaction as a sleek new machine from Detroit, though it would be interesting to see what could be accomplished with a public advertising and sales effort comparable to that staged each year by the automobile manufacturers.

Still another economic obstacle is the prior existence of spread cities. One constantly hears that densities in cities such as Los Angeles simply make mass transit impossible, no matter what its advantages. It is characteristic to cap this argument by pointing out that such facilities would operate at a loss, given present densities—a statement tantamount to sounding the death knell for mass transit, in the eyes of many. But this is circular and fallacious logic. Cities cannot develop high density without mass transit, and so it is asserted they cannot have mass transit because they do not have sufficient density! Present densities were created by the auto; new densities would be created by mass transit.

If mass transit systems are to be introduced in our cities, our political institutions must carry the burden. Yet, our political institutions are superbly designed to block any meaningful change. Several reasons account for the politician's unwillingness to provide effective leadership, including the cozy relationship between the politician and the highway lobby, the strength of pro-highway interests in the political process, and the checks and balances of our government.

If one had to design the structure for an effective interest group, one could do no better than model it after the highway lobby. Although some interest groups exert strong pressures at only one level of government, the highway lobby is persistent at every level of government. Obviously, the major auto producers and the petroleum associations are the prime spokesmen at the federal level, and political contributions (although illegal in some cases) attest to their desire to keep federal elected officials happy. But if the highway lobby exercises power at the federal level, it is even more visible at the state and local level. Construction companies and their union and auto associations are ubiquitous lobbies of state legislatures. At the local level, there is a plethora of business interest groups, including the auto dealers, gas station owners, local construction companies, and parking lot owners.

What makes the highway lobby so effective is the distribution formula for highway funds. In a mass transit system, funds can be allocated in only a few areas of a state, but in allocating funds for highways, every section of the state is likely to get a slice of the pie.

Although urbanization has been the dominant characteristic of American society in the past three decades, it is certainly not reflected in our political system. Before the one-man-one-vote rule, the cities were grossly under-represented in our legislatures. But by the time the equal representation decision was made, the center cities were declining in population, and the suburbs were growing at fantastic rates. In other words, the political power of cities was limited before the decision as a consequence of malapportionment; after the decision, the suburbs became the prime beneficiaries, not the center cities.

In our suburban areas the "car is king," and it is therefore understandable that the suburban representatives would line up with the rural representatives on transportation issues. Illustrative of the suburban-rural coalition was the recent controversy in the Dallas–Fort Worth region concerning the composition of a regional transportation commission. Although the cities of Fort Worth and Dallas were accorded a greater number of representatives in the original plan, the suburbs and the counties (representing the rural areas in the region) lined up against the proposed plan. A compromise was worked out whereby any decision to divert highway funds to mass transportation would require a two-thirds vote. In sum, the fate of transportation for center cities without any autonomous funding mechanism and in a minority position in the decision-making councils is left to the mercy of the suburbanites and the rural representatives.

Finally, the checks and balances of our system of government result in political immobilization. It is a well-known feature of our government that it is easier for opponents to block some measure than for proponents to pass it. At any stage in the political process, any innovative policy can either be blocked or emasculated. A mass transit system of the type discussed here certainly deviates markedly from the mind-set of our elected representatives, and it appears that once again, change will be instituted not through political leadership but as a consequence of another crisis. This argument is best illustrated by the most recent energy crisis, which clearly exemplifies the inability of government to do anything more than react.

It has been frequently pointed out that ours is a government of crisis: the only time anything happens is when a crisis occurs (or is created). That we have survived so many crises can be attributed to the genius of our political system or to pure luck. Yet, we believe that urban transportation can be restructured to accommodate the needs of the city—of its people, its neighborhoods, and its environment. The first step, of course, is to drastically curtail our heavy reliance on the auto in the city by developing a "full-price" costing system and by limiting auto traffic. We recognize that these changes will not come easily. As we have tried to point out, our political and economic institutions are the principal conduits for change, but these institutions—except under crisis conditions—have largely been unresponsive to the needs of urban America. If it takes another crisis to generate institutional change, then we can only hope that the next crisis will not be the last.

10

EPILOGUE

In a recent article in a futuristic series, the *Wall Street Journal,* if it is correct, achieved two singular accomplishments.[1] It pronounced the death sentence on alternative forms of urban transportation in the United States within this century and in so doing it may have guaranteed sales of this book until the end of the century. According to the *Journal*'s crystal ball the bases of the American ground transportation system will continue to be the car and truck at least through the year 2000 and probably beyond. Citing rapidly escalating costs for the construction of mass transit facilities and the unwillingness of Americans to get out of their cars to use these facilities as the two principal obstacles to alternative ground transport, the *Journal* article also discounts the impact of such things as oil prices and oil shortages on continued auto use. While some changes might be expected, such as a trend to slightly smaller and lighter vehicles, the *Journal* predicts annual auto sales of 17 to 18 million vehicles by 2000. Mass rail transit, according to several sources cited in the article, has no significant place in the foreseeable future of American ground transportation.

Futurists a decade ago had one thing pegged right in their outlook for transportation. Well into the next century, they said, most people would still depend on the automobile and the airplane to move about.[2]

Some of the arguments used by "experts" cited in the article are spurious, such as the aerospace corporation planner who pronounced rail mass transit infeasible because you simply cannot pick up a rail line and subsequently move it as conditions change. Who ever heard of a six lane freeway being moved in response to changed conditions? Nonetheless, without some rather significant changes in the institutional system which supports present transportation developments—the theme of this book—we are inclined to agree with the *Journal's* predictions in substance if not in detail.

The usual assortment of experts is trotted out to confirm the obvious—that they expect no important changes in federal policy toward ground transportation. Further, barring any sustained policy shift, the private sector cannot be expected to come up with any significant changes on its own. So where does this leave us?

When this book was originally conceived it was not our intention to provide a blueprint for the overhaul of the American urban transportation system. Our aims were considerably more modest: 1) to fill in what we perceived to be an important gap in the literature dealing with the social and economic consequences of the urban transportation system, and 2) to draw more attention to the political and economic institutions which propel policy in this arena. We were content to organize, taxonomize, and analyze a series of serious systemic problems which would have to be overcome if we were ever going to structure our urban transportation system in more humane and socially desirable ways. We were satisfied to suggest the broad, yet only very general conceptual framework of ecological holism as the only viable long-term basis for urban transportation development. We also just did not have any ready answers to a lot of the seemingly intractable problems, and our imaginations failed. But we, and our students, we hope, have learned a great deal from the exercise. Partly at their urging—graduate students have an insistent, nagging way of saying: "This is all very well as far as proposals go, but how do we actually get from here to there?"—we have decided to add an epilogue. It contains several suggestions (none of which is original with us) which we feel have merit in fostering a more suitable institutional environment for the kind of urban transportation system we believe it will be necessary to develop in the United States.

These suggestions are contained in an exhaustively researched study by Bradford C. Snell presented to the Subcommittee on Antitrust and Monopoly of the Senate Committee on the Judiciary in 1974. Basically, Mr. Snell outlines a procedure for breaking up the automobile and truck industries into their constituent elements and for the divestiture by General Motors of its bus and locomotive production facilities. His proposals would restore competition in the industry and destroy the concentrated locus of power, the ill effects of which we have attempted to document in this book. Approximately the final third of Mr. Snell's study is accordingly reproduced as an appendix.

APPENDIX

An Extract From

AMERICAN GROUND TRANSPORT
A Proposal for Restructuring the Automobile, Truck, Bus, and Rail Industries

BY

BRADFORD C. SNELL
(Financing Provided by the Stern Fund of New York)

––––––

PRESENTED TO THE

SUBCOMMITTEE ON ANTITRUST AND MONOPOLY

OF THE

COMMITTEE ON THE JUDICIARY
UNITED STATES SENATE

FEBRUARY 26, 1974

Notes are not included in this appendix.

III. RESTRUCTURING GROUND TRANSPORTATION : A FIRST APPROXIMATION

As demonstrated in part II, the anticompetitive structure of the automobile, truck, bus, and rail industries enabled General Motors, Ford, and Chrysler to suppress price, product, and technological competition in motor vehicle production and to restrain practical alternatives to motor vehicle transportation. This section considers a first approximation at restructuring these industries. In brief, it proposes reorganization of the automobile and truck industries into their constituent elements and divestiture of General Motors' bus and locomotive production facilities. The objectives are threefold : To restore competition and innovation to the motor vehicle industries; to promote a balanced and technologically advanced ground transportation system comprising low-pollution cars, trucks, and buses, as well as high-speed rail transport; and to secure the additional social advantages of energy conservation, expanded employment, and a more favorable balance of trade.

A. Restructuring the Motor Vehicle Industries: Automobiles and Trucks

The economic analysis in part II concluded that high structural concentration, extensive vertical integration, multinationalization, and insuperable barriers to entry precluded the longrun survival of competitive conduct and performance in motor vehicle manufacturing.[341] Conversely, a competitively structured industry, with numerous firms at each stage of automobile production both at home and abroad, would behave more competitively and perform more satisfactorily. It is recommended, therefore, that this industry be restructured to permit the maximum feasible number of competitors, the minimum feasible degree of vertical integration, and the maximum feasible degree of ease of entry at every level of domestic and foreign production.[342]

Application of these guidelines would require dissolution of General Motors, Ford, Chrysler, and, to facilitate competition in the postreorganization environment, American Motors. More specifically, these four multinational enterprises would be reorganized into their constituent car and truck assembly, manufacturing, distribution, financing, and related automotive as well as nonautomotive facilities.

The basis for reorganization is inherent in the decentralized method of operations adopted by the four automakers. Their economists and engineers apparently have decided that efficiency in production is maximized by assigning different functions to geographically separate and distinct facilities. Motor vehicle assembly, engine production, body stamping, and dozens of other major automotive manufacturing processes, therefore, are undertaken in hundreds of physically distinct and geographically disparate plants throughout the United States and other parts of the world. As shown in table 1, the four American automakers operate more than 300 domestic facilities in 32 different States. This study assumes the wisdom of such an arrangement. It would leave unaltered the number, size, and physical location of these plants. Instead, it would recommend a change in their ownership: each plant or group of plants now separate in fact, would become separate in law as well.

TABLE 1

LOCATION OF AUTOMOTIVE PLANTS IN THE UNITED STATES AND PUERTO RICO CURRENTLY OWNED BY GENERAL MOTORS, FORD, CHRYSLER, AMC

Location	Assembly plants	Body and engine components production facilities	R. & D. facilities[1]	Parts depots	Total
Alabama		1		1	2
Arizona			3		3
California	[2]5	1	1	11	18
Colorado			1	4	5
Connecticut		1			1
Delaware	2			1	3
Florida			1	4	5
Georgia	3			4	7
Illinois	2	3		4	9
Indiana		16	1	2	19
Kansas	1	1		4	6
Kentucky	1			1	2
Louisiana				1	1
Maryland	[3]1			1	2
Massachusetts	1			5	6
Michigan	11	74	5	13	103
Minnesota	[3]1			4	5
Missouri	[4]5			3	8
Nebraska				1	1
New Jersey	[4]3	3		4	10
New York	1	13		6	20
North Carolina				2	2
Ohio	[5]3	29		8	40
Oklahoma				1	1
Oregon				3	3
Pennsylvania		1		5	6
Puerto Rico		1			1
Tennessee		1		4	5
Texas	1			8	9
Virginia	1			4	5
Washington				1	1
West Virginia				1	1
Wisconsin	[4]2	3	1	2	8
Total	44	148	13	113	318

[1] Includes technical centers and proving grounds.
[2] Includes 2 which assemble trucks also.
[3] Assembles trucks also.
[4] Includes 1 which assembles trucks also.
[5] Includes 1 which assembles trucks also and 1 which assembles Jeeps.

Source: Motor Vehicle Manufacturers Association, "Plants of U.S. Motor Vehicle Manufacturers in the United States" (February 1973); "Annual Reports," GM, Ford, Chrysler, AMC.

As summarized in table 2, all of the American auto industry's 44 assembly plants and 148 of its most important automotive components facilities, including all of its body stamping and engine production plants, are owned by General Motors, Ford, Chrysler, and American Motors. In addition, virtually all of its 25,000 retail car outlets are contractually tied to the 4 automakers.[343] Many of these facilities were once independent entities which competed with one another in the production and distribution of motor vehicles.[344] Now they are all owned or controlled by four corporations which eschew competition in the American automobile market. Reorganizing these corporations into their constituent parts would create enable as many as 44 assembly companies. They could produce automobiles with improved performance capabilities assembled from the body and engine components of competing suppliers, and retailed through independent dealers. This study, of course, does not attempt to specify the exact number of existing facilities which might be separately incorporated. Further investigation might reveal that some automotive plants would operate best if jointly owned. No preliminary studies, however, have demonstrated this to be the case. In any event, reorganization along these general lines would allow for a greater degree of competition at every significant level of automobile production and distribution.

Table 2.—*Automobile industry reorganization: Ownership status of U.S. automobile facilities at each level of production*

Components production:

GM	73
Ford	39
Chrysler	31
American Motors	5
Total [1]	148

Final assembly:

GM	22
Ford	15
Chrysler	6
American Motors	1
Total [2]	44

Retail distribution (U.S. makes):

GM	12, 045
Ford	6, 684
Chrysler	5, 406
AMC	1, 947
Total [3]	25, 427

[1] Does not include R. & D. facilities or parts depots.
[2] Plants may also include some manufacturing operations.
[3] Big Four breakout includes 655 intercorporate duals.

SOURCE: 1972 annual reports for General Motors, Ford, Chrysler, and American Motors; various statistical reports compiled by the Motor Vehicle Manufacturers Association.

Likewise, in truck manufacturing, 19 of the industry's 41 assembly plants, many of its major component facilities (particularly GM's diesel engine plants at Detroit and Grand Rapids, Mich.) and most of its wholesale and retail outlets are owned by or contractually tied to the Big Three automakers.[345] Fourteen of the Big Three's 19 assembly plants produce both light trucks and automobiles. As light trucks (compact pickups) are fundamentally a variety of personal automobiles and are often run on the same assembly line as autos, there would appear to be no reason to separate their production. Accordingly, these 14 plants could become independent car/truck corporations pursuant to the auto industry reorganization. In addition, unpacking the automakers' remaining all-truck assembly plants, truck body and components facilities and retail outlets might contribute to renewed competition at each level of truck production.

Supplemental measures would be necessary to provide the newly incorporated motor vehicle assemblers and automotive components suppliers with equal access to research, engineering, and design services. GM, Ford, Chrysler, and AMC each maintain automotive design, research and engineering centers, and proving grounds.[346] These facilities could be reorganized into independent corporations to compete with other consulting groups in providing auto assemblers and components suppliers with design, research, and engineering assistance. In light of the critical role of these functions in automobile manufacturing, however, it is assumed that auto (and truck) assemblers might decide to undertake some of them in-house.[347]

The new assemblers and components suppliers as well as retail dealers would also require wholesale parts distribution services. Currently the four automakers own more than 100 automotive parts depots and operate an indeterminate number of wholesale distribution outlets. To insure that assemblers, suppliers, and dealers have adequate access to wholesale parts services, these facilities might be reorganized into independent corporations in the automotive wholesale and after-market (replacement parts) trade.

Moreover, steps should be taken to insure that independent retail dealers have equal access to adequate financing services. Currently, each of the automakers maintains a wholly owned finance company. In fact, General Motors Acceptance Corp., with assets in excess of $12 billion, is the largest finance unit in the Nation.[348] Reorganizing the automakers' finance subsidiaries into several regional corporations might best serve the interests of local dealers while increasing competition in regional lending markets.[349]

The disposition of automobile brand names (GM, Chevrolet, Ford, Dodge, et cetera) would also affect the viability of the new car and truck assemblers. Retention of brand names currently associated with the four automakers might handicap some assemblers while favoring others. Their dedication to the public domain, therefore, would insure that no one assembler, by retaining the exclusive right to use a popular brand name (such as, Chevrolet), would enjoy an unfair advantage over another.

Our paramount concern for national security and long-term economic stability would seem also to require the eventual release of foreign automotive facilities from control by domestic makers. As the analysis in part I demonstrated, the construction abroad of motor vehicle plants can compromise U.S. national security and can undermine national economic policies. The relative ease with which automotive facilities can be converted to warplane, tank, and military transport production makes this category of multinational investment particularly hazardous to national security and foreign policy. In light of the enormous contribution of motor vehicle manufacturing to domestic employment and overall industrial growth, its movement abroad threatens domestic economic stability more than the multinational ventures of any other industry. By contrast, the sale abroad of products and services by competitively structured, nationally based motor vehicle firms would contribute immensely to domestic employment, economic stability, and a favorable balance of trade, while preserving our legitimate interests in national security. At the same time, such an arrangement would permit the sale of technological services and managerial/production know-how to less developed countries.

General Motors, Ford, Chrysler, and AMC own car and truck assembly, parts manufacturing, distribution, and finance subsidiaries in 44 foreign countries. To generate new competition in the world automobile market, discourage the export of American capital and jobs abroad, and protect our national interests in the event of international conflicts, these subsidiaries should be sold to holders of U.S. dollars abroad. United Auto Workers President Leonard Woodcock strongly supports this plan. He has suggested that the U.S. Government "encourage foreign owners of dollars to use them to acquire the assets of the subsidiaries of U.S.-based MNC's (multinational corporations) operating within their respective national boundaries." "Those subsidiaries," he said, "would then become independent national competitors of their parent MNC's, thus reversing—at least temporarily—the trend toward world oligopoly." Woodcock's proposal would also benefit this country's balance of payments. "At the same time," he added, "a substantial part of the dollar overhang would be removed as an obstacle to reform of the international monetary system." [350]

In general, the management, shareholders, and employees of the four automakers, as well as consumers, would all benefit from the proposed reorganization of the motor vehicle industries. For the first time the management of hundreds of facilities formerly controlled by four corporations would now command their own companies. No longer would they be subject to the mind-dulling bureaucratization of a giant organization which, in the words of one formerly high-ranking auto executive, is "totally inconsistent with any thoughtful and creative originality." [351] Instead, they would decide what prices to charge, what products to make, which innovations to pursue. The assembler executives, in particular, would enjoy complete technological flexibility. They could build rotary cars, electric cars, steam cars, Freon cars, fuel-cell cars; they could stress fuel economy, or safety, or pollution control as well as style. Competition, moreover, would drive them seriously to assess technological alternatives and marketing strategies which might win consumers away from other assembler-rivals.

Nondominant shareholders would also benefit. They would maintain their continuity of stock interests in a diversified range of smaller, more aggressively competitive companies rather than in only 4 increasingly bureaucratic, moribund and unimaginative monoliths. To avoid ownership interlocks, however, dominant shareholders, directors and executives would be required to dispose of their interests in all but one of the newly created automotive companies.

Employees would also be expected to benefit from the proposed reorganization. The return of competition, particularly with respect to the automotive export market, would very likely increase production and hence employment. Competition might spur these new companies to seek novel ways of raising worker productivity, such as through the less dehumanizing production technique of team assembly or possibly through worker participation in some phases of management decisionmaking. [352] In short, the opportunity to work for a smaller, more innovative company should enhance employee satisfaction.

A motor vehicle industry composed of competing assemblers, independent suppliers and a network of independent retail dealers, moreover, should provide consumers with better automotive transportation. The same plants which today assemble monopolistically priced and virtually unchanged cars and trucks would after reorganization be forced to adapt to a new, competitive environment. The emergence of price and technological competition in turn should result in the development of energy-conserving, economical, safer, low-pollution vehicles powered by innovative propulsion systems. This is the quality of industry performance reorganization should engender.

B. Restructuring the Bus and Rail Industries

The economic analysis in part II demonstrated that the automakers' lobbying against rail transit and General Motors' diversification into bus and rail transportation very likely restrained these alternative forms of transport from effective competition with cars and trucks. A reduction in the automakers' resources for anticompetitive political lobbying and termination of GM's conflicting involvement in competing ground transport industries would appear, therefore, to be essential prerequisites to achieving a balanced system of ground transportation. In this regard, a three-part structural remedy is suggested. First, deconcentration of the motor vehicle industries in the manner already proposed would reduce their ability to pass on the costs of antirail lobbying to consumers in the form of higher priced cars and trucks. Second, reorganization of GM's bus and rail divisions into independent corporations would enable them to operate free from the conflict of interest which may have seriously hampered their development under GM ownership. Third, the facilitation of entry by a number of new bus and rail enterprises would provide this country with the competitive manufacturing capability necessary for the production of modern passenger and freight transport systems.

Reorganization of the automobile and truck industries as recommended would virtually eliminate the automakers' current power to raise substantial revenues for lobbying. They would no longer be able to contribute vast sums to fight rail transit by charging higher-than-competitive prices for their motor vehicles. Instead, the return of competition to this industry should force prices back into line with actual production costs. Of course, the new car and truck producers might continue to contribute some funds for antirail lobbying through an industrywide trade association. But lacking the Big Three's prior monopolistic control over prices, they would be reluctant as individual competitors to raise their costs appreciably for this nonessential purpose. Moreover, in a competitive environment, there would probably be some firms which by refusing to contribute could reduce their prices and increase their share of the market. This form of competitive discipline, therefore, would very likely bring the lobbying resources of the auto interests into more approximate balance with those of the rail interests, a situation which would better serve the public interest.

Reorganization of General Motors' bus and rail divisions into independent corporations would appear to be both desirable and precedented. It would enable these bus and rail manufacturers to develop free from the conflicts of interest which quite possibly restrained them from effective competition with cars and trucks. Separation of these facilities from the world's largest motor vehicle manufacturer, moreover, is precedented. As summarized in part I, the policy of Congress for nearly 60 years has been to maintain competition among operators of competing modes of transport by prohibiting their common control. This was the rationale underlying the Panama Canal Act of 1912 (now part of section 5 of the Interstate Commerce Act), the Motor Carrier Act of 1935, the Civil Aeronautics Act of 1938, and the Transportation Act of 1940. Segregation of GM's bus, rail, and motor vehicle facilities into independent corporations, therefore, would be in harmony with well-established pre-existing congressional policy.

Furthermore, there is some precedent for applying this congressional policy to manufacturers as well as operators of transport equipment. In 1934 Congress passed the McKellar-Black Air Mail Act, which prohibited the common ownership of aviation manufacturing and aviation transport companies. As revealed in the floor statements of its cosponsor Senator Black, the act was specifically designed to preclude GM's control of the aviation industry. Senator Black warned that unless the proposed legislation were enacted "our aviation industry is definitely headed for General Motors' . . . control." [353] At the time, GM held substantial interests in both aircraft manufacturing and air transport companies, including Eastern Air Lines, Western Air Lines, TWA, and United Air Lines (aviation transport) and Douglas Aircraft, Bendix Aviation, B/J Aircraft, Allison Engineering and General Aviation Manufacturing Co. (aviation manufacturing).[354] Although GM's common control of competing highway, rail, and air transportation was not formally raised as an issue during the congressional debates, GM Chairman Sloan subsequently implied that it had entered the aviation industry to protect its interest in the promotion of automobiles. "[W]e got into aviation because we thought the . . . airplane would be an important competitor of the automobile . . . and we felt that we had to gain some protection by 'declaring ourselves in' the aviation industry." [355] Pursuant to the mandate of the 1934 act, GM disposed of its interests in the four airlines.[356] In sum, a reasonable reading of the policies embodied in the Panama Canal-Motor Carrier-Civil Aeronautics Acts and in the Air Mail Act would seem by analogy to prohibit the common ownership of competing ground transport manufacturing facilities.

Reorganization of GM's bus and rail facilities would be relatively uncomplicated. In general, the company has combined bus and truck manufacturing within the same facilities. Specifically, it manufactures both bus and truck diesel engines at its Detroit Diesel-Allison plant; and it engages in the final assembly of buses as well as trucks at its GMC complex in Pontiac, Mich.[357] These and other bus facilities, therefore, would be separated from GM ownership simultaneously with the proposed reorganization of the truck industry discussed earlier.[358] With regard to rail production, GM produces diesel locomotives and railcars at facilities located in LaGrange and Chicago, Ill.[359] These plants could be easily reorganized into independent rail manufacturing corporations.

Reorganization of GM's bus and rail facilities alone, however, cannot provide this country with the productive capacity and degree of competition requisite for a balanced system of transportation. As discussed earlier, GM has eliminated virtually all competing bus and train locomotive producers and, through joint lobbying activities and other means, has very likely restrained the growth of these and other nonautomotive methods of travel. Moreover, its own plants produce a relatively small number of bus and rail vehicles for domestic service. A third measure, Government encouragement of entry by new ground transport firms, is therefore recommended. This would involve, for example, the provision of guaranteed Government loans, tax incentives and other benefits to newcomers.

Absent GM's domination of bus and rail production and given a reduction in the automakers' antirail lobbying capabilities, these incentives should induce entry by new firms. The approximate number of additional companies needed to provide us with an adequate bus and rail building capacity may be roughly discerned by comparing the number of firms producing this transport hardware in the technologically advanced countries of West Germany, France, and Japan. Significantly, for purposes of comparison, the combined population of these three countries roughly equals that of the United States. Their systems of ground transportation, however, as discussed later in this study, are far superior to anything available in this country.[360] As indicated in figure 3, these three nations contain more than 85 competing manufacturers of bus and rail vehicles. or more than 10 times as many as America.

TABLE 3

BUS AND RAIL INDUSTRIES: TOTAL NUMBER OF PRODUCERS[1] IN UNITED STATES AND WEST GERMANY-FRANCE-JAPAN[2]

	United States	West Germany-France-Japan
Buses: City and intercity; diesels and electric_____	3	26
Railcars: Streetcars, interurbans, subway, elevated, rapid transit, commuter railroad__	3	23
Train locomotives: Diesels and electric_____	2	33
Totals_____	8	82

[1] Includes established manufacturers of production-line and revenue-service vehicles. Excludes firms solely engaged in the limited production of experimental or prototype equipment.
[2] Comparative indices (1972 population): United States, 203,000,000; West Germany-France-Japan (combined), 213,-000,000.

As in the proposed reorganization of the automakers' motor vehicle facilities, management and employees as well as the riding public would be expected to benefit substantially from reorganization of GM's bus and rail plants into independent corporations. Management would not only be in control of their own plants, but they would also have the opportunity and incentive to experiment with more efficient production techniques and, perhaps, with innovations in motive power including steam turbine, electric and Freon engines which have been developed both here and abroad. In short, for the first time since the acquisition by GM of Yellow Coach and Electro-Motive more than 40 years ago, management would be free to promote the sale of transport vehicles without regard for the conflicting interests of a parent motor vehicle corporation. Likewise, employees should welcome the opportunity to work for a corporation whose growth and ability to innovate are unrestrained. Stockholders should also benefit through their holdings in an aggressive group of new transport companies.

Whether the automakers' nontransport facilities should also be reorganized is a question clearly beyond the scope of this study. It is recommended, therefore, that pending further investigation these facilities should continue to function as operating units of four multiproduct enterprises. Thus, General Motors' household appliance (Frigidaire), aerospace, Earth-moving machinery (Terex), real estate, and other nonautomotive divisions would comprise one such enterprise; Ford's properties, including its household appliance and electronics division (Philco-Ford), and its steel, glass, and tractor production subsidiaries would constitute a second; Chrysler's glass, marine, air conditioning (Airtemp), real estate, and defense-space businesses a third; and American Motors' properties, including its computer services (AM Data Systems), car leasing (American Motors Leasing), and nonautomotive injected-molded plastics (Windsor Plastics) subsidiaries would comprise a fourth.

The proposed restructuring of the ground transport sector is based on a fundamental premise: the presence of many competing manufacturers of buses, trains, subway cars, and rapid transit vehicles as well as automobiles and trucks would help to achieve the genuinely balanced system we so desperately need. We need smaller, less-expensive cars powered by low-pollution, energy-efficient engines for use outside of central cities. We need technologically attractive bus and rapid rail equipment which can provide downtown commuters with viable alternatives to driving their own cars. We also need improved forms of rail freight delivery to reduce the number of noxious, fuel-guzzling diesel trucks on city streets. Restoring competition to those industries which produce our transportation hardware is an important prerequisite to meeting these several needs.

C. The Mechanics of Reorganization

The actual mechanics of reorganization are relatively uncomplicated. Nevertheless, some of the more salient details are set forth in this section. As discussed earlier, the basic objectives are fundamentally two-fold in nature: first, to create independent and viable corporations for each physically distinct manufacturing, assembly, distribution, and financial unit currently owned by General Motors, Ford, Chrysler, and American Motors; and second, to separate foreign subsidiaries from control by these four corporations.

Before reviewing the mechanics involved in acomplishing these two objectives, some general observations should be made concerning concentrations of stock ownership and transitional planning. An effective reorganization plan must insure that the new corporations created are genuinely independent of the interests which controlled the original enterprises. Shares in the new corporations, therefore, should be distributed in such a way as to eliminate old, and preclude the emergence of new, concentrations of control in any individual or group.

In addition, it is anticipated that advance planning would minimize interference with the physical operation of plants during the transition from old to new organizational structures. Contractual arrangements with future suppliers and purchasers, reassignments of engineering, marketing and administrative personnel from central headquarters to decentralized assembly and component plants, and other transitional matters should be negotiated well in advance of the actual reorganization date. The tax and financial consequences of the recommended restructuring transactions, moreover, could be anticipated at an early stage and, through proper planning, could be used as incentives to encourage current management to contribute to the creation of independent and viable enterprises.

The creation of new corporations and severance of control over foreign subsidiaries would require seven contemporaneous transactions: [361] (1) Stock merger of all domestic subsidiaries into their four respective parents; (2) sale of assets of foreign subsidiaries to foreign owners of U.S. dollars; (3) proportionate assignment of all the assets and liabilities of the parents to the prospective new companies; (4) actual formation and capitalization of the new companies; (5) issuance and exchange of shares in the new companies for the assets and liabilities proportionately assigned them by the parents; (6) solicitation of parent shareholders to determine which new company (or companies) shares they wish to receive in exchange for their old parent shares, and, to the extent possible, allocation of the new shares on the basis of shareholders' preferences, with any balance allocated by lottery; (7) complete liquidation of parents by an exchange of securities in which the shares of the new companies are exchanged for those of the old parent corporations.

Although these seven transactions might appear complex, they would amount in essence to the creation of a number of new, viable corporations to receive the current business of the four automakers. Some explanatory comments, however, are necessary. The stock merger of domestic subsidiaries into parents would result in only one set of equity securities outstanding covering each parent and its respective subsidiaries. This would facilitate the subsequent transactions: The solicitation of parent shareholders would permit the allocation of shares in the new companies to be based on the expressed preferences of shareholders. Some GM shareholders, for example, might prefer to have shares in one or more auto assembly companies; others might prefer stock participation in the new independent bus and rail corporations. To the extent that conflicts might arise in shareholder preferences, the allocation of new company shares could be determined by lottery. Provision could also be made for the tax-free exchange or sale by shareholders who are dissatisfied either with the lottery outcome or otherwise. In this fashion, shareholders might exchange their new company shares for those in companies formerly owned by any of the four automakers. A Chrysler shareholder, for example, would have the opportunity to negotiate a tax-free exchange of shares in properties formerly owned by Chrysler for those in properties formerly owned by Ford. Alternatively, shareholders would have the option of a tax-free sellout.

The sale of assets of foreign automotive subsidiaries to foreign owners of U.S. dollars, contained in transaction (2), would sever parent control over these foreign-based enterprises. It would also serve to remove a portion of the dollar overhang. In short, it would eliminate the economic disadvantages of multinationalization while contributing to international monetary stability.

Under current law, most of these transactions would be nontaxable. For example, the merger of domestic subsidiaries with the present parent companies, the transfer of assets by the parents in exchange for the stock of the new corporations, and the distribution of that stock to the present company stockholders in exchange for their old stock would all represent nontaxable transactions. Some transactions taxable under current law, however, could occur. To that extent, appropriate amendments to the Internal Revenue Code would be advisable.

Additional measures would be needed to insure the effectiveness of the reorganization. In particular, precautions would have to be taken to preclude officers, directors, and large shareholders of the new companies from attempting to reconstitute the prior anticompetitive structures. This might require, for example, that officers, directors, and large shareholders of the new companies, as well as the companies themselves, be prohibited from owning shares in any other ground transportation company. At the same time, tax and other financial incentives should be considered as a means of encouraging management, directors, and employees to dedicate their energies to the new companies. In this regard, profit-sharing, tax-delaying stock options, deferred compensation, generous pension plans, and numerous other devices could be used effectively to link both executives and employees closely to the success of the reorganization.

Tax incentives, moreover, could be provided the new corporations to induce their modernization of production and their commitment to innovation. For the first purpose, special investment credits, accelerated depreciation, or additional first-year depreciation for plant and equipment acquired might be warranted. For the latter, special credits and amortization deductions could be granted automotive companies which engage in the development of low-emission propulsion systems. Similar incentives could be extended to nonauto ground transport firms which undertake research and development aimed at improving America's bus and rail systems.

D. Some Considerations Regarding Feasibility

Reorganization of these four ground transportation industries would appear to be feasible in light of their early structure and performance in this country, their comparative structure and performance abroad, and the subsequent experience of transport companies formerly owned by General Motors.

1. Early Structure and Performance of the Ground Transportation Industries.—Reorganization of these industries is feasible, first, because it would restore them to their naturally competitive states. The early automobile industry, for instance, comprised numerous firms which competed at every level of production: manufacturing, assembly, and distribution. Automobile producers were primarily assemblers of bodies and engines purchased from independent suppliers specializing in automotive parts production. Since producers had access to parts from external suppliers, they were not compelled to integrate upstream into components production.[362] Moreover, the availability of interchangeable replacement components obviated any need for integration downstream into extensive networks of franchised dealers with specialized repair and maintenance capabilities.[363] The industry's emphasis upon purchasing from external suppliers and distributing through external outlets generated two competitively beneficial effects: ease of entry and technological flexibility.

The absence of vertical integration greatly reduced the amount of initial investment required for entry and survival in the early auto industry.[364] The Ford Motor entry was typical. The company was incorporated in 1903 with only $28,000 in cash (or about $139,000 in 1973 dollars).[365] This ease of entry was reflected in the low level of industry concentration. In 1921, for example, 88 assemblers competed in the sale of 1.5 million passenger cars.[366] In 1972, by comparison, industry sales amounted to 9 million, or six times as many.[367] Restructuring this vastly enlarged industry into half the number of assembler-producers as existed in 1921, therefore, would not seem unreasonable.

The absence of vertical integration also provided early assemblers with a high degree of technological flexibility. The lack of enormous capital investments in components production allowed these firms virtual freedom to experiment with the alternative technological offerings of external body and engine manufacturers. As a result, the early auto industry was noted for its wide variety of fundamentally different motor vehicles. There were, for example, assemblers of electric and steam as well as gasoline-powered vehicles.[368] This technological competition, in turn, greatly accelerated the pace of innovation, particularly with regard to alternative propulsion systems. In fact, the development of pollution-free electric cars had advanced during the 1920's to the point where the Federal Oil Conservation Board recommended in a 1928 report to the President that the economy and operating advantage of "the present type of storage-battery electric vehicle as compared with the gasoline car" warranted the substitution of electric for gasoline automobiles.[369] Likewise, as early as 1907, steam cars capable of speeds in excess of 190 miles per hour were available which would have met the 1975–76 clean air standards.[370]

Then, suddenly, the industry became collectively monopolized, and the development of alternative propulsion systems was halted. In the course of 3 years, from 1923 to 1926, 43 assemblers left the market.[371] By 1935, only 10 firms were producing automobiles.[372] Today, only four remain, with three highly integrated firms accounting for 97 percent of domestic production. General Motors, Ford, and Chrysler invested billions of dollars integrating upstream into the production of internal combustion engines.[373] Due to their complexity (15,000 moving parts) and high cost of replacement, it is probable that these engines contributed more to Big Three profits than would the simpler and relatively inexpensive electric or steam systems. In the process, these alternative forms of motive power vanished. To protect their substantial investments in internal combustion systems, therefore, it is suspected that the Big Three vigorously pursued the elimination of competing electric and steam car producers.[374] Nonetheless, GM, Ford, and Chrysler have continued cautiously to experiment with these displaced power sources (for example, the SE–101 steam and XEP–1A electric car by GM, gas turbine cars by Chrysler, and Ford's electric "commuta" car). But these projects have reportedly been undertaken primarily to enable the three automakers to claim "good faith" efforts before inquiring congressional bodies and to deter entry by prospective manufacturers of these alternative propulsion systems.[375]

In light of its earlier competitive structure and satisfactory performance, there is reason to believe that the industry could once again be reorganized as proposed. This would involve not a departure from precedent but a return to earlier competitive conditions. In fact, the current structure of this industry might best be perceived as a historical aberration. The trend toward concentration was the result not of natural economic forces, but rather of four artificial, concentration-increasing factors set in motion by the Big Three automakers: Acquisition of competitors, components integration, annual style change, and exclusive franchised distribution. A brief review of these factors should demonstrate that because it seeks no more than to restore competition to this industry, the reorganization proposed is well-founded.

The first concentration-increasing activity initiated by the Big Three automakers was the acquisition of competitors. At the outset, General Motors attempted to acquire all the major auto manufacturers, in the manner of Standard Oil, American Tobacco, and other great trusts of the period.[376] By the end of 1909, it controlled nine formerly independent automobile assemblers (including Buick, Cadillac, Oldsmobile, and Pontiac) and its board of directors had authorized the purchase of a tenth, Ford.[377] Although Ford rejected its takeover bid, GM went on to acquire 12 more assemblers by 1920 and to make an unsuccessful bid for Dodge in 1925.[378] Meanwhile, Ford acquired Lincoln (1922), Chrysler acquired Chalmers (1923) and Dodge (1928), and Nash (which later merged with Hudson to form American Motors) purchased Lafayette (1922).[379] By 1928, these firms had acquired a total of 25 independent automobile asemblers.

The Big Three's integration upstream into components production constituted a second concentration-increasing activity. By the start of World War I, GM had acquired more than a dozen parts suppliers and Ford was busily constructing in-house components facilities. Later, Chrysler also began to purchase parts manufacturers.[380] By 1937, GM alone had acquired more than 40 independent producers of key automotive components.[381] In this fashion, the Big Three deprived unintegrated assemblers of the access to independent sources of body and engine components which was requisite for survival.

General Motors' introduction of annual style change in 1923, and the interdependent adoption of this practice subsequently by Ford and Chrysler, was a third artificial factor leading to increased concentration.[382] As a marketing weapon, annual style change severely disadvantaged smaller volume producers by encouraging them to integrate upstream while forcing them prematurely to scrap prohibitively expensive tools, dies and jigs. Specifically, an inevitable result of the Big Three drive to produce "all-new" cars annually was intensification of the industry trend toward components integration. The annual need to produce uniquely styled vehicles, including redesigned bodies and rearranged (although not necessarily improved) engines, encouraged producers to internalize an increasing proportion of body and engine production.[383] This shift from assembly of body and engine components to their integrated fabrication on an annually restyled basis, however, greatly increased the scale of production necessary for optimum efficiency.[384] Integrated production of annually redesigned vehicles at optimum efficiency required an annual volume of at least 250,000 units.[385] Operation below that volume resulted in higher average costs through the premature scrapping of expensive tools, dies and jigs which, although physically still useful, could not be used again for next year's restyled models. On the other hand, integrated operation at or above the 250,000-unit level of output required vast sums of capital. After the introduction of annual style change, therefore, entry and survival in this industry was barred to all but large, completely integrated enterprises.[386]

The Big Three's integration downstream into exclusive franchised distribution was a fourth factor responsible for industry concentration. Prior to 1925, there was little need for automakers to establish exclusive retail outlets. Independent retailers provided adequate sales and service for a wide variety of automobiles.[387] Since at least 1925, however, General Motors, Ford, and Chrysler pursued a tacit policy of prohibiting their respective dealers from handling automobiles manufactured by competing firms.[388] This "exclusive dealing" practice effectively foreclosed smaller assemblers from distributing their cars through thousands of previously independent dealers. In early 1933, for instance, Continental attempted to enter the automobile industry by distributing its cars through already established dealers. GM Sales

Committee Chairman Grant responded at once to the threat of new entry. On January 4, 1933, he ordered his sales representatives to block Continental's access to dealers: "* * * Continental, which is attempting to get distribution through already established dealers, should not be permitted to get a foothold with General Motors dealers." [389] By the end of 1934, Continental was forced to withdraw from the industry.[390]

Moreover, the emergence of annual style change as an industry practice precluded small firms from sharing whatever independent dealers remained. Periodic restyling required differentiation of even the most minute components, which led in turn to a decline in interchangeable replacement parts.[391] As a consequence, automakers were required to establish nationwide dealer networks with specialized repair and maintenance capabilities, a project which small volume producers could ill afford to undertake.

By pursuing these four activities (acquisition of competitors, components integration, annual style change, and exclusive franchised distribution), the Big Three revolutionized the industry's structure. They transformed a naturally competitive industry of nearly 100 competing assemblers, thousands of parts suppliers, and tens of thousands of independent retail dealers into one dominated by three highly integrated monopoly sharing firms. They also closed the door to new competitors by raising the capital costs of entry tenfold. To enter and survive in the vertically integrated, style-changing industry of the 1970's, a prospective firm would need an estimated $1 billion for the in-house production of specialized body and engine components, annual style changes, and a nationwide network of franchised dealers.[392] By contrast, had the Big Three not restructured the industry, a new firm could enter as an assembler at a cost of $55 million, or less than one-fifteenth as much.[393]

Nevertheless, it has been urged that efficiency in automobile production can only be achieved by a highly concentrated, integrated industry.[394] It has been argued, for instance, that horizontal concentration of assembly operations in a few giant firms maximizes productive efficiency.[395] The preponderance of economic literature and the actual distribution of assembly facilities in the industry are to the contrary. Bain, for example, has concluded that an assembler achieves maximum efficiency within a production range of from 60,000 to 180,000 cars per year.[396] In their study of the British motor car industry, Maxcy and Silbertson found that scale efficiencies in assembly operations were exhausted at the 100,000 unit level; whereas Rhys has suggested that the figure might reach 200,000 units.[397] Reviewing German automobile production, Jurgensen and Berg stated that maximum efficiency in assembly could be realized at output levels of 25,000–50,000 units.[398] Significantly, these estimates of efficient production levels are no larger than the average-size American assembly plant, which in 1972 produced 200,000 cars.[399]

The actual distribution of American assembly operations also belies the purported need for horizontal concentration. The four automakers assemble cars not in 4 but in 44 geographically separate plants. Concentration, therefore, is limited to ownership and does not extend to production. If physically combining assembly plants enhanced efficiency, the four automakers most certainly would have combined them.

It would appear, therefore, that each of these 44 plants might be able to operate efficiently as an independent assembler of passenger cars. Others have maintained that efficiency in automobile manufacturing requires vertical integration upstream into components and downstream into distribution.[400] The available literature and actual industry plant structures, however, contradict this argument. In his definitive studies of vertical integration in the American auto industry, Crandall concluded that integration was not required for optimal efficiency. More specifically, he stated that the presumed advantages of coordination and control often cited in support of integration could be realized as effectively through long-term contracts between assemblers and independent suppliers and distributors.[401] Moreover, at least one other student of the industry suggested that efficiency would have been enhanced had the automakers undergone "vertical disintegration" in the early 1930's.[402]

The actual distribution of parts manufacturing facilities in this industry also indicates that integration is, at best, unrelated to efficiency. The four automakers maintain physically separate establishments for assembly, body stamping, engine casting, transmission assembly, and myriad other parts production activities. If physical integration enhanced efficiency, the four automakers would have integrated plants as well as ownership. It is not unreasonable to propose, therefore, that these facilities, now separate in fact, could become separate in law without any loss in productive efficiency.

Likewise, the early American truck industry operated in a competitive environment. At one time, it comprised more than 100 producers which, like their counterparts in the auto industry, were primarily assemblers.[403] By means of acquisition, components integration, elimination of auto firms which also produced trucks, and other concentration-increasing activities, however, the Big Three automakers restructured this industry.[404] Today, 84 percent of total production is concentrated in the Big Three's truck divisions.[405] This study therefore recommends nothing more than restoring the industry's previously competitive environment.

The early bus and rail industries were also structured more competitively than today. They were not concentrated. At one time, there were more than 150 competing manufacturers of bus and rail vehicles.[406] In addition, they were not characterized by interindustry diversification. More specifically, neither industry was dominated by motor vehicle manufacturers.[407] It was during this earlier period that the development of technological alternatives flourished. There were builders, for example, of steam- and electric-powered buses, double-deck and articulated (multiple-unit) buses, electric streetcars and high-speed electric interurban trains.[408] The technological development of these vehicles, however, stopped suddenly in the 1930's. By this time, as carefully documented above, General Motors had diversified into bus and rail production and, with Ford, Chrysler, and other highway interests, had begun to lobby against rail transit. Since then the bus and rail industries have been largely untouched by technological progress.[409] By separating out GM's bus and rail facilities, reducing the automakers' lobbying capacities, and encouraging entry by new ground transport firms, therefore, the proposed reorganization would attempt to reconstruct the competitive conditions which generated an earlier and apparently more innovative era.

In sum, all four industries once functioned effectively within competitive structures similar in principle to those now advocated. Their departure from these structures was largely the result of concentration-increasing activities undertaken by the Big Three automakers. In light of available evidence, it may be strongly argued that the competitive reorganization of these industries would not impair productive efficiency and would very likely contribute to technological progress. This then is the first ground upon which a claim of feasibility is maintained.

2. Structure, Conduct, and Performance of These Industries Abroad.—It is feasible to reorganize America's ground transport industries into smaller, independent, less integrated units for a second reason: the more advanced transport industries of Europe and Japan are largely organized in this fashion. In terms of structure, they are generally less concentrated, less integrated, and, in an interindustry sense, less diversified than in the United States. In fact, several of the most innovative European and Japanese firms reflect some of the size and organizational characteristics recommended in this study for American transport firms. In terms of conduct and performance, moreover, many experts believe that these industries are superior to those operating in this country. A brief review of the structure, conduct, and performance of automobile, truck, bus, and rail industries abroad follows.

With the exception of the Big Three foreign subsidiaries, automobile manufacturing in most of Europe and Japan is characterized by lower levels of structural concentration and integration than in America. For example, in West Germany, France, and Japan, whose combined population and motor vehicle output approximate those of the United States, there are 20 competing producers of passenger cars.[410] Most of these producers are also considerably less integrated than General Motors, Ford, and Chrysler. They buy rather than make a large proportion of automobile parts.[411] This permits them to take advantage of the economies of volume realized by a parts supplier that produces interchangeable parts for the entire industry. A few, such as Germany's Porsche and Japan's Suzuki, operate primarily as assemblers, buying in all major body and engine components.[412] In addition, European and Japanese automakers generally distribute their products through nonexclusive independent outlets.[413]

The more competitively structured auto industries of Europe and Japan seem to behave and perform more satisfactorily than the American auto industry. Due to the larger number of firms, price, product and technological conduct is aggressively competitive. There is, for example, a noticeable absence of the interdependent or collusive pricing, product imitation, and suppression of technology which characterize the American Big Three. Instead, prices fluctuate in a more competitive manner, products vary remarkably in terms of both design and performance features, and advances in automotive technology are more rapidly introduced.[414]

This degree of competitive conduct, in turn, has resulted in a more satisfactory record of performance in terms of efficiency, progressiveness, and international competitiveness. European and Japanese manufacturers appear to have achieved high levels of efficiency through their use of common, interchangeable components and their stead-fast avoidance of the prohibitively expensive American practice of annual model changes.[415] Their progressiveness in several areas of public concern, particularly emission control and safety, has also become widely acknowledged. Japan's Toyo Kogyo (Mazda), Honda, Daihatsu, and Suzuki have all produced low-pollution cars which either meet or are expected to meet the 1975–76 U.S. emission standards.[416] Sweden's Volvo was the first to introduce safety belts, crash-absorption bumpers, interior crash padding, and collapsible steering columns as standard equipment.[417] Germany's Porsche has developed a "long life" car designed to last for 20 years.[418]

High levels of efficiency and progressiveness have also enhanced the international competitiveness of European and Japanese car industries. Both Germany and Sweden, for example, export more than half of the automobiles they produce.[419] Japan generally exports 20 percent of its passenger car production.[420] By contrast, due in large part to their extensive multinational operations, American automakers sell less than 1 percent of the cars they produce here abroad.[421]

Furthermore, major technological breakthroughs have been achieved by European and Japanese firms structured in a manner closely resembling that which is recommended by this study. The Wankel rotary engine, hailed by many as the most significant development in automotive propulsion since the invention of the internal combustion engine, was the product of two small, nonintegrated companies: NSU of Germany and Toyo Kogyo of Japan. When NSU first developed its rotary car in 1957, it was an unintegrated assembler producing 17,000 vehicles a year.[422] When Toyo Kogyo ("Mazda") began marketing an improved Wankel rotary car in 1967, the firm was primarily an assembler of only 129,000 vehicles annually.[423]

Likewise, Porsche's recent development of a long-life 20-year car built of materials which can later be recycled constitutes a significant breakthrough in automotive technology.[424] Yet, this firm is one of the world's most compact and least integrated automakers. In 1972, it produced slightly more than 14,000 cars from components nearly all of which were bought-in.[425] In other words, the proposed reorganization would create new auto-assembly companies which in terms of output (average of 220,000 units per annum) and absence of vertical integration would compare favorably with the most innovative producers operating abroad.

Although considerably smaller in annual output than the 220,000-unit level suggested as optimum, Porsche exemplifies the organizational model advocated by this study. It is primarily an assembler of bought-in components. It distributes its cars through a contractual arrangement with the Volkswagen distribution system.[426] Its only production facilities other than an assembly plant consist of a first-rate research and development center, a sheet metal pressing shop, and an administration building.[427] Its major production activity consists of engineering, inspecting, and assembling the parts it purchases.[428] As an assembler, it avoids the technological lock-in which accompanies vertical integration. "Integration," according to one high-placed Porsche executive, "is a barrier to cost reduction and technological development; it eliminates that competition among automotive parts suppliers which is essential for maximum efficiency and innovation."[429]

Porsche builds high-cost sport cars at a relatively low annual level of output. But the same structural advantages of deconcentration and nonintegration apply to the production of any other class of passenger car. The relevant variables are unit cost and level of output: the lower the unit cost, the higher the volume of output required to achieve economies of scale. For Porsche's high-cost sport cars, that volume would appear to be around 15,000 units a year. For lower cost passenger cars, the figure would probably reach the 220,000 annual unit level.[430] Higher outputs and/or vertical integration, however, cannot be justified in terms of efficiency or technological innovation. Why then have some European and Japanese firms recently increased their outputs through mergers and integrated vertically? One high-ranking Porsche executive suggested three possibilities: first, imitation of the American Big Three and their foreign subsidiaries ("if American firms are gigantic and fully integrated, then perhaps we should organize ourselves in this fashion . . ."); second, the failure to include a proper allowance for overhead costs in "make-buy" (vertical integration) decisions; and, third, the drive by management to increase their personal salaries and prestige through otherwise inexplicable corporate expansion.

Truck manufacturing in Europe and Japan is generally less concentrated and less integrated than in the United States. In West Germany, France, and Japan, for example, whose combined population and production of trucks approximate that of the United States, there are 19 competing producers, or nearly three times the number of American firms.[431] European and Japanese truckmakers also rely more heavily on external component suppliers and independent distributors.[432] This more competitive structure has generated an enviable record of performance. The Japanese, for example, were the first to develop the light utility vehicle; in fact, the Japanese firms of Isuzu and Toyo Kogyo produce GM's "LUV" and Ford's "Courier," respectively.[433] Toyo Kogyo is also marketing the world's first rotary-powered light trucks.[434] Meanwhile, Germany's Daimler-Benz, Messerschmitt, and Volkswagen have produced electric-powered trucks and vans. [435] The effectiveness of these less concentrated, less integrated industrial structures demonstrates in a general way the feasibility of the proposed reorganization of American truck manufacturing.

Ground transportation in Japan and most of Europe is far superior to anything available in the United States. This is due, at least in part, to the ability of their bus and rail industries to compete effectively with each other and with manufacturers of cars and trucks. Competition within the bus and rail industries is enhanced by the large number of firms involved. In West Germany, France, and Japan alone, there are 26 builders of buses, 23 producers of rail transit cars, and 33 manufacturers of locomotives.[436] By contrast, in America three firms assemble GM buses, only three firms still produce rail transit cars and two firms manufacture locomotives. [437] Competition between these industries and the motor vehicle industries is also vigorous due to the lower level of interindustry diversification and the more even distribution of political power. West Germany, France, and Japan, for example, are free of the American dilemma where a single automobile manufacturer dominates both bus and rail production. Although a few automakers such as Daimler-Benz, Toyota, and Nissan also produce buses, none of them accounts for more than 30 percent of these three countries' total bus output.[438] Likewise, Mitsubishi of Japan produces trains as well as automobiles, but it dominates neither industry.[439] The level of interindustry diversification in these countries, therefore, is sufficiently low so as to preclude automakers from restraining competition with nonautomotive forms of ground transportation.

There is also a more equal distribution of political power between auto manufacturers and competing transport interests in Europe and Japan. This is due in large part to the presence of competition in the auto industries and the absence of automaker domination of bus and rail production. The more balanced lobbying capacities of these divergent transport interests are reflected in the legislative determination regarding use of motor vehicle taxes. Unlike America, these countries are largely free of devices such as highway trust funds, which earmark moneys exclusively for highways and deprive rail systems of essential public funding. Instead, they levy motor vehicle taxes which are spent for both highways and rail systems. West Germany, for example, has a special gasoline and diesel fuel tax whose revenues are split 60 percent for highways and 40 percent for rail transit.[440] Roughly one-half of that country's total transportation budget, moreover, is allocated to rail systems.[441]

Largely as a consequence, Europe and Japan have achieved a more balanced system of ground transportation, particularly in urban areas. "All during the late 1940's, 1950's, and 1960's, while American transit systems have been allowed to decay," noted one transportation specialist, "European systems have been expanding and improving and preparing for the inevitable competition with private automobiles." [442] He added: "While American cities have been talking about balanced transportation, European cities have been achieving it by means of building new rapid transit lines and a network of modern highways." [443] No fewer than eight rapid rail systems are currently under construction in West Germany alone.[444]

The more competitively structured ground transport sectors of Europe and Japan perform appreciably better in terms of efficiency and progressiveness than their American counterpart. As compared with America, overall transport efficiency in West Germany, France, and Japan, for instance, is enhanced by a more balanced and workable allocation of passenger and freight traffic between highways and rails. In metropolitan areas such as Paris and Tokyo, where travel by auto is least efficient, technologically attractive bus and rail vehicles transport 80 and 90 percent, respectively, of the commuting work force.[445] By comparison, nonauto transportation accounts for but 50 percent of the journey to work in Metropolitan New York, and less than 15 percent in Metropolitan Los Angeles.[446] Likewise a larger proportion of European and Japanese freight moves by rail rather than by truck.[447] In short, due to their extensive use of energy-efficient, cost-saving rail systems, these foreign nations have achieved balanced systems of ground transportation far superior to anything available in the United States.

Performance is also a function of progressiveness, or the rate of technological innovation. Transport technology in Japan and most of Europe is flourishing; moreover, it is being applied. MAN and Daimler-Benz, for example, have developed noiseless, pollution-free electric buses which are already on the streets of several German cities.[448] Likewise, Japanese and French producers, including Naniwa Koki and Société Sovel are producing modern electric-powered buses and trolley coaches.[449] Other European manufacturers build modern double-deckers and electric "flywheel" stored-energy buses.[450]

Rail technology in these countries is equally impressive. ANF-Frangeco, Brissoneau, and Altshom of France manufacture RTG and TGV turbine-powered intercity trains designed for speeds in excess of 150 miles per hour.[451] Five Japanese firms (Hitachi, Kawasaki, Kinki, Tokyu, and Nippon Sharyo Seizo) build the incredibly fast, quiet, and pollution-free electric "bullet trains" which operate without vibration on the Tokaido line at speeds of 125–150 miles per hour.[452] Germany's Krauss-Maffei and Messerschmitt-Bolkow-Blohm, acknowledged leaders in the development of high-speed trains powered by 250–350 miles per hour electric linear induction motors, will soon construct operational systems in Germany and Canada.[453] Linke-Hoffman-Busch and Düwag, also of Germany, are producing advanced light rail vehicles, and CIMT, Alsthom, M.T.E., and Brissoneau of France are building exceptionally well-engineered, rubber-tired cars for the Paris, Montreal, and Mexico City Metros.[454] There are, moreover, manufacturers abroad of a whole range of transportation alternatives including streetcars, trolley coaches, and interurban electric trains, which in this country were displaced years ago by General Motors.

As compared with the efficiency and performance of industrialized countries overseas, America is a second-rate Nation in ground transportation. The proposed reorganization would reverse that situation. It would restore competition to motor vehicle manufacturing; it would release the bus and rail industries from General Motors' domination; and it would reduce the Big Three's antirail lobbying capabilities. It would also encourage entry by new ground transport firms which, through the resulting competition, would contribute to the rebuilding of a technologically advanced and balanced system of transportation for this country. The comparative structure and performance of this sector in Japan and most of Europe demonstrates the feasibility of such a reorganization.

3. Subsequent History of Companies Formerly Owned by General Motors.—The financial success of companies formerly owned by General Motors provides a third measure of this proposal's feasibility. Reorganization is a natural and frequent occurrence among corporate enterprises. Accordingly, GM has disposed of a great number of companies which it once effectively controlled. With few exceptions, these companies have prospered subsequently. TWA, Eastern Airlines, Bendix, North American-Rockwell, and Hertz, for example, have all experienced spectacular growth since their separation from General Motors in 1936, 1938, 1948 (2), and 1953, respectively.[455] TWA has increased its operating revenues from a mere $6.2 million in 1936 to $1.1 billion in 1969; Eastern Airlines has grown from operating revenues of only $3.8 million in 1938 to $649 million in 1969; Bendix net sales have risen from $162.4 million in 1948 to $1.6 billion in 1971; North American-Rockwell has expanded from a sales volume of $11.7 million in 1948 to $2.2 billion in 1971; and Hertz has grown from gross vehicle revenues in 1953 of $20.1 million to more than $600 million last year.[456]

Executives, shareholders, and employees as well as consumers mutually benefited from the release of these companies from General Motors' control. The history of Hertz Rent-A-Car is illustrative. General Motors acquired Hertz in April 1925.[457] For the following 28 years, GM operated this company in a manner which frustrated the efforts of Hertz executives to expand operations, and, as a consequence, was contrary to the best interests of GM employees and shareholders as well as the consuming public. From 1925 until August 1953, GM imposed requirements on Hertz which virtually insured that the company would grow no more than 10–15 percent a year.[458] The requirements were basically twofold in nature: First, Hertz was instructed to borrow money only from GM, and was expressly prohibited from seeking any "outside" funds; second, the company was required to pay to GM an annual dividend payment out of retained earnings. By refusing to lend Hertz any funds and by gaging the required dividend payment to absorb all but a fixed portion of retained earnings, GM was able to limit Hertz' growth to 10–15 percent per annum.[459]

The motives underlying GM's limitation of Hertz' growth are not entirely clear. One explanation, however, seems at least plausible. During the period of GM ownership (1925–53), consumers leased cars and trucks as a less expensive alternative to buying them. In its 1958 annual report, for example, the Hertz Corp. stated that while GM owned Hertz, "the industry was patronized by non-car owners who rented for occasional local usage or vacation travel." [460] Conceivably, GM saw Hertz' growth as a threat to its more profitable sale of cars and trucks, The 1958 report went on to state that due principally to the growth of commercial airline operations, the industry emphasis after GM's ownership of Hertz "shifted in favor of a national market—the car-owning traveler who required an automobile at locations distant from his home." [461] There is reason to suspect, therefore, that GM restricted the growth of Hertz leasing concern in order to protect its sale of cars and trucks, and that in 1953 it disposed of the company because the motor vehicle rental industry no longer threatened motor vehicle sales.

The impact on executives, employees, stockholders, and consumers was considerable. GM's growth restrictions utterly frustrated the efforts of Hertz executives to expand the company's leasing business. As one former Hertz official remarked, "GM allowed us no freedom of action; Hertz was held back." [462] Restricted growth also resulted in restricted revenues, reduced employment, and diminished contributions to GM shareholders. In addition, Hertz' inability to expand meant that a great number of consumers were deprived of the benfits of leasing rather than owning motor vehicles.[463]

GM's sale of Hertz inured to the benefit of all concerned. A review of the company's growth before and after reorganization roughly demonstrates what happens to an enterprise when it becomes an independent entity. After 28 years of oppressive GM ownership, Hertz executives at last were in command of their own company. At once they began to match their marketing skills against their competition. Successfully obtaining a $13 million line of credit, they set out to turn Hertz into an aggressive nationwide transportation enterprise.[464] The results were remarkable. During the last 5 years of GM ownership (1948–52), the company's annual revenue had increased from $11 million to $17.9 million, or by an average of only 13 percent a year. By contrast, 5 years of independent operation saw Hertz revenues soar from $20.1 million in 1953 to $78.9 million in 1957, or an average increase of about 42 percent a year.[465] Some of this growth could be attributed to acquisitions, but in large measure the company grew through internal expansion. In short, a dynamic group of previously frustrated executives had transformed a sluggish corporate stepchild of GM into a fast-growing independent concern.

An independent Hertz had a salutary effect on both employment and stock values. As it expanded nationwide, it employed more workers. The effect on stock values was also impressive. In 1958, the company reported that a holder of 100 shares since 1953 would have realized $997 in cash dividends and a threefold appreciation in the book value of his original holdings.[466] Hertz had also benefited the consumer by increasing the number of cities served by car rental agencies. For the 5-year period from 1948 to 1952, GM-owned Hertz managed to augment the number of cities served by 3, from 27 to 30. By comparison, during the 5-year post-GM period of 1953–58, Hertz secured representation in 118 additional cities, or an increase from 30 to 148.[467]

The experience of Hertz and other companies following their separation from General Motors suggests that reorganizing GM, as well as Ford and Chrysler, into smaller, autonomous units would enable new companies to prosper in a competitive environment previously denied them. In particular, the possibility that GM may have suppressed Hertz in order to sell more motor vehicles underscores the critical need to liberate GM's bus and locomotive divisions, whose probable suppression more than likely has enhanced GM's sale of cars and trucks.

E. Implementation

There are several conceivable methods of implementing this proposal. Executives of the auto companies, for instance, might themselves welcome the opportunity not only to revitalize their own industry but also to contribute to the public's interest in technologically advanced and balanced transportation. If the automakers failed to act voluntarily, the Department of Justice or Federal Trade Commission could sue under the antitrust laws to enforce the proposed reorganization of our ground transport industries. Alternatively, Congress might consider passage of legislation specifically designed to bring about a restructuring of this and other highly concentrated industrial sectors.

1. *The Prospects for Voluntary Reorganization.*—Voluntary reorganization by enlightened executives of the Big Three motor vehicle manufacturers is possible but, absent tremendous public and governmental pressures, highly unlikely. In 1956, for example, Assistant Attorney General Stanley N. Barnes suggested that General Motors ease the trend toward economic concentration by voluntarily divesting itself of some motor vehicle, bus, home appliance (Frigidaire), and finance (GMAC) operations. GM president Harlow H. Curtice termed the Antitrust Division chief's suggestion "nonsense." [468] Two years later, in 1958, American Motors President George Romney testified before the Senate Antitrust Subcommittee that the Big Three automobile companies should cooperate with the Government in formulating an industry dissolution plan which would restore competition to automobile manufacturing. He stated that reorganizing the Big Three into several new companies "would be in the interest of stockholders, ex-

ecutives, employees, dealers, customers, competitors, communities, States, and the Nation." He appealed directly to his industry colleagues: "If the men who have built the success of General Motors and Ford would really think it through * * * what I am proposing is a means by which those who excel can continue their effort to excel without restraint." [469] GM President Curtice rejected Romney's suggestion, claiming instead that his company's dominant position in ground transport was "a healthy situation for the country and the industry in general." [470]

With but one significant exception, the automakers have demonstrated a steadfast resistance to voluntary reorganization. In 1967, the Department of Justice seriously contemplated a suit to break up General Motors' passenger car operations. The giant automaker's response reportedly was to draft a secret, detailed plan which would have divested it of Chevrolet assembly plants and supporting parts manufacturing facilities. [471] When Attorney General Donald A. Turner decided against the suit, however, GM shelved its divestiture proposal. [472] Since 1967, the automakers have taken affirmative steps to preclude and Government-imposed reorganization. By 1971, GM President Edward N. Cole confirmed that he had centralized and otherwise scrambled operations to "make it tougher for the Justice Department to break up the corporation." [473]

2. The Failure of Antitrust Enforcement.—The Department of Justice and the Federal Trade Commission share responsibility for enforcing this Nation's antitrust laws. At least with respect to the ground transportation sector, however, they have compiled a strikingly unimpressive record. Although they possess the legal authority to restructure the auto, bus, truck, and rail industries as proposed, they have failed to exercise it. This past paralysis of will, casts considerable doubt on their future ability to succeed. [474] The Department of Justice, for example, has filed a total of 13 cases to date against General Motors for alleged violations of the antitrust laws; the Federal Trade Commission has filed three. Nine of the cases brought by Justice and all of those filed by the FTC dealt with anticompetitive behavior rather than monopoly structure; they attacked only the symptoms of concentrated economic power without ever assaulting the existence of power itself. Thus, GM was forced to pay nominal fines for charging monopolistic prices on such products as ball bearings, clutch facings, and brake linings. [475] The shared monopoly structure which enabled GM to charge monopolistic prices on these and other automotive products, however, was never assailed. It is also doubtful that these fines affected GM's subsequent behavior. Given the absence of price competition in motor vehicles, fines imposed on General Motors were ultimately passed on to consumers in the form of higher-priced cars and trucks.

Of the four "structural" cases filed against General Motors by the Department of Justice, only two could be termed successful and neither of these involved GM's control of the auto, truck, bus, and rail manufacturing industries. In *du Pont-GM*, the Supreme Court ordered du Pont to divest itself of its 23 percent stock interest in General Motors. [476] In *Euclid*, a consent decree was entered requiring GM to sell its Euclid off-highway earthmoving equipment division to White Motor Co. [477]

Although the two remaining structural cases did involve ground transport, neither was prosecuted to a successful conclusion. On July 6, 1956, Attorney General Herbert Brownell, Jr., announced on national television the filing of a suit against GM for monopolization of the bus industry. At that time GM accounted for more than 85 percent of bus production. The Government's complaint charged that GM had used this monopoly power to drive scores of competitors from the market. For the succeeding 9 years, the case moved through a seemingly endless series of pretrial maneuvers. Finally, on November 30, 1965, just a few days before trial was to begin, Assistant Attorney General Donald Turner authorized acceptance of a consent decree which permitted General Motors to retain its bus monopoly.[478]

Likewise, structural suits brought against GM for monopolization of the locomotive industry were subsequently abandoned. On April 12, 1961, Attorney General Robert F. Kennedy announced that a Federal grand jury had indicted General Motors for monopolization of the locomotive industry. At that time GM accounted for 100 percent of passenger locomotives and 77 percent of all types of locomotives manufactured in the United States. The Government's complaint alleged that GM had used this monopoly power to eliminate its competitors. Two years later, on January 14, 1963, the Department followed with a civil antitrust action brought under section 2 of the Sherman Act and section 7 of the Clayton Act. After several years of protracted litigation, the Government abandoned both suits.[479] Since then, GM has successfully eliminated Alco Products, the country's first manufacturer of diesel-electric locomotives. By 1972, GM not only retained 100 percent of passenger locomotive production, but it also had increased its monopoly share of all types of locomotives manufactured from 77 to 83 percent.[480]

Significantly, not one of the many cases filed against the Big Three automakers dealt with the problem of shared monopoly in the automobile industry. In fact, the only monopoly case ever brought in this industry was filed against Checker Motors more than 25 years ago for its alleged monopolization of the taxicab market.[481]

The failure of both Justice and the FTC to reorganize our anti-competitively structured ground transport manufacturing sector would appear to proceed from two interrelated factors: Political paralysis and the inherently protracted nature of litigation under the existing antitrust laws. A brief review of the Justice Department's ill-fated attempt to reorganize General Motors is illustrative.

Beginning in the late 1940's, the Antitrust Division of the Department of Justice became sharply divided with respect to how General Motors might be competitively restructured. One group of staff attorneys advocated the filing of a comprehensive "big case" against GM which would seek to reorganize that corporation into more manageable and competitive parts. Another group favored bringing a series of "peripheral" cases which would seek to obtain piecemeal divestiture of selected GM facilities.[482]

Initially, promoters of the "big case" predominated. They sought to restructure General Motors through a two-stage process: First, separation of GM from outside control by Du Pont; and, second, dissolution of the corporation into its constituent elements. In 1949 they persuaded Attorney General Tom C. Clark to bring suit to divest Du

Pont of its 23 percent stock interest in the giant automaker. Subsequently, they began to prepare for the filing of an overall divestiture case against GM for monopolization of what they described as a "land transportation market," which included automobiles, trucks, buses, and locomotives.[483] In 1954, however, after an exhaustive trial, the District Court ruled against the Government in *Du Pont-GM* and dismissed the case.[484] The adverse decision was a serious setback to "big case" supporters. Three years later, in 1957, the Supreme Court would reverse and ultimately, in 1961, would order divestiture of Du Pont's stock holdings in General Motors. But in the meantime, the "big case" concept was shelved.

After the trial court's adverse ruling in *Du Pont-GM*, the Antitrust Division changed direction. It embarked upon a series of peripheral cases relating to General Motors' city and intercity bus manufacturing operations. At the time, many in the Division felt that the relatively large scope of *Du Pont-GM* may have contributed to the Government's defeat at trial. They urged, moreover, that the filing of less comprehensive cases might be more acceptable politically. In 1956 the Department of Justice sued GM for monopolization of the bus industry and requested divestiture of its bus production facilities.

GM-Bus was a failure. In the words of one former Justice official, it "was a failure before it started because there was no relief." [485] More specifically, General Motors had combined bus and truck manufacturing within the same facilties. Divestiture of GM bus production, therefore, would necessarily have entailed divestiture of GM truck production as well. For a judge ruling on a comprehensive ground transport case which included autos, buses, trucks, and rails, an order for divestiture of GM's combined bus/truck facilties may have been appropriate. But the judge in *GM-Bus* did not have that case before him. Rather he was confined to ruling exclusively on GM's bus operations. As a result, he lacked the power to order divestiture of GM's combined bus/truck facilities.

In short, the narrow scope of *GM-Bus* effectively precluded the achievement of adequate relief. As one veteran of *GM-Bus* subsequently observed, "it would have been much easier to dissolve General Motors as a corporation than to divest it of its bus business." [486] In 1965, after 9 years of protracted litigation, the Department disposed of the case by reluctantly accepting an innocuous consent decree, whose principal provisions were drafted, at least in part, by GM's antitrust attorneys.[487]

Three years after *GM-Bus* was filed, the Antitrust Division revived consideration of the "big case." In 1959 a large, comprehensive complaint was drafted with separate counts for each of General Motors' separate transport equipment divisions. That same year a Federal grand jury was convened in New York City to investigate GM's overall operations, including its involvement in the automobile, truck, bus, and rail equipment industries. Almost immediately, the investigation was halted. Amid what one former Department attorney described as "mysterious and unprecedented circumstances," the judge refused to allow the Government to subpena any of GM's records.[488] Holding as "extravagant" the Government's request for certain policy documents, District Judge McGohey denied it access even to GM's corporate identification papers.[489] Eventually the Government was able to subpena some information relating principally to GM's locomotive operations.

This setback renewed the Antitrust Division's interest in bringing peripheral cases. Despite the unsatisfactory progress of *GM-Bus* and with the "full recognition," as one Justice attorney noted later, "that adequate relief would be difficult, if not impossible, to obtain," it brought the abortive *GM-Locomotive* cases described earlier. By 1967 both had been abandoned.

The Department never again seriously considered the multi-industry big case. Instead, its focus shifted to the automobile industry, and to the prospect of bringing yet another peripheral case against GM. This time, however, the Department rejected the possibility of securing any structural relief. Unlike its posture in the bus and locomotive cases, it sought to punish "bad" corporate practices. Accordingly, it disregarded repeated recommendations from high-level staff that the auto industry be restructured. In 1966, for example, Eugene J. Metzger assembled a massive 106-page complaint which recommended reorganization of General Motors into the dozens of automotive assembly and parts production facilities which it had previously acquired.[490] That same year, Breyer and Comanor recommended reorganizing GM into "two or three separate companies."[491] In 1968 a staff memorandum authored by Baker, Shepherd, and Hunter proposed a shared-monopoly case which would reorganize GM, Ford, and Chrysler into more manageable and competitive units. That same year, former Assistant Attorney General Donald A. Turner and Gordon Spivack separately recommended that the Department bring structural antitrust action at least against General Motors and Ford.[492] None of these proposals was ever acted upon.

Instead, the Department filed suits against the automobile industry which related to monopolistic symptoms rather than to the monopolistic structure which caused them. In 1969 it brought the *Smog* case, which sought to penalize the automakers for allegedly conspiring to retard the development of pollution control devices. In 1972 it sought in the *Fleet Lease* case to prevent them from allegedly conspiring to fix prices on motor vehicles sold to the car and truck lease market.[493] Both cases were directed at monopolistic conduct. Neither was aimed at the essential element underlying this industry's anticompetitive behavior and unsatisfactory performance: shared monopoly structure.

The Department of Justice as well as the Federal Trade Commission, therefore, have failed for more than three decades to restore competition to one of this Nation's most important economic sectors: ground transportation. To accommodate political pressures, they have avoided bringing the multi-industry suits necessary for adequate relief and have opted instead for protracted and ultimately ineffectual peripheral litigation. "They have only nibbled around the edges," observed one veteran Justice official, "bringing little piecemeal cases which consumed an enormous amount of time, which dragged on for years and years, and which ended up with a two-bit consent decree that really didn't mean anything."[494]

3. The Potential for Congressional Action.—The best chance for implementation of the proposed restructuring, therefore, may rest with Congress. By passing legislation specifically aimed at this problem, it could bypass the dual problems of political paralysis and protracted litigation which have hampered antitrust enforcement in the past. In this regard, several high-level staff members in the Antitrust Division conceded recently that reorganization of highly concentrated industries would require new congressional action.[495]

In the past, however, Congress has failed to take any substantive action to restructure the highly concentrated ground transport industries. Instead, it has attempted to regulate their anticompetitive behavior and thereby to alter their unsatisfactory performance. In short, it has combined Government bureaucratic planning with private monopolistic decisionmaking to create the worst of all possible situations.

With respect to the auto industry, for example, Congress has sought to remedy unsatisfactory performance through pervasive Government control and participation. Dozens of Federal agencies have become involved in the actual design and production of automobiles and trucks. The epicenter of automotive activity, many would contend, has shifted from Detroit to Washington. Federal legislation already affects a wide range of auto and truck components including bumpers, braking systems, seatbelts, headlamps, emission control equipment, tires, ignition systems, doors, power windows, head restraints, accelerator mechanisms, steering columns, door locks, seats, windshields, wheels, and fuel tanks.[496] In addition, other Federal agencies are engaged in the development of advanced automotive engines.[497] Meanwhile, the monopoly structure responsible for the car and truck industries' unsatisfactory performance has been left intact.

Likewise, with regard to the bus and rail manufacturing industries, Congress has sought to regulate rather than to restructure. More specifically, it has authorized Federal agencies to participate in these industries to a degree which approaches nationalization. For instance, it has provided the Urban Mass Transportation Administration (UMTA) and Federal Railroad Administration (FRA) with more than one-half billion dollars to design, develop, and produce standardized buses, rail transit cars, and trains, which would become the industry standard for all federally financed equipment purchases.[498]

UMTA's Transbus project is illustrative of the Government's involvement in both bus and rail transportation. It has as its objective the formulation of a Federal bus design which "will be incorporated into an industry standard for future urban buses purchased under UMTA's capital grant program." [499] Eventually, Transbus will become the only bus available to the riding public. Since UMTA contemplates no change in the monopolistic structure of bus manufacturing, moreover, it is likely that GM will continue to dominate this field. In short, Transbus represents that unique blend of public and private monopoly which often presages the death of free enterprise and the onset of nationalization.

With respect to ground transport, therefore, the choices open to Congress are fundamentally two: competition or public ownership. The first requires new structural legislation to reorganize the auto, truck, bus, and rail industries. The second will naturally evolve in the absence of such legislation. If Congress prefers competition to monopoly, public or private, it will reverse its emphasis on regulation and take action to restructure these industries.

Structural reform, however, is only part of the solution. The long-term process of shifting our emphasis from highway to rail transport, for example, will require a major effort on the part of industry and Government as well as the public. Reorganizing the Big Three motor vehicle manufacturers cannot by itself bring us balanced and efficient transportation; rather it is an essential first step in this direction.

The proposals outlined in this study are not lightly conceived. They are founded on the fundamental tenet of our system of free enterprise, competition; and they are designed to help restore what this country has lacked for years, balanced transportation. Their disregard could result in a development as abhorrent as it is otherwise imminent; Government ownership of the automobile, truck, bus, and rail manufacturing industries.[500]

NOTES

PREFACE

1.   Robert L. Lineberry and Ira Sharkansky, *Urban Politics and Public Policy* (New York: Harper and Row, 1971), p. 270.
2.   George M. Smerk, *Urban Transportation: The Federal Role* (Bloomington: Indiana University Press, 1963), p. 35.

CHAPTER 1: APPROACHES TO URBAN TRANSPORTATION

1.   A sampling of some of these is contained in a recent bibliography by the authors entitled *Urban Transportation: The Social Dimensions: An Annotated Bibliography* (Monticello, Ill.: Council of Planning Librarians, Aug. 1973).
2.   The concept of ideology has a long and controversial history, and no rigorous definition will be offered here. For an extensive analysis of this concept, see Willard A. Mullins, "On the Concept of Ideology in Political Science," *American Political Science Review*, 66 (June 1972), pp. 498–510.
3.   See, for example, Robert S. Friedman, "State Politics and Highways," *Politics in the American States*, ed. Herbert Jacob and Kenneth N. Vines (Boston: Little, Brown, 1965).
4.   Dallas County Commissioner Roy Orr recently observed that if "those socialists" thought they were going to divert the money paid by motorists for better roads to undermine the great American automotive industry, they were dead wrong.
5.   Francis C. Turner, former Federal Highway Administrator, is an enthusiastic advocate of this approach. See, for example, his "Moving People on Urban Highways," *Traffic Quarterly*, 24 (July 1970), pp. 321–333.
6.   Italics added. The apparent inconsistency produced by the fact that it is the public highway department and not motorists who determine where the roads go does not appear disturbing to the proponents.
7.   An interesting, informative, and amusing assessment of the logic of this position is contained in an article by Ezra J. Mishan, "Pangloss on Pollution," *Swedish Journal of Economics* (Mar. 1971) pp. 113–120.
8.   Prime illustrations of these views may be found in W. Norman Kennedy, "The Urban Form and Transit," and Vergil G. Stover, "The Capabilities and Cost Effectiveness of Transit," papers delivered at the Symposium on Urban Transportation jointly

sponsored by Southern Methodist University's Urban Institute and the Dallas Central Business District Association at the Statler-Hilton Hotel in Dallas, Texas, Oct. 26, 1972.

9.   The classic work which epitomizes this approach is the American Academy of Arts and Science, *Conference on Poverty and Transportation* (Springfield, Va.: National Technical Information Service, 1968).

10.   Sumner Myers, "Personal Transportation for the Poor," in American Academy of Arts and Sciences, *Conference on Poverty and Transportation* (Springfield, Va.: National Technical Information Service, 1968).

11.   Cordell K. Ballard, "Transportation Dependents," *Traffic Quarterly,* 12 (Jan. 1967), pp. 83–90.

12.   Gerald Kraft and Thomas A. Domencich, "Free Transit," in American Academy of Arts and Sciences, *Conference on Poverty and Transportation* (Springfield, Va.: National Technical Information Services, 1968).

13.   Helen Leavitt, *Superhighway-Superhoax* (Garden City, N. Y.: Doubleday, 1970).

14.   A. Q. Mowbray, *Road to Ruin* (N. Y.: Lippincott, 1968).

15.   Edward Ayres, *What's Good for GM* (Nashville: Aurora Publishers, 1970).

16.   See, for example, Delbert A. Taebel, "Citizen Groups, Public Policy and Urban Transportation," *Traffic Quarterly,* 27 (Oct. 1973), pp. 503–515. Also see Ben Kelley, *The Pavers and the Paved* (New York: Brown, 1971).

17.   The Conservation Society and subsequently the Sierra Club fought the San Antonio freeway battle for 13 years. And the latter was involved in suits against the Environmental Protection Agency over air quality standards stemming from potential auto pollution.

18.   See, for example, William B. Furlong, "Profile of an Alienated Voter," *Saturday Review of the Society,* 55 (July 1972), pp. 48–51.

19.   Emma Rothschild, "The Great Transpo Expo," *New York Review of Books* (July 20, 1972).

20.   George Smerk, "The Urban Transportation Problem: A Policy Vacuum," *Urban Transportation Policy: New Perspectives,* ed. David R. Miller (Lexington, Mass.: Heath, 1972), p. 41.

21.   An interesting and useful exposition of the main features of the externalities problem is contained in an article by Ralph Turvey, "Side Effects of Resource Use," in Henry Jarrett, ed., *Environmental Quality in a Growing Economy* (Baltimore: Johns Hopkins, 1966).

22.   See, for example, Robert Goodman, *After the Planners* (New York: Simon and Schuster, 1971).

CHAPTER 2: THE URBAN TRANSPORTATION SYSTEM IN RETROSPECT

1.   For a detailed discussion of transportation in the United States, see Charles Luna, *The UTU Handbook of Transportation in America* (New York: Popular Library, 1971), pp. 5–16.

2.   Richard C. Wade, *The Urban Frontier* (Cambridge, Mass.: Harvard University Press, 1959), p. 40.

3.   Ibid., p. 190.

4.   Sam B. Warner, Jr., *Streetcar Suburbs* (Cambridge, Mass.: Harvard University Press and MIT Press, 1962), p. 15.

5.   Glen E. Holt, "The Changing Perception of Urban Pathology," *Cities in American History,* ed. Kenneth T. Jackson and Stanley K. Schultz (New York: Knopf, 1972), pp. 324–343.

6.   Ibid., p. 328.

7.   See George Smerk, "The Streetcar: Shaper of American Cities," *Traffic Quarterly,* 21 (Oct. 1967), p. 570.

8.   Ibid., p. 573.

9.   Warner, op. cit., p. 16.

10. Holt, op. cit., p. 333.
11. Ibid., p. 338.
12. Harian W. Gilmore, *Transportation and the Growth of Cities* (Glencoe, Ill.: Free Press, 1953), p. 116.
13. Kenneth T. Jackson, "The Crabgrass Frontier: 150 Years of Suburban Growth in America," *The Urban Experience: Themes in American History,* ed. Raymond A. Mohl and James F. Richardson (Belmont, Calif.: Wadsworth, 1973), p. 215.
14. James H. Johnson, *Urban Geography* (New York: Pergamon Press, 2d ed., 1972), p. 43.
15. Kenneth R. Schneider, *Autokind vs. Mankind* (New York: Schocken, 1972), p. 58.
16. Colin Clark, "Transport—Maker and Breaker of Cities," *Town Planning Review,* 28 (1957–58), p. 248.
17. For an interesting study on the development of the automobile and its impact on American society, see James J. Flink, *America Adopts the Automobile, 1895-1910* (Cambridge, Mass.: MIT Press, 1970).
18. Luna, op. cit., p. 22.
19. As cited in Ben Kelley, *The Pavers and the Paved* (New York: Scribner's, 1971), p. 7.
20. Helen Leavitt, *Superhighway-Superhoax* (Garden City, N. Y.: Doubleday, 1970), p. 38.
21. John B. Rae, *The Road and the Car in American Life* (Cambridge, Mass.: MIT Press, 1971), p. 66.
22. Wilfred Owen, *The Accessible City* (Washington, D. C.: Brookings Institution, 1972), p. 6.
23. For a brief summary of some of the more deleterious effects, see Edgar M. Hoover, *Motor Metropolis: Some Observations on Motor Transportation in America* (Pittsburgh: Center for Regional Economic Studies, 1965).
24. U. S. Department of Housing and Urban Development, *Tomorrow's Transportation* (Washington, D. C.: U. S. Government Printing Office, 1968), p. 11.
25. See Barry Benepe, "Pedestrian in the City," *Traffic Quarterly,* 19 (Jan. 1965), p. 29.
26. One ray of hope is that bicycle sales in 1972 exceeded automobile sales for the first time, 13 million to 10 million. See *Harper's Magazine,* 246 (Apr. 1973), p. 12.
27. Owen, op. cit., p. 27.
28. C. West Churchman, *The Systems Approach* (New York: Delta, 1968), p. 29.

CHAPTER 3: PUBLIC POLICY AND URBAN TRANSPORTATION

1. David Easton, "An Approach to the Analysis of Political Systems," *World Politics,* 9 (1957), pp. 383-400.
2. Part of this discussion is drawn from Thomas R. Dye, *Understanding Public Policy* (Englewood Cliffs, N. J.: Prentice Hall, 2d ed., 1975), pp. 17-38.
3. Arthur F. Bentley, *The Process of Government* (Bloomington, Ind.: Principia Press, 1935).
4. David B. Truman, *The Governmental Process* (New York: Knopf, 1951).
5. Michael Lipsky, "Street-Level Bureaucracy and the Analysis of Urban Reform," *Urban Affairs Quarterly,* 6 (June 1971), pp. 391-409.
6. Orion F. White, "The Dialectical Organization—An Alternative to Bureaucracy," *Public Administration Review,* 29 (Jan.-Feb. 1969), pp. 32-42.
7. For a rather extensive discussion of this process, see Yehezkel Dror, *Public Policy-Making Re-examined* (San Francisco: Chandler, 1968).
8. Charles E. Lindblom, "The Science of Muddling Through," *Public Administration Review,* 19 (Spring 1959).
9. See, for example, Louis C. Gawthrop, *Administrative Politics and Social Change* (New York: St. Martin's, 1971), esp. pp. 41-56; and Gordon Fellman, *The Deceived*

Majority: Politics and Protest in Middle America (New Brunswick, N. J.: Transaction Books, 1973).

10.   See David Easton, *A Framework for Political Analysis* (Englewood Cliffs, N. J.: Prentice Hall, 1965).

11.   See, for example, M. Margaret Conway and Frank B. Feigert, *Political Analysis* (Boston: Allyn and Bacon, 1972), esp. chap. 9, "Systems Analysis."

12.   Irving Louis Horowitz, ed., *The Use and Abuse of Social Science* (New Brunswick, N. J.: Transaction Books, 1971), pp. 112–113.

13.   The Federal Aid Highway Act of 1970 also contains some provisions for certain kinds of improvements to city streets.

14.   This section relies heavily on Donald Dewees et al., *Mass Transit and the Highway Trust Fund* (NTIS, PB 190 951) Jan. 1970.

15.   Jay Stanford, *Local Government Fiscal Structure in Texas* (Arlington, Tex.: Texas Urban Development Commission, 1972), p. 17.

16.   Douglass B. Lee, Jr., *The Costs of Private Automobile Usage in the City of San Francisco* (National Technical Information Service, PB-220 222) Apr. 1972.

17.   Ibid., p. 31.

18.   Theodore W. Kheel, "The Port Authority Strangles New York," in David M. Gordon, ed., *Problems in Political Economy: An Urban Perspective* (Lexington, Mass.: Heath, 1971), p. 448.

19.   Ibid.

20.   Ibid., p. 445.

21.   U. S. Department of Transportation, *A Progress Report on National Transportation Policy,* May 1974, p. 38.

22.   Dewees, loc. cit.

23.   John K. Higgins, "Whose Free Ride? Transit Subsidies," *New Republic* (May 6, 1972), pp. 13 ff.

24.   Carter Goodrich, *Government Promotion of American Canals and Railroads, 1800–1890* (New York: Columbia University Press, 1960).

25.   George M. Smerk, *Urban Transportation: The Federal Role* (Bloomington: Indiana University Press, 1965), p. 119.

26.   As cited by *Environmental Action,* May 29, 1971.

27.   Wilfred Owen, *Strategy for Mobility* (Washington, D. C.: Brookings Institution, 1964), p. 133.

28.   Charles L. Dearing, *American Highway Policy* (Washington, D. C.: Brookings Institution, 1941), p. 99.

29.   Herman Mertins, Jr., and David R. Miller, *Urban Transportation Policy: Fact or Fiction* (Syracuse, N. Y.: Urban Transportation Institute Occasional Paper No. 2, 1970), p. 4.

30.   For an excerpt of the act, see George M. Smerk, ed., *Readings in Urban Transportation* (Bloomington: Indiana University Press, 1968), pp. 231–234.

31.   For a more extended discussion of the act, see Smerk, op. cit., pp. 131–139; Mertins and Miller, op. cit., pp. 5–7; Ben Kelley, *The Pavers and the Paved* (New York: Brown, 1971), pp. 21–38.

32.   Section 108, Public Law 84-627. For an excerpted version of this act, see Smerk, op. cit., pp. 234–236.

33.   The hypocrisy of this claim is developed by Kelley, op. cit., pp. 9–10.

34.   Mertins and Miller, op. cit., p. 5.

35.   Smerk, op. cit., p. 131.

36.   As cited by Nancy Hubby, "Transportation Legislation 1960–70: Evolution, Perhaps Revolution," *Planning Comment,* 8, no. 2.

37.   Smerk, op. cit., pp. 48–61.

38.   For a further discussion of the act, see Hubby, op. cit., p. 4.

39.   "The Transportation System of Our Nation," message from the President of the United States, 87th Congress, 2nd Session, House of Representatives Document No. 384, April 5, 1962.

40.   For an excerpted version of the act, see Smerk, op. cit., pp. 310–318.

41.   In Congress, it is easier to promise than to give, and although $75 million was authorized, only $60 million was appropriated for the first year.

42.   For a discussion of the Federal Aid Highway Act of 1970, see *Environmental Action,* May 29, 1971.

43.   Federal Aid Highway Act of 1972, Report of the Committee on Banking, Housing and Urban Affairs to accompany S. 3939, Report No. 92-1103, 92nd Congress, 2nd Session (Washington, D. C.: Government Printing Office, September 8, 1972), p. 5.

44.   For an extensive analysis of this act, see Robert Cassidy, "The Highway Act: More Platypus than Policy," *Planning* 39 (Sept. 1973), pp. 21–23.

45.   George M. Smerk, "The Urban Transportation Problem: A Policy Vacuum?" *Urban Transportation Policy: New Perspectives,* ed. David R. Miller (Lexington, Mass.: Lexington, 1970), p. 15.

CHAPTER 4: THE ECONOMIC SYSTEM AND URBAN TRANSPORTATION PRIORITIES

1.   Under a more comprehensive definition of mass transit—i.e., one that encompassed the function performed and the impact on urban life rather than focusing solely on the technological characteristics of the vehicles involved—the bus would not be considered mass transit at all, merely a hardware appendage to the auto system with the capacity to carry somewhat more passengers. See, e.g., James Cornehls and Delbert Taebel, "Mass Transit: What Are the Limits?" *Consulting Engineer* (Mar. 1974).

2.   An article in *American Motorist* (June 1969), the official magazine of the American Automobile Association, assured its readers that despite the various anti-auto propaganda attacks, the average American's "love affair with the automobile continued to be ardent." A two-page drawing of a young couple surrounded by hearts and embracing one another across the hood of a new car was used to illustrate this argument. See Ben Kelley, *The Pavers and the Paved* (New York: Brown, 1971).

3.   Frank Ikard, president of the American Petroleum Institute, in "Where Oilmen Stand on Roads and Cars," *Highway User* (Feb. 1969).

4.   Although the significance of the point seems to escape the survey takers, more people prefer public transit (subways, commuter trains, and so forth) in areas where such facilities exist—and have existed for some time—than in areas where they do not. The ultimate in the myopia involved here is to be found in the statement that "Westerners have a greater preference for the automobile than do Easterners."

5.   Kelley, op. cit., pp. 152-153 et seq.

6.   See, e.g., Louis Kohlmeier, Jr., "The Federal Highway Program," reprinted in Robert Haveman and Robert Hamprin, eds., *The Political Economy of Federal Policy* (New York: Harper and Row, 1973), pp. 226–230.

7.   See, e.g., William G. Shepherd, *Market Power and Economic Welfare* (New York: Random House, 1970), pp. 232–234. While the recent gasoline shortage and the accompanying boom in small car sales produced an unusually large profit for American Motors, no one really expects this to be more than a short-term windfall.

8.   Shepherd, op. cit., p. 238.

9.   "GM Year-End Profits Up in '75," *Fort Worth Star-Telegram* (Feb. 1, 1976), p. 6A.

10.   Senate Committee on Public Works, Subcommittee on Air and Water Pollution, Air Pollution 1970, Part 5 (GPO, 1970), pp. 1609–1610. The logical traps into which the present indirect methods of raising tax revenues can lead are nowhere more aptly demonstrated than in Mr. Iacocca's remarks regarding the taxes generated by the automobile and truck industry. Cars do not pay taxes; makers of cars pay taxes. This statement, a very effective scare tactic, assumes that if people were not making cars they would be sitting around doing nothing and hence not generating any taxable income. Income is of course income whether it comes from making autos or pollution

control equipment. If production shifts from the former to the latter, then pollution control equipment could become a larger generator of tax revenue.

11.   U. S. Department of Commerce, Office of Business Economics, *Survey of Current Business*, 53 (April. 1973), pp. 13–14.

12.   The principal factors that distinguish these key industries can be summarized as follows:

1. *Industrial Interdependence-Backward and Forward Linkage.* A number of industries have extensive backward linkages (their purchases form a significant part of the sales of other industries) and forward linkages (their output makes up a significant part of the purchases of other industries). Their importance thus derives not only from their own output and employment but from that of all the other industries that are significantly related to them.

2. *Price-Cost Effect Industries.* Certain products that are used as inputs by other industries have a strong impact on the cost structures of those other industries. The latter industries, in turn, "pass on" those cost increases together with an additional markup equal to their accustomed margin, thus producing a second round of price-pressure effects. The steel industry, for example, has long been regarded as the one that has the most significant of these price-cost "pyramiding" effects.

3. *Growth Industries.* An industry that grows at an especially high rate from year to year and hence contributes significantly to the overall rate of growth of GNP is an important industry indeed.

4. *Wage-Setting Demonstration Effect.* Wage rates won by workers in the key industries tend to set the pattern for later settlements in other sectors of the economy.

5. *Full-Employment Bottleneck Industries.* Not all industries expand at the same rate during periods of rapid economic advancement: i.e., demand grows more rapidly in some industries than in others. Once full employment is reached in these rapid-growth industries, their inability to produce further supplies for other industries and/or consumers can create shortages and thus further price pressures. See Robert T. Averitt, *The Dual Economy* (New York: Norton, 1968), pp. 38-42.

13.   John Kenneth Galbraith, *The New Industrial State* (Boston: Houghton Mifflin, 1967), pp. 9–10.

14.   Averitt, op. cit., p. 7.

15.   Metal cutting and metal forming machine tools, plus internal combustion engines. Idem.

16.   *Fortune 500: The Largest U. S. Industrial Corporations* (May 1973), pp. 222–224.

17.   "Input-Output Matrix of the United States Economy," *Fortune* (1966). The Fortune input-output table for the U. S. economy was compiled in 1966. The dollar figures used are in 1966 dollars and hence grossly understate the absolute importance of the motor vehicle industry. Though the tables are now somewhat dated, the coefficients on which the interindustry relationships are based are generally believed to change only very slowly. In addition, the principle of interrelatedness, which is what we wish to illustrate, is not affected by the lag. If anything, the total effect is greater now than in 1966.

18.   Bradford C. Snell, *American Ground Transport: A Proposal for Restructuring the Automobile, Truck, Bus and Rail Industries.* Testimony presented to the Subcommittee on Antitrust and Monopoly of the Committee on the Judiciary, U. S. Senate (Washington, U. S. Government Printing Office, 1974), p. 27. This entire section relies heavily on this exhaustively documented study.

19.   Ibid., p. 30.

20.   *United States* vs. *National City Lines*, 1951 Trade Cases.

21.   Snell, op. cit., p. 31.

22.   *Bus Transportation* (May, 1974), p. 80.

23.   An interesting and instructive set of readings on the subject of how regulatory agencies are converted into tools of the industry supposedly being regulated is contained in Samuel Krislov and Lloyd Musolf (eds.), *The Politics of Regulation* (Boston:

Houghton Mifflin, 1964). See also Ralph Nader, "Efficiency and Regulatory Policy," in Robert Haveman and Robert Hamprin (eds.), *The Political Economy of Federal Policy* (New York: Harper and Row, 1973), pp. 267-272.
24. Cited in S. Lazarus and L. Ross, "Rating Nader," *New York Review of Books* (June 28, 1973), p. 31 (Emphasis added.)
25. See, e.g., Senator Lee Metcalf's description of how a Civil Aernoautics Board Advisory Committee, one made up almost exclusively of persons with the interests of the airlines in mind, dispensed with the formality of meeting at the CAB's own offices and convened, instead, at One Chase Manhattan Plaza, the office of the Advisory Committee's chairman, a gentleman who was also Chase Manhattan's vice-president in charge of airline finances. Not surprisingly, the Committee suggested that the federal government provide the airlines with a large subsidy to improve their liquidity position. Lee Metcalf, "The Vested Oracles: How Industry Regulates Government," in Haveman and Hamprin, note 18, supra, p. 53.
26. Cited in Edward Ayres, *What's Good for GM* (Nashville: Aurora, 1970), p. 66.
27. Ibid., pp. 66-67.
28. See Jerry Landauer, "Milk Scandal Is Threatening to Blow Up Any Day," *Wall Street Journal* (Nov. 5, 1973) and Edward Morgan, "ITT: The Real Scandal," *The Progressive* (May 1972), pp. 3-10.
29. "The US's Lopsided Transportation Budget," *Forbes* 102 (Oct. 1968), pp. 40-51.
30. Sam Bowles, "Economists as Servants of Power," *American Economic Review* (May 1975), pp. 129-132.

CHAPTER 5: THE POLITICAL ESTABLISHMENT

1. The strongest arguments are voiced by David B. Truman, *The Governmental Process* (New York: Knopf, 1951).
2. See Lester W. Milbrath, *The Washington Lobbyists* (Chicago: Rand McNally, 1963). For a more current overview, see Thomas P. Murphy, *Pressures upon Congress: Legislation by Lobby* (Woodbury, N.Y.: Barron's Educational Service, Inc., 1973).
3. For an interesting discussion of the highway lobby, see Ben Kelley, *The Pavers and the Paved* (New York: Brown, 1971) chap. 3; John Robinson, *Highways and Our Environment* (New York: McGraw-Hill, 1971) chap. 20; Gordon Fellman, *The Deceived Majority: Politics and Protest in Middle America* (New Brunswick, N. J.: Transaction Books, 1973), pp. 175-184.
4. George Denison and Kenneth Y. Tomlinson, "Let's Put the Brakes on the Highway Lobby," *Reader's Digest*, 94 (May 1969), pp. 97-102.
5. As quoted in Kelley, op. cit., p. 40.
6. Robinson, op. cit., p. 292.
7. "The US's Lopsided Transportation Budget," *Forbes* 102 (Oct. 1968), pp. 40-51.
8. Edward Ayres, *What's Good for GM* (Nashville: Aurora, 1970), pp. 66-68.
9. David R. Hyde and Payson Wolff, "The AMA: Power, Purpose and Politics in Organized Medicine," *Yale Law Journal*, 63 (May 1954), pp. 938-947.
10. Emmette S. Redford et al., *Politics and Government in the United States* (New York: Harcourt, 1965), p. 212; For a concise account of factors accounting for the strength of interest groups, see Fellman, op. cit., pp. 170-190.
11. Robinson, op. cit., p. 321.
12. Richard Herbert, "How the AAA Uses Its Members to Pave the Way for More Freeways," *Washingtonian*, June 1970.
13. For a discussion of these interest groups, see Edmond L. Kanwitt, "The Urban Mass Transportation Administration: Its Problems and Promise," *Urban Transportation Policy: New Perspectives*, ed. David R. Miller (Lexington, Mass.: Lexington, 1972), pp. 98-99.
14. *The Texas Observer*, Feb. 15, 1974, p. 10.

15. Daniel P. Moynihan, "New Roads and Urban Chaos," *Reporter* (Apr. 14, 1960).

16. David Hapgood, "The Highwaymen," *Inside the System*, ed. Charles Peters and Timothy J. Adams (New York: Praeger, 1970), pp. 140–141.

17. Ibid., pp. 142–143.

18. See Douglas Cater, *Power in Washington* (New York: Random House, 1964).

19. J. Leiper Freeman, *The Political Process: Executive Bureau-Legislative Committee Relations* (Garden City, N. Y.: Doubleday, 1955).

20. Daniel M. Berman, *In Congress Assembled* (New York: Macmillan, 1964), p. 126. Recent changes in the House of Representatives, however, may modify the power of committee chairmen.

21. David E. Rosenbaum, "Panel Bars Road Funds for Building Mass Transit," *New York Times*, Aug. 10, 1972.

22. "Transit Amendment Voted Down after Intense House Campaign," *The Concrete Opposition*, May 1973, p. 4.

23. "Suburbia: Potential but Unrealized House Influence," *Congressional Quarterly*, Apr. 6, 1974, pp. 878-880.

24. As cited by Fellman, op. cit., p. 176.

25. This fragmentation was resolved to some extent in 1975 when most transportation matters were shifted to the Public Works Committee, which was renamed the Public Works and Transportation Committee under H Res 988. The Banking and Currency Committee lost its jurisdiction over mass transit, and the Interstate and Foreign Commerce Committee was stripped of its jurisdiction over civil aviation. The latter committee, however, retained control over railroads.

26. "Highway Boys Win Another One," *Wall Street Journal*, Oct. 10, 1972.

27. Herman Mertins, Jr., "National Transportation Planning: Dimensions and Challenges," *Public Administration Review*, 30 (May/June 1971), p. 361.

28. For an evaluation of the efforts by the first secretary of transportation, see Robinson, op. cit., p. 296. Also see Alan S. Boyd, "The Federal Department of Transportation," *Traffic Quarterly* 21 (Oct. 1967), pp. 467–470.

29. For a discussion of the activities of various department agencies, see Grant M. Davis, *The Department of Transportation* (Lexington, Mass.: Heath, 1970), p. 119. Also see Kanwit, op. cit., pp. 77-124. The functions of the Bureau of Public Roads *as an official agency* were absorbed by the Federal Highway Administration in 1970.

30. Robinson, op. cit., p. 295.

31. As cited by Kelley, op. cit., p. 4.

32. Peter Woll, *American Bureaucracy* (New York: Norton, 1963), p. 134.

33. Kelley, op. cit., p. 17.

34. Emma Rothschild, "The Great Transpo Expo," *New York Review of Books* (July 20, 1972), p. 27.

35. Ibid.

36. Colin Buchanan, "Urban Transportation: The Scope of the New Technology," *Future Directions for Research in Urban Transportation* (Paris: OECD, 1969), p. 96.

37. Ibid.

38. Rothschild, op. cit.

39. Richard Barshess, "The Department of Transportation: Concept and Structure," *Western Political Quarterly* (Sept. 1970), p. 500.

40. Robert S. Friedman, "State Politics and Highways," *Politics in the American States*, ed. Herbert Jacob and Kenneth Vines (Boston: Little, Brown, 1965), p. 411.

41. Alan Lupo, Frank Colcord, and Edmund P. Fowler, *Rites of Way: The Politics of Transportation in Boston and the U. S. City* (Boston: Little, Brown, 1971), p. 181.

42. As cited in the *Texas Observer*, May 11, 1973, p. 13.

43. "State Highway Trust Funds under Heavy Attack," *The Concrete Opposition* (Mar. 1972), pp. 1-2.

44. Ibid.

45. Friedman, op. cit.

46. Ibid., p. 421.

47. Ibid., p. 423.
48. Ibid., p. 421.
49. Frank C. Colcord, "Decision-Making and Transportation Policy," *Southwestern Social Science Quarterly*, 48 (Dec. 1967), p. 396.
50. This fragmentation, apparent in many cities, is hardly the case in New York, where through the efforts of Robert Moses a gigantic and monolithic organization was developed which exercised a stranglehold on the city's transportation system. For an extensive analysis, see Robert A. Caro, *The Power Broker: Robert Moses and the Fall of New York* (New York: Knopf, 1974).
51. Lupo, Colcord, and Fowler, op. cit., pp. 210ff.
52. For a discussion of the various subroles which planners may assume and the ideological basis of these roles, see Susan S. Fainstein and Norman I. Fainstein, "City Planning and Political Values," *Urban Affairs Quarterly*, 6 (Mar. 1971), pp. 341–362.
53. Colcord, "Decision-Making and Transportation Policy," p. 394.
54. Lupo et al., op. cit., p. 182.
55. For a discussion of how such elections fared in five American cities, see Matthew A. Coogan, et al., *Transportation Politics in Atlanta* (Washington: National Technical Information Service, 1970).
56. See Edward C. Banfield and James Q. Wilson, *City Politics* (New York: Vintage, 1963), pp. 18–32.

CHAPTER 6: THE OUTSIDERS

1. Louis Wirth, "Urbanism as a Way of Life," *American Journal of Sociology*, 44 (July 1938), pp. 8–20.
2. Ibid., p. 16.
3. Lewis M. Schneider, *Marketing Urban Mass Transit* (Boston: Harvard University Press, 1965), p. 27. There is very little systematic, continuous compilation of data (such as a census) which reflect the impact of the transportation system on various subgroups, e.g. the poor, the elderly, and minorities. Such data are usually found only in one-time studies dealing with a particular population in a specific place. As a result, not all of the data contained in this chapter are for the same years, and several of the studies cited have not been updated recently. Where we have used data which are several years out of date, we do so with the understanding that nothing in recent history that has come to our attention would contradict the conclusion derived.
4. U. S. Department of Commerce, Bureau of the Census, *Statistical Abstract of the United States, 1973* (Washington, D. C.: 1973), p. 332; and John F. Kain and John R. Meyer, "Interrelationships of Transportation and Poverty: Summary of Conference on Transportation and Poverty," in American Academy of Arts and Sciences, *Conference on Poverty and Transportation* (Springfield, Va.: National Technical Information Service, 1968), p. 5.
5. National Advisory Commission on Civil Disorders, *Report of the National Advisory Commission on Civil Disorders* (New York: Bantam Books, 1968), p. 114.
6. The Governor's Commission on the Los Angeles Riots, *Violence in the City—An End or a Beginning?* (Los Angeles: State of California, 1965), p. 65.
7. National Advisory Commission on Civil Disorders, op. cit., p. 392.
8. Ibid., p. 418.
9. Transportation Research Institute, *Latent Demand for Urban Transportation* (Pittsburgh: Carnegie-Mellon University, 1968), pp. 60–61.
10. U. S. Department of Commerce, Bureau of the Census, *Statistical Abstract of the United States, 1973* (Washington, D.C.: U. S. Government Printing Office, 1973), p. 17.
11. David Greytak, *Residential Segregation, Metropolitan Decentralization, and the Journey to Work* (Springfield, Va.: National Technical Information Service, 1970), p. 3.
12. Ibid., p. 9.

13. Ibid.
14. The following discussion is based on Janet S. Rankin, *Commuting: Transportation for Workers in Houston's Central City* (Houston: U. S. Department of Labor, 1970).
15. Transportation Research Institute, op. cit., p. 71.
16. S. J. Bernstein, "Mass Transit and the Urban Ghetto," *Traffic Quarterly*, 27 (July 1973), p. 436.
17. Ibid., p. 436.
18. Ibid., p. 440.
19. The following discussion is based on Transportation Research Institute, op. cit., pp. 12–38.
20. Cordelle K. Ballard, "Transportation Dependents," *Traffic Quarterly*, 21 (Jan. 1967), pp. 86–87.
21. Bernstein, op. cit., pp. 436–437.
22. U. S. House Committee on Public Works, Sub-Committee on Public Buildings and Grounds, Hearing to consider accommodation for Handicapped on Metro System, June 29, 1972 (Washington, D. C.: U. S. Government Printing Office, 1972), pp. 32-34.
23. Transportation Research Institute, op. cit., p. 48.
24. Ibid., p. 51.
25. Sumner Myers, "Personal Transportation for the Poor" in American Academy of Arts and Sciences, *Conference on Poverty and Transportation* (Springfield, Va.: National Technical Information Service, 1968).
26. Kain and Meyer, op. cit., p. 10.
27. Myers recognizes this problem and offers a companion solution which we will deal with later.
28. Myers, op. cit., p. 22.
29. S. Rosenbloom, "Taxis, Jitneys and Poverty," in American Academy of Arts and Sciences, *Conference on Poverty and Transportation* (Springfield, Va.: National Technical Information Service, 1968), p. 28.
30. Ballard, op. cit., p. 89.
31. For a critical discussion of this proposal, see Gerald Kraft and Thomas A. Domencich, "Free Transit," in American Academy of Arts and Sciences, *Conference on Poverty and Transportation* (Springfield, Va.: National Technical Information Service, 1968). For discussions of increased subsidization for public transportation, see Sumner Myers, "Turning Transit Subsidies into 'Compensatory Transportation,' " *City*, 6 (Summer 1972), pp. 17-21; Allan Altschuler, "Transit Subsidies: By Whom, For Whom?" *AIP Journal*, 35 (March 1969) pp. 84–89; and John K. Higgins, "Whose Free Ride? Transit Subsidies," *New Republic*, 166, No. 19 (May 6, 1972), p. 13.
32. Kraft and Domencich, op. cit., p. 18.
33. Ibid., p. 4.
34. For a further discussion of this point, see Kain and Meyer, op. cit., p. 14.

CHAPTER 7: URBAN DESIGN AND THE ENVIRONMENT

1. Ian McHarg, *Design with Nature* (Garden City, N. Y.: Doubleday, 1971), pp. 24–26.
2. Richard F. Muth, *Urban Economic Problems* (New York: Harper, 1975), p. 32.
3. Ibid., pp. 56–59.
4. Peter Wolf, *The Future of the City: New Directions in Urban Planning* (New York: Whitney Library of Design, 1974), p. 19.
5. Raymond Murphy, *The American City: An Urban Geography* (New York: McGraw-Hill, 1966), p. 219.
6. University of Texas at Arlington, *Linear City: Rapid Transit as a Determinant of Urban Form* (Arlington: Department of Architecture, 1973), pp. 10–11.
7. Ibid., pp. 10–12.
8. Examples of these may be found in Sam Bass Warner, Jr., *Streetcar Suburbs*

(Cambridge, Mass.: Harvard University Press, 1962), and Robert M. Fogelson, *The Fragmented Metropolis* (Cambridge, Mass.: Harvard University Press, 1967).

9.   Cambridge, Mass.: MIT Press, 1960.

10.   Ibid., p. 96.

11.   Ibid., p. 47.

12.   Joseph Dechiara and Lee Koppelman, *Urban Planning and Design Criteria* (New York: Van Nostrand, 2d ed., 1975), p. 239.

13.   One of the sad ironies of the quest to reduce congestion by building ever greater numbers of larger urban freeways, which in time helped destroy the essence of the city, is that the quantity and quality of roadways apparently bears no relation to traffic congestion. Predictions that traffic would "grind to a halt" were not borne out, nor were predictions that traffic speed would be improved. In a recent study, J. Michael Thomson has produced data which show that average traffic speeds in widely diverse world cities with differing car populations and unlike road systems tend to settle at about 10 miles per hour.

Average Traffic Speeds Recorded in City Centers during Peak Hours

	Miles per hour
London	10
Paris	10
Calcutta	7–10
New York	10
Athens	9–12
Manila	7
Birmingham (England)	13

Note: *Methods of Traffic Limitation in Urban Areas* (Paris: Organization for Economic Cooperation and Development, 1972), p. 89.

14.   Wilfred Owen, *The Accessible City* (Washington: Brookings Institution, 1972), p. 9, citing Ada Louise Huxtable.

15.   From "L. A. Freeway," a song by Guy Clark.

16.   While the number of autos registered increased two and one-half times from 1940 to 1973, the number of trucks and buses expanded almost four times.

17.   J. R. Meyer, J. F. Kain, and M. Wohl missed the point of the influences of the decentralized urban transportation system when they argued that there should be a negative correlation between city transit and the decentralization trend. *The Urban Transportation Problem* (Cambridge, Mass.: Harvard University Press, 1965), p. 44. Since the skilled labor force is mobile and can go anywhere in the city or on the fringe, and the need for locating near a central transportation terminal is removed, the incentive to central location is gone. Thus it is not the demise or decline of rapid transit systems which leads to sprawl. The correct way to phrase the hypothesis is to observe if there is a correlation between the extensiveness of the auto-highway system between cities and their degree of decentralization.

18.   Wolf, op. cit., p. 21.

19.   Ibid., p. 25.

20.   Ibid., p. 27.

21.   Ibid., p. 31.

22.   Ibid., p. 25.

23.   See R. U. Ayres and M. L. Walker, *An Aggregated Impact Model for Environmental Pollutants* (Washington: International Research and Technology Corp., 1970).

24.   A. Q. Mowbray, *Road to Ruin* (Philadelphia: Lippincott, 1969), pp. 36–39.
25.   Recently, this issue has come to the fore in a struggle between environmentalists and the real-estate-interest-dominated San Antonio City Council over efforts to continue urban fringe development of a 129-acre shopping mall in the middle of the Edwards aquifer and hence directly over the city's water supply. Earlier developments included the siting of the University of Texas San Antonio campus directly over the recharge zone and the subsequent tentative approval of a plan to build Ranch Town, a community for 8,000 people, over the recharge area. "San Antonio Citizens Challenge Development over Aquifer," *The Texas Observer,* 68, no. 1 (Jan. 16, 1976), p. 6.
26.   Ecotones are transitional zones between natural geographic areas where changes in botanical characteristics take place. These areas are critical in the maintenance of plant and wildlife.
27.   John Esposito, *Vanishing Air* (New York: Grossman, 1970), p. 28.
28.   Philip Nobile and John Deedy, eds., *The Complete Ecology Factbook* (Garden City, N. Y.: Doubleday, 1972), pp. 195–198.
29.   Esposito, op. cit., p. 13.
30.   J. Clarence and Barbara S. Davies, *The Politics of Pollution* (Indianapolis: Pegasus, 2d ed., 1975), pp. 56–57.
31.   As early as 1967, an interdepartmental committee of experts established by the secretary of commerce and chaired by Dr. Richard S. Morse of MIT concluded that the steam engine was such an alternative and would produce very little pollution: 2 percent of the hydrocarbon, 2.5 percent of the nitrogen oxides, and 1.5 percent of the carbon monoxide emissions produced by the internal combustion engine.
32.   U. S. Council on Environmental Quality, U. S. Department of Housing and Urban Development and the Environmental Protection Agency, *The Costs of Sprawl* (Washington: U. S. Government Printing Office, 1974) vol. 2, p. 134.
33.   Quoted in Esposito, op. cit., p. 21.
34.   Organization for Economic Cooperation and Development, *Urban Traffic Noise–Strategy for an Improved Environment* (Paris: Organization for Economic Cooperation and Development, 1970), p. 13.
35.   See Kenneth Orski, "The Impact of the Automobile on the Environment," *OECD Observer* (Aug. 1971), p. 31.
36.   Melville C. Branch, "Outdoor Noise, Transportation, and City Planning," *Traffic Quarterly* (Apr. 1971), p. 169.
37.   Ibid., pp. 169–170.
38.   OECD, *Urban Traffic Noise,* p. 27.
39.   Ibid.
40.   See U. S. Department of the Interior, *Mining and Minerals Policy, 1973* (Washington: U. S. Government Printing Office, 1973).
41.   Stanford Research Institute, *Patterns of Energy Consumption in the United States,* prepared for the office of Science and Technology, Executive Office of the President, 1972, pp. b–13 and p. 145.
42.   W. G. Dupree, Jr., and John S. Corsentino, *United States Energy Through the Year 2000* (Revised) U. S. Department of the Interior, Dec. 1975, p. 57.
43.   Gerald Leach, *The Motor Car and Natural Resources* (Paris: Organization for Economic Cooperation and Development, 1973), p. 1.
44.   William J. Ronan, "Energy Conservation and Public Transit," *Transit Journal,* 1, no. 2 (May 1975), p. 3.
45.   Robert C. Weaver, "Planned Communities," in *Highway Research Record Number 97* (Washington: Highway Research Board of the National Academy of Science, 1965), p. 1.
46.   *The Costs of Sprawl* (Washington: U. S. Government Printing Office, 1974), 2 vols.
47.   McHarg, op. cit., p. 7.
48.   Ibid., p. 197.

CHAPTER 8: CITIZEN REACTION

1. See William B. Furlong, "Profile of an Alienated Voter," *Saturday Review of the Society*, 55 (July 1972), pp. 48–51.

2. "Halting the Highway Men," *Business Week* (July 19, 1969), p. 37.

3. Jack Linville, "Troubled Urban Interstates," *Nation's Cities*, 8 (Dec. 1970), p. 10.

4. There are several case studies which deal with citizen involvement, including "Fighting the Freeway," *Newsweek*, 71 (Mar. 25, 1968), pp. 64–65); Gordon Fellman, Barbara Brandt, and Roger Rosenblatti, "Dagger in the Heart of Town," *Transaction*, 7 (Sept. 1970), pp. 38–47; Ben Kelley, *The Pavers and the Paved* (New York: Donald W. Brown, 1971), esp. pp. 91–178; Alan Lupo, Frank C. Colcord and Edmund P. Fowler, *Rites of Way: Politics of Transportation in Boston and the U. S. City* (Boston: Little, Brown, 1971). The most extensive case study and analysis, especially from a sociological perspective, is developed by Gordon Fellman, *The Deceived Majority: Politics and Protest in Middle America* (New Brunswick, N.J.: Transaction Books, 1973).

5. For a comparative analysis as to the issues which generated highway controversies, see Lupo, Colcord, and Fowler, op. cit., pp. 226–232.

6. Kelley, op. cit., pp. 127–150; and Daniel Zwerdling, "How to Stop a Highway," *Saturday Review of the Society*, 1 (Feb. 17, 1973), pp. 60–61.

7. Kelley, op. cit., p. 129.

8. Elliott Arthur Pavlos, "Chicago's Crosstown: A Case Study in Urban Expressways," *Urban Transportation Policy: New Perspectives*, ed. David R. Miller (Lexington, Mass.: Heath, 1972), pp. 57–66.

9. Kelley, op. cit., pp. 130–131.

10. Fellman, op. cit., pp. 57ff.

11. For a summary review of these procedures, see Angus Macbeth and Peter W. Sly, "Federal-Aid Highways: Public Participation in the Administration Stages or How to Hold up the Highwaymen," *The Concrete Opposition* (Mar. 1972), pp. 3–4.

12. Zwerdling, op. cit., p. 61.

13. David Hapgood, "The Highwaymen," in Charles Peters and John Rothchild, eds., *Inside the System* (New York: Praeger, 1970), p. 153.

14. *The Concrete Opposition* (Mar. 1972), p. 3.

15. Ibid., p. 1. For those interested in the legal aspects, see B. A. Brown, "Citizen Opposition to a Suburban Freeway, A Semi-Hypothetical Scenario: The Seattle Experience," *Urban Law Annual*, 1972 (St. Louis: The School of Law, Washington University, 1972), pp. 105–130.

16. Hapgood, op. cit., 151.

17. E. E. Schattschneider, "The Scope and Bias of the Pressure System," *Public Policies and Their Politics*, ed. Randall B. Ripley (New York: Norton, 1966), p. 23. Citizen groups without any power sources appear to follow a similar pattern. See, for example, Michael Lipsky, "Protest as a Political Resource," *American Political Science Review*, 62 (Dec. 1968), pp. 1133–1158.

18. Hapgood, op. cit., p. 158.

19. For discussion of the regulatory process, see Samuel Krislow and Lloyd D. Musolf, eds., *The Politics of Regulation* (Boston: Houghton-Mifflin, 1964).

20. See, for example, Victor A. Thompson, *Modern Organization* (New York: Knopf, 1961).

21. Francis E. Rourke, *Bureaucracy, Politics, and Public Policy* (Boston: Little, Brown, 1969), pp. 39–61.

22. See, for example, Edward C. Banfield and James Q. Wilson, *City Politics* (New York: Vintage, 1963), pp. 187–203.

23. For a penetrating analysis of citizen participation, see Jerre S. William, "An Evaluation of Public Participation in the Location of Public Facilties," *Public Affairs Comment*, 19 (Nov. 1972), pp. 1–6.

24.   See Donald N. Dewees et al., *Mass Transit and the Highway Trust Fund* (Springfield, Va.: National Technical Information Service, 1970).

25.   This proposal was presented to the research staff of the Texas Senate Interim Committee on Urban Affairs. One of the authors served as staff director for the committee.

26.   See advertisement, "The Geography of Survival," American Trucking Association Inc., *Harper's Magazine*, 243 (Oct. 1971), pp. 38–39.

27.   The kind of organization into which the Anti-Crosstown Action Committee is developing appears to represent this change in citizen groups. See Furlong, op. cit.

CHAPTER 10: EPILOGUE

1.   Todd Fandell and Charles Camp, "Transportation in 2000 to Rely on Equipment Much like Today's, *Wall Street Journal* (Apr. 1, 1976), p. 1 ff.

2.   Ibid., p. 1.

BIBLIOGRAPHY

MAJOR WORKS

Altschuler, Allen. "Transit Subsidies: By Whom, For Whom?" *AIP Journal* (March 1969), pp. 84–88.

Urban transit subsidies are needed to enhance the mobility of the poor and the physically handicapped whose relative mobility has been steadily decreasing. Analysis of the overall transit situation suggests that such subsidies should be specifically tailored to needy individuals rather than to transit companies. Transportation user charges, including highway user tax payments, offer one logical source for subsidies.

Benede, Barry. "Pedestrian in the City," *Traffic Quarterly,* 19 (Jan. 1965), pp. 28–42.

Traces the development and decline of consideration of pedestrians in urban transport networks and sets criteria for planning for pedestrian use of streets on various street networks.

Bishop, Bruce A. *Socio-Economic and Community Factors in Planning Urban Freeways* (Ann Arbor: University Microfilms, 1969).

Approaches planning of freeways in a more comprehensive, people-oriented manner. Special emphasis is on quantitative and qualitative measures and on user and nonuser effects of freeway location.

Branch, Melville. "Outdoor Noise, Transportation and City Planning," *Traffic Quarterly* (April 1971).

The major thrust of the article is that noise is registered by and affects the unconscious mind and central nervous system as an irritant. This is perhaps the reason why land adjacent to airports and freeways experiences blight and decay. Land use control, noise regulations and screening are the three suggested ways to control the effects of noise. Some of the legislative suggestions are: establish an office responsible for noise emission and control, set accoustical insulation standards for

207

residences in noise designated areas, provide mandatory noise warnings to home buyers when their dwelling is in a noise pollution area.

Dewees, Donald N., et al. *Mass Transit and the Highway Trust Fund* (Cambridge: Harvard University Press, 1970).

This study focuses on the Highway Trust Fund and discusses the appropriateness of the fund for mass transit expenditures. The material has been organized into (1) major characteristics of the Highway Fund with a view to suggesting the kinds of judgments required to decide whether some proposed extensions of the highway fund are appropriate; (2) use of this analysis to examine various proposals to extend the Highway Fund to cover certain highway costs not presently financed in this way; (3) a look at the problems of mass transit using the previous analysis to consider three alternative proposals: first to fund mass transit capital expenditures out of a special mass transit trust fund; second to fund them out of the Highway Fund itself; and to establish a multi-modal transportation trust fund. Finally direction for public policy.

Fitch, Lyle C. *Urban Transportation and Public Policy* (San Francisco: Chandler Publishing Co. 1964).

This text was written prior to the Urban Mass Transportation Act of 1964, when the federal role was minimal. The work is important historically, as it cites the major reports which gave impetus to emerging federal involvement. It also details congressional political battles over urban transportation. Many of Fitch's suggestions in the chapter "Recommendations for the Future" have become reality—for example, formulation of an urban mass transit administration and the increasing federal role in research and development.

Ganz, Alexander. "Emerging Patterns of Urban Growth and Travel," *Highway Research Record,* no. 229 (1968), pp. 27–37.

The trend towards dispersal of travel away from the central city is discussed with reference to land use, travel patterns, and mode of travel.

Heilbroner, Robert, et al. *In the Name of Profit* (Garden City: Doubleday and Co. 1972).

In the Name of Profit is a series of case studies which illustrate various instances of irresponsibility by business corporations. The major chapter of interest for the transportation system is Chapter 2, "Deciding to Cheapen the Product," which outlines certain actions by General Motors aimed at reducing the quality of their product to maintain profit percentages.

Hilton, George W. "Rail Transit and the Pattern of Modern Cities: The California Case," *Traffic Quarterly,* 21 (July 1965), pp. 379–393.

A study of the relation between the geographical pattern, the technology of urban transportation, and the other forces at work on the form of American cities, with emphasis on San Francisco and Los Angeles.

Hoover, Edgar M. *Motor Metropolis: Some Observations on Motor Transportation in America* (Center for Regional Economic Studies 1965).

Given the mass ownership of private automobiles and the revolutionary changes in the physical layout of cities which characterize modern society, Hoover analyzes the dysfunctional costs associated with automobile use on a massive scale: (1) increased congestion and distances to work; (2) the greater expense of the automobile for work trips; (3) urban sprawl and poor land use; (4) increased city tax burdens with a corresponding decrease in taxable land; (5) massive pollution; (6) political competition between cities and suburbs; and (7) homogeneity of "automobile suburbs."

Kelley, Ben. *The Pavers and the Paved* (New York: Donald W. Brown 1971).

As the first director of the Federal Highway Administration's Office of Public Affairs, the author is able to provide a penetrating analysis of national transportation problems. The author divides the book into two parts. The first section deals with the road builders and administrators who tended to act without taking the needs and desires of the urban dwellers into account when the routes for the freeways were established. The second part of the book reviews some of the efforts to oppose the highway program. Some of the areas include San Francisco, North Nashville, and Washington, D. C. For opponents to unwarranted freeway construction, the author provides some useful advice.

Leavitt, Helen. *Superhighway–Superhoax* (Garden City, N. Y.: Doubleday and Co. 1970).

This book outlines the growth of highways and the highway bureaucracy in the United States from Colonial America to the present day. Pro-highway interest group pressures are discussed, as are anti-highway citizen group activities. Methods of dealing with the transportation problem, and alternatives to the use of the automobile in urban areas are suggested.

Levinson, H. S. "Transportation and Conservation," *Traffic Quarterly* (Jan. 1969).

Transportation can be used as an aid to help conservation. For example a rapid transit brought into a downtown area can revitalize a deteriorating core. If freeways are not planned properly, freeways can be disastrous to the retail value of the CBD. The author says this can be prevented by using the total environmental approach. Highways can either work for or against conservation when they go through open space areas. The controversial San Antonio Freeway is an example of how roads can endanger open space whereas the Natches Trace Parkway is an example of how open space is preserved and enjoyed.

Luna, Charles. *The U. T. U. Handbook of Transportation in America* (New York: Popular Library 1971).

This is a source for the governmental role in transportation from an historical stance. It deals with transportation in the U. S. dating back to the 18th century. It places an emphasis on inter-city transportation rather than intra-city. The book is useful in defining the federal role in transportation in three areas: investment, promotion, and regulation.

Mertins, Herman. *National Transportation Policy in Transition* (Lexington, Mass.: D. C. Heath and Co. 1972).

This book offers a general background of federal involvement in transportation policy. Although urban transportation is not covered extensively, state and federal governments' roles in developing canal, rail, and highway systems are more thoroughly discussed. Restrictive controls, beginning with the Act to Regulate Commerce, are seen as challenging the modern economy.

Mertins, Herman. *Urban Transportation Policy: Fact or Fiction?* (Syracuse, N. Y.: Syracuse University Press 1970).

> Perhaps the most important work in the area of federal urban transportation policy, it first reviews federal highway legislation in terms of its impact on urban transportation policy. After reviewing legislation that pertains to urban mass transportation, discussing the effects of federal organization on policy, and evaluating the interactions of federal policy and urban transportation problems, Mertins concludes that policy is a piecemeal series of responses to particular crises rather than an integrated national policy.

Meyers, Sumner. "Personal Transportation for the Poor," *Traffic Quarterly* (Apr. 1970), pp. 191–206.

> Examines the transportation plight of low income groups in relation to employment and other social goals, and explores a number of alternatives for meeting the mobility needs of the poor. Among those alternatives discussed is the "New Volks for Poor Folks" plan to help poor people purchase and maintain their own cars.

Mowbray, A. Q. *Road to Ruin* (Philadelphia: J. B. Lippincott 1969).

> This book reviews the first ten years of progress and controversy since the establishment of the Interstate Highway System Act in 1956. Among the highlights of the controversies is the fight between President Lyndon Johnson and the highway lobby over Johnson's attempts to cut back on highway funding. The success of the highway builders over a variety of the cities and protest groups is documented. Organizational changes brought about by establishing the Department of Transportation are also analyzed.

Moynihan, D. P. "The War Against the Automobile," *The Public Interest,* 3 (Spring 1966), pp. 10–26.

> Moynihan examines the forces which oppose serious traffic safety policy. The automobile industry is shown to be notably opposed to producing safer cars, and the psychological role played by the automobile in Amerian life suggests why nothing has been done. The author suggests that mass volume can be reduced. He elaborates on the new forces that are gathering to support traffic safety, and mentions new federal legislation which may combat the safety problem.

O'Leary, Jeremiah, Jr. "Evaluating the Environmental Impact of an Urban Expressway," *Traffic Quarterly* (July 1969).

> Although primarily concerned with the proposed Riverfront Expressway in New Orleans, this study indicates an approach and method of impact analysis that should be of value to other communities. The method developed to systematically weight the expected results of a proposed expressway on urban areas directs efforts in favor of corrective action to allay disastrous environmental mistakes.

Orski, Kenneth. "The Impact of the Automobile on the Environment," *OECD Observer* (Aug. 1971).

> Examines what many countries are beginning to do in establishing controls on the automobile to respect the broader range of human needs. Among the controls mentioned are: (1) Safety programs; (2) Emission reductions; (3) Noise level reductions; (4) New equipment requirements to force prices up and reduce automobile demand; (5) "Local-specific" restraints on auto use; (6) Traffic bans; (7) Encouraging mass transit use; and (8) Other problem controls.

Owen, Wilfred, *The Accessible City* (Washington, D. C.: The Brookings Institution, 1972).

Surveys many of the changes needed in the design of our cities if they are to cope with automobile and mass transit. The dysfunctional nature of our cities is as much to blame for the urban crisis as the automobile itself. Alternative means of travel are stressed and explored. Presents an overview of European systems for comparison with our present position.

Owen, Wilfred. *The Metropolitan Transportation Problem* (Washington, D. C.: The Brookings Institution, 1972).

The role of public and private transportation in urban areas is compared by costs and trends of the industry. The problems presented by urbanization and the inability of transit to adjust to its changes are the prime focus.

Sexton, Burton H. "Traffic Noise," *Traffic Quarterly* (July 1969).

Discusses noise control features which should be designed into sections of expressways near quiet urban areas. Masonry walls, plantings, and slope cuts are some of the best methods of reducing the decibel level of ambient noise.

Smerk, George M. "An Evaluation of Ten Years of Federal Policy in Urban Mass Transportation," *Transportation Journal* (Winter 1971), pp. 45–57.

Research and demonstration projects from various legislative acts passed in the 1960's have failed largely because of transit mismanagement. Program development has been hindered because no reasonable, workable objectives or long-range purposes have been set. Adequate provision of money, real organization, and formulation of workable objectives are detailed in a specific set of suggestions to improve mass transit programs.

Smerk, George M., ed. *Readings in Urban Transportation* (Bloomington: Indiana University Press, 1968).

This work reviews various aspects of the urban transportation problem and proposes methods for its solution. The most valuable section of the reference is the section on "Automobile Use and Its Cost." Of most value was the review of the relevant costs of getting to work by all modes of transportation. In assessing the fixed and variable costs, the article concludes that the automobile is generally the most expensive way to get to work.

Smerk, George M. *Urban Mass Transportation: A Dozen Years of Federal Policy* (Bloomington: Indiana University Press, 1974).

This book follows much the same line as "An Evaluation of Ten Years of Federal Policy in Urban Mass Transportation" (1971). After detailing the shortcomings of each piece of urban mass transit legislation, Smerk offers detailed alternatives to foster improvements. The need for goals and objectives within a specific time frame, money, and proper management principles are mentioned. Subsidies for improvements, goals of quality service, increased mobility, and a "consumer-oriented" management program that focuses on marketing functions are among the many detailed suggestions that Smerk offers.

OTHER WORKS

American Academy of Arts and Sciences. *Conference on Poverty and Transportation* (Springfield, Va.: National Technical Information Service, 1968).

American Automobile Association. *American Motorist* (June 1969).

Ayres, Edward. *What's Good for G. M.* (Nashville: Aurora Publishers, 1970).

Ballard, Cordelle K. "Transportation Dependents," *Traffic Quarterly*, 21 (Jan. 1967), pp. 83–90.

Barloon, Marvin. J. "The Interrelationship of the Changing Structure of American Transportation and Changes in Industrial Location," *Land Economics*, 41 (May 1965), pp. 169–179.

Barsness, Richard. "The Department of Transportation: Concept and Structure," *Western Political Quarterly*, 23 (Sept. 1970), pp. 500–515.

Bernstein, S. J. "Mass Transit and the Urban Ghetto," *Traffic Quarterly*, 27 (July 1973), pp. 431–449.

Boyd, Alan S. "The Federal Department of Transportation," *Traffic Quarterly*, 21 (Oct. 1967), pp. 467–470.

Brown, B. A. "Citizen Opposition to a Suburban Freeway, A Semi-Hypothetical Scenario: The Seattle Experience," *Urban Law Annual, 1972* (St. Louis: The School of Law, Washington University, 1972), pp. 105- 130.

Buchanan, Colin. "Urban Transportation: The Scope of the New Technology," *Future Directions for Research in Urban Transportation* (Paris: OECD, 1969).

Bunge, William. "Toward a General Theory of Movement," *Theoretical Geography* (Lund, Sweden: C. W. K. Gleerup, 1962), pp. 108–129.

Burby, John. *The Great American Motion Sickness* (Boston: Little, Brown and Co., 1971).

Cassidy, Robert. "The Highway Act: More Platypus than Policy," *Planning*, 39 (Sept. 1973), pp. 21–23.

Clark, Colin. "Transport—Maker and Breaker of Cities," *Town Planning Review*, 28 (1957).

Colcord, Frank C. "Decision-Making and Transportation Policy," *Southwestern Social Science Quarterly*, 48 (Dec. 1967), p. 383–397.

Coogan, Matthew A., et al. *Transportation Politics in Atlanta* (Washington: National Technical Information Service, 1970).

David, Grant M. *The Department of Transportation* (Lexington, Mass.: Heath Lexington Books 1970).

Denison, George, and Kenneth Y. Tomlinson. "Let's Put the Brakes on the Highway Lobby," *Reader's Digest*, 94 (May 1969), pp. 97–102.

Dupree, W. G., Jr., and John S. Corsentino. *United States Energy Through the Year 2000* (U. S. Department of the Interior, rev. Dec., 1975).

Fellman, Gordon. *The Deceived Majority: Politics and Protest in Middle America* (New Brunswick, N. J.: Transaction Books, 1973).

Flink, James J. *America Adopts the Automobile, 1895-1910* (Cambridge, Mass.: MIT Press, 1970).

Friedman, Robert S. "State Politics and Highways," *Politics in the American States*, ed. Herbert Jacobs and Kenneth N. Vine (Boston: Little, Brown, 1976).

Gilmore, Harian W. *Transportation and the Growth of Cities* (Glencoe, Ill.: The Free Press, 1953), p. 116.

Goodman, Robert. *After the Planners* (New York: Simon and Schuster, 1971).

Goodrich, Carter. *Government Promotion of American Canals and Railroads, 1800-1890* (New York: Columbia University Press, 1960).

Greytak, David. *Residential Segregation, Metropolitan Decentralization, and the Journey to Work* (Springfield, Virginia: National Technical Information Service, 1970).

Hapgood, David. "The Highwaymen," *Inside the System,* ed. Charles Peters and Timothy J. Adams (New York: Praeger, 1970).

Herbert, Richard. "How the AAA Uses Its Members to Pave the Way for More Freeways," *Washingtonian* (June 1970).

Higgins, John K. "Whose Free Ride? Transit Subsidies," *New Republic* (May 6, 1972), pp. 13ff.

Holt, Glen E. "The Changing Perception of Urban Pathology: An Essay on the Development of Mass Transit in the United States," *Cities in American History,* ed. Kenneth T. Jackson and Stanley K. Schultz (New York: Knopf, 1972).

Hubby, Nancy. "Transportation Legislation, 1960–70: Evolution, Perhaps Revolution," *Planning Comment,* 8, no. 2.

Jackson, Kenneth T. "The Crabgrass Frontier: 150 Years of Suburban Growth in America," *The Urban Experience: Themes in American History,* ed. Raymond A. Mohl and James F. Richardson (Belmont, Calif.: Wadsworth, 1973).

Kheel, Theodore, W. "The Port Authority Strangles New York," in *Problems in Political Economy: An Urban Perspective,* ed. David M. Gordon (Lexington, Mass.: Heath, 1971).

Lansing, John B. and Eva Miller. "Residential Location and Urban Mobility," *Highway Research Record,* no. 106 (1966), pp. 77–96.

Leach, Gerald. *The Motor Car and Natural Resources* (Paris: Organization for Economic Cooperation and Development, 1973).

Lee, Douglas B., Jr. *The Costs of Private Automobile Usage in the City of San Francisco.* (National Technical Information Service, April 1972).

Lupo, Alan, Frank Colcord and Edmund P. Fowler. *Rites of Way: The Politics of Transportation in Boston and the U. S. City* (Boston: Little, Brown, 1971).

McHarg, Ian. *Design With Nature* (Garden City, N. Y.: Doubleday, 1971).

Mertins, Herman. "National Transportation Planning: Dimensions and Challenges," *Public Administration Review,* 30 (May / June 1971).

Meyer, J. R., J. F. Kain and M. Wohl. *The Urban Transportation Problem* (Cambridge: Harvard University Press, 1966).

Meyers, Sumner. "Turning Transit Subsidies into 'Compensatory Transportation,' " *City,* 6 (Summer 1972), pp. 17–21.

Miller, David R., ed. *Urban Transportation Policy: New Perspectives* (Lexington, Mass.: Lexington, 1972).

Moynihan, Daniel P. "New Roads and Urban Chaos," *Reporter* (Apr. 14, 1960).

Nelson, James C. "Government's Role Toward Transportation," *Transportation Journal* (Summer 1972).

Norton, Hugh S. *National Transportation Policy: Formation and Implementation* (Berkeley: McCutchan Publishing, 1966).

Ornati, Oscar A. *Transportation Needs of the Poor* (New York: Praeger, 1969).

Owen, Wilfred. *Strategy for Mobility* (Washington, D. C.: The Brookings Institution, 1964).

Parente, Francis R. *D. C. Transportation Controversies, Values and Integration of Communities* (Springfield, Va.: National Technical Information Service, 1970).

Pignataro, Louis J. and John C. Falcocchio. "Transportation Needs of Low Income Families," *Traffic Quarterly* (Oct. 1969), pp. 505–526.

Rae, John B. *The Road and Car in American Life* (Cambridge, Mass.: MIT Press, 1971).

Research and Policy Committee. *Developing Metropolitan Transportation Policies: A Guide for Local Leadership* (Committee for Economic Development, April 1965).

Robinson, John. *Highways and Our Environment* (New York: McGraw-Hill, 1971).

Schneider, Kenneth R. *Autokind vs. Mankind* (New York: Schocken, 1972).

Sheperd, William G. *Market Power and Economic Welfare* (New York: Random House, 1970), 232-243.

Smerk, George M. "The Streetcar: Shaper of American Cities," *Traffic Quarterly,* 21 (Oct. 1967).

Smerk, George M. "Subsidies for Urban Mass Transportation," *Land Economics* (February 1965).

Smerk, George M. *Urban Transportation: The Federal Role* (Bloomington: Indiana University Press, 1965).

Thiel, Floyd I. "Social Effects of Modern Highway Transportation," *Highway Research Bulletin,* 327 (1962), pp. 1-20.

Transportation Research Institute. *Latent Demand for Urban Transportation* (Pittsburgh: Carnegie-Mellon University, 1968).

U. S. Department of Housing and Urban Development. *Tomorrow's Transportation* (Washington, D. C.: 1968).

U. S. Department of Transportation. *Background Information on the Urban Mass Transportation Administration* (Washington, D. C.: U. S. Government Printing Office, 1972).

Urban Mass Transportation Administration, *Policy on Major Urban Mass Transportation Investment* (U. S. Department of Transportation, March 1976).

Veatch, James F. "Federal and Local Urban Transportation Policy," *Urban Affairs Quarterly,* 10, no. 4 (June 1975).

Wade, Richard C. *The Urban Frontier* (Cambridge, Mass.: Harvard University Press, 1962).

Warner, Sam B., Jr. *Streetcar Suburbs* (Cambridge, Mass.: Harvard University Press, 1962), p. 15.

William, Jerre S. "An Evaluation of Public Participation in the Location of Public Facilities," *Public Affairs Comment,* 19 (November 1972).

INDEX

Administered prices: and automotive industry, 61-62, 70
Agencies, social welfare, 8
Agnew, Spiro, 75
Air quality, 123-125
American Association of State Highway Officials, 138
American Medical Association, 81
American Motors, 62, 64, 164
American Road Builder's Association, 85
American Transit Association, 71
Anti-Crosstown Action Committee, 135
Antitrust Division, U. S. Department of Justice, 75
Antitrust enforcement, failure of, 186
Appleyard, Donald, 118-119
Approaches to urban transportation, 1
Architecture, 121
Assembly lines, 21
Auto apologists, 4, 7
Auto dealers, and local policies, 77
Auto industry: and price leadership, 61-62; and self-regulation, 62, 74; and profitability, 62; and jobs, 62; and key industries, 64; and principle of collective economic inaction, 66; and Greyhound Corporation, 71; and resource use, 113; restructuring of, 164; and brand name, 167; mechanics of reorganization, 172; and sale of foreign interests, 173
Auto monopolists, 4
Auto power, uses of, 70
Automotive society, 21
Averitt, Robert, 64

Balancers, 4, 10
Ballard, Cordelle, 108
Baltimore and Ohio Railroad, 18
Bay Area Rapid Transit, 24, 110, 157
Bentley, Arthur F., 31
Bowles, Sam, 78
Brinegar, Claude, 44, 54
Buchanan, Colin, 90
Bureau of Public Roads, 41, 88
Bureaucratic role in transportation, 143
Bus industry, restructuring of, 168
Business Week, 136

Campaign contributions, 76
Canals, 17
Capital costs: of automobiles, 47; and auto industry, 162
"Center economy," 64
Central Business District, 14, 94, 114, 158
Centrifugal force of transportation system, 20
Centripetal force of transportation system, 19
Chicago Tribune, 50
Chrysler: 64; and clean air package, 125, 164
Citizen action groups, 135
Citizen interest groups, strategies, 135-139
Civil Aeronautics Act, 169
Clayton Act, 187
Clean Air Act, 124
Colcord, Frank, 93
Collective economic inaction, principle of, 66
Collusion, tacit, and auto industry, 68
Commoner, Barry, 126
Commuter trains, 23-24
Competition, elimination of; and General Motors, 70-72
Comprehensive planning, 12
Concentration in auto industry: factors accounting for, 175-176
Concrete Opposition, The, 9
Congestion, vii, Center city, 7
Congressional committees: role of chairman, 85; and constituents, 86; House Ways and Means, 87
Congressmen: Pro-Highway, 86; Constituents, 87
Conner, John T., 75
Consumer sovereignty, 59
Costs of transportation, 22, 36
Crime, 153

Darwinian Capitalism, 14
Diseconomies, external, 7
Democraticization of urban transportation, 156
Department of Transportation, 23, 87-88, 109